The New Standards

Methods for Linking
Business Performance and
Executive Incentive Pay

RICHARD N. ERICSON

WILEY

John Wiley & Sons, Inc.

Library of Congress Cataloging-in-Publication Data:

Ericson, Richard N.

  The new standards : methods for linking business performance and executive incentive pay / Richard N. Ericson.
    p. cm.
  Rev. ed. of: Pay to prosper. c2004.
  Includes index.
  ISBN 978-0-470-55989-5 (cloth)
  1. Incentives in industry. 2. Executives–Salaries, etc. 3. Chief executive officers–Salaries, etc. 4. Stock options. 5. Employee motivation. I. Ericson, Richard N. Pay to prosper. II. Title.
  HF5549.5.I5E62 2010
  658.4'07225–dc22

                                                                        2009046292

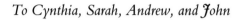
To Cynthia, Sarah, Andrew, and John

Contents

Preface

A tiny portion of the world's population largely directs the affairs of commerce. A typical Fortune 500 company has a few hundred of these people. Medium-sized companies have between a few and a few dozen. They are senior-level members of company management. And they, either alone or working within a team, have a material impact on the value of a private or public business enterprise or a business unit of either.

Edmund Burke said people in important posts must be "formed to the greatest degree of vigilance, foresight, and circumspection in a state of things in which no fault is committed with impunity and the slightest mistakes draw on the most ruinous consequences . . ."[1] Senior management roles carry this sort of impact. The well-being of many stakeholders hinges on their decisions. But, in the case of most of the bigger companies, they don't own the businesses they run. Instead, they manage these enterprises at the behest of shareholders and their board representatives.

This book is about how to design senior management incentive plans. It asserts that companies should use senior management's incentive pay as a proactive instrument of business governance, one specifically designed to increase business performance. Companies have been moving in that direction in recent years. Most revamped their incentive structures in reaction to the onset of new option expensing rules. In the past, they delivered almost all their long-term incentive (LTI) pay in the form of stock options, and LTI is the largest element of pay at the top of the house. They did this because typical options did not require expense recognition in the income statement. Option grants appeared to be free, and companies overused them wildly. Companies now make heavier use of other kinds of LTI:

- *Restricted stock.* These are grants of shares that vest over time, typically, but may have at least modest performance contingencies associated with granting, vesting, or both. These grants sometimes are made as stock *units*—deferred share-based awards paying out in shares or cash.
- *Performance units.* Also known as performance cash plans, these are awards earned based on attainment of multiyear goals (most often based on preset financial performance goals). *Performance shares.* These are like performance

units, but awards are denominated in shares of company stock. Actual payment of performance shares or units may be in cash or shares.

- *Phantom stock.* These grants are meant to resemble stock options or restricted stock, but usually are based on the value of a nonpublic company or a business unit and are paid out in cash rather than actual shares. Stock appreciation rights (SARs) are a kind of phantom option, but one normally issued against shares of a public company as a substitute for stock options, and paying out either in cash or shares.

Before option expensing, options appeared costless in the P&L, so most companies used little else. Now they face big-ticket, complex choices about matters such as what should be the mix of cash, shares, and options within the overall structure of LTI and what LTI goals and metrics to use. And the decision-making environment—conditions in capital markets, the business outlook, the demands of pay and governance critics—has become more complex and uncertain, compounding the difficulties involved in getting things right in this important area. The balance of incentive pay takes the form of annual bonuses. These have grown in importance, and they continue to be troubled by the difficulties of target setting, metric selection, and payout calibration.

Problems with the traditional incentive structure have been plain for many years. Incentives pose enormous costs. They carry high stakes in terms of potential business impact. Designed and run properly, they can help drive high-quality business decision making and better business results. However, incentive policy at many companies is not merely a poorly designed matter but also is an episodic, unstable, and continually reactive one. The result is that senior management's incentives pose astoundingly high costs and don't contribute adequately to business performance.

Things don't have to be this way. Incentive structures can be set up to endure. They can adapt to a wide range of business conditions and market events. They can stand vigil through all business conditions, continually encouraging the best performance and consistently serving shareholder interests. Many companies should step back and think fundamentally about what role senior management's incentives should play and about how, precisely, they should be designed for greatest business impact and return on investment.

This book is meant to assist in that process and to do so in decisive and specific terms. It sets forth the case for activist incentive policy, providing insights and techniques along with examples of how to implement them. The book is called *The New Standards* because it emphasizes that management incentives should now respond to new, tougher standards. These new standards originate from several sources. Shareholders and their activist representatives demand that executive pay costs be spent in exchange for real performance. They expect incentives to meet high quality standards for prudence in design and administration. They expect incentives to be used actively in governance and effectively as performance devices.

The new market situation obliges companies to do a better job of setting performance standards themselves. Capital markets impose standards, ones that identify conditions for value creation and shareholder returns. In the new environment around executive pay, capital market standards should be examined and implemented explicitly in matters like incentive structure, target setting, metric selection and payout calibration.

The business world gets tougher and more competitive each year, and standards for business performance ratchet ever upward. All elements of business operations have been under great pressure to improve.

Almost all elements, that is. Where executive incentives were concerned, the situation for many years was that "free" option accounting caused options to grow to dominate the executive incentive structure. During that time, this very limited menu caused market practices in incentive pay to be less responsive than they should have been to business performance exigencies. Bookkeeping rules had the effect of stunting the evolution of these potentially critical performance devices. Now, companies feel much freer to choose. They can craft their designs after looking at a broad menu. They can do so fully in pursuit of potential business advantage in their own particular setting. The pace of "catch-up" and change has been rapid and will continue to be so. This book strives to support such changes in a way that responds closely to the new standards.

Chapter 1 is an overview of the book. The typical incentive structure does not consistently encourage good, value-creating business performance. It can often reward senior management for bad business decisions. At other times, it can leave them indifferent. Incentives at most companies should be restructured based on principles of business governance and value creation. Chapter 1 is written to the chief executive officer (CEO), since it is in the CEO's interest to adopt better-working incentives as a way to pursue better business results for shareholders. Further, most companies really can't enact this sort of change without CEO support.

To design incentive plans, an organization does not have to specify from scratch the linkages among business decisions, business results and value creation. Rather, as Chapter 2 shows, it can draw on the techniques of business valuation, where the relevant rules have been set out in a clear and compelling way for many decades. Chapter 3 describes common incentive structures in the market. We find they often connect actions of key decision makers only weakly with the results they drive and they may reward advancement up the ranks much more clearly than anything else.

You can't set up incentive plans properly unless you have a set of objectives against which to make the many important choices involved in design. Chapter 2 provided some concrete guidance here by setting out clearly the linkages between business decisions, business results, and value creation. Chapter 3 provided a range of market perspectives. Chapter 4 reviews a range of additional inputs regarding proper incentive policy, sourced from a wide sample of shareholder activists and governance commentators. Overall findings are synthesized in Chapter 4 into a set of design principles.

Senior managers are in the "decision" business. Their jobs involve not only managing business operations, but making material, long-term, and often irrevocable commitments of shareholder resources. And they do so under conditions of uncertainty, or risk. Chapter 5 addresses the many ways in which incentive structures can bias management against reasonable risk taking or encourage them to gamble too freely with shareholder money. It then details a range of ways in which incentives can assist in the critical matters of risk management and balanced business risk taking.

Hundreds of approaches to incentive plan design exist. What distinguishes them most is their basis for rewards—the methods and media used to capture management's performance. Chapter 6 hones in on the most effective approaches for senior management teams, focusing on the importance of linking pay decisively to sustained business results that create value. Most bonus pay is delivered based on a few common financial yardsticks like earnings per share, net income, return on equity, and revenue. Deficiencies in these metrics are among the main problems with bonus plans, since they allow many poor business decisions to be rewarded. Chapter 6 continues by using valuation-based principles to examine the full range of financial metrics and to show how to use them properly within incentive plans.

Value-based metrics such as economic value added, cash flow return on investment, and total business return have been in and out of the spotlight for two decades, promising to help improve business results and create more value. Economic value added is the best known of the group. Most companies took a close look at it in the 1990s, but its prevalence is only around five percent today. So, its rejection rate has been very high, with its complexity being implicated most often. Chapter 7 demystifies value-based metrics and makes them easier to assess. It proves that they all have the same roots. They can be put in place simply and effectively, without the clutter of metric adjustments and odd incentive plan designs, and without turning the whole company upside down. Also, Chapters 6 and 7 prove out a key assertion of this book—that companies wishing to implement value-focused *incentives* do not have to use value-based *metrics* at all.

Most goal-based incentive plans use performance targets and ranges that stem from an internal, negotiated process. Most bonus goals are based on budgets, for example. This can lead to internal battles, mediocre performance expectations, and managed business results. Companies don't have to do things this way, and Chapter 8 lays out a set of solutions.

Most companies base incentive pay heavily on corporate results: stock price movements that drive gains on stock and option grants, for example, and corporate-level metrics such as earnings per share. In contrast, most of the value of a typical company—as well as most of its executives and most of the business decisions that it might hope to improve through better incentives—are found in business units like groups, sectors, divisions, profit centers, and joint ventures. Chapter 9 shows how to tie incentives to business-unit results in effective, fair, and prudent ways. It also looks closely at the related matter of LTI design in private companies.

Since the onset of option expensing, companies have been making far fewer option grants and instead are using other forms of stock-based pay. This has been a fundamental shift in how incentive pay is used and also a very big-ticket move since so much of senior management pay, until just a few years ago, came in the form of stock option grants. Chapter 10 establishes a framework for stock-based incentive design, reviewing the most pertinent choices at issue. It encourages companies to examine in a clear-eyed way what stock-based pay can accomplish for a company and what it cannot, and to put it to its highest and best uses.

One of the platitudes of incentive design is that proper communication of incentive plans is pivotal to their success within a business. What's said less often, though, is that the plans themselves are important communication media. When we talk about communication of incentive plans for senior management, the most important thing to recognize is that the medium is the message. Formal communication initiatives will not work if the plan design itself is ineffective. Chapter 11 addresses plan communication, part and parcel with the incentive plan design process.

▪ NOTE

1. "Letter from the New to the Old Whigs" (1791), Selected Prose of Edmund Burke, edited and introduced by Sir Philip Magnus (1948).

Acknowledgments

A great number of professional colleagues contributed to this book, directly or indirectly. I'd like to acknowledge in particular: Steve Davies, Michael Welsh, Steve Sahara, Paula Todd, Doug Friske, Gary Locke, Robert Grams, Mike Grund, Brian Blackwood, Katie Williams, Scott Olsen, Rob Greenberg, Ben Stradley, Mark Yango, Jeff Kridler, Henry Erlich, Steve Faigen, Andy Restaino, Ted Jarvis, Allen Jackson, Tina Gay, Roger Grabowski, Pat Finegan, Diana Scott, David Kelly, Max Smith, and Russell Hall.

To the CEO

Management incentive plans cost a ton of money and often do not work very well. At most medium to large companies, a group of executives numbering from a few dozen to a few hundred make most of the big-ticket decisions on the part of shareholders. Yet, for many, the linkage from performance to payout is too muted and inert to be called an *incentive*. Instead, most of the money in variable rewards is delivered as a kind of vague results-sharing arrangement, one administered distantly and after the fact.

There's also just a lot of wasted money. Executives often discount their incentive opportunities. To them, an incentive plan with a likely cost of a dollar might seem like it is worth only a quarter or two. The rest is an avoidable waste of corporate assets, one sometimes called an *agency cost*.

Incentives are supposed to link senior management's interests and shareholder interests very closely. Often, they do not. In many important ways, they can leave open the possibility of paying people to make poor business decisions. Poorly designed incentives may do the following:

- Consistently favor short-term results over the long-term ones that weigh much more heavily in value creation.

- Encourage executives to manage expectations for their performance more than to deliver the best possible results.

- Contribute to common failures in mergers and acquisitions and other pivotal investing activities by biasing the selection and evaluation processes and systemically weakening accountabilities.

- Drive excessive risk-taking or risk aversion.

- Encourage talented people to do whatever is involved in moving up the career ladder—not always the same thing as making their best contributions in roles they fill along the way.

These shortcomings persist despite a significant restructuring of senior management incentives that has occurred in the marketplace in recent years in response to pressing concerns such as option expensing and shareholder activism. Here's a current snapshot:

- The biggest part of executive incentives is in stock-denominated long-term incentive grants. Purely stock-based incentives—stock options, restricted stock—do not come with instructions on how to create value. It's a stretch to expect executives in a stock-heavy incentive structure to readily understand how to optimize the share price. Valuation is complex, and stock prices can bewilder investors. Tellingly, executives themselves do not demonstrate a consistent edge in their timing of option exercises and share purchases and sales. Corporate experience with acquisitions does not testify to valuation expertise, either.

- Annual incentive and performance-based long-term incentive (LTI) plans often are not much help, either. They often feature payout schedules that permit a range of imprudent actions to be rewarded. Metrics are drawn from a short list of the usual suspects. Goals flow from a difficult targeting process that begs mediocre outcomes. A common result is an overwhelmingly short-term focus.

The big management incentives are not in formal incentive plans, anyway. Stock and cash incentive gains can move up and down a lot, but most of senior management cannot affect most of that. The payouts that one *can* control have to do with advancing up the organizational ladder. Pay rises hugely when people get bigger and bigger jobs. Division chief executive officer (CEO) pay is twice that of the division's head of manufacturing. The corporate CEO earns many times what the division CEO does. What the executive rewards system says to most of its participants is just to do whatever is involved in moving up. When you come down to it, the efficacy of performance-based pay relies extremely heavily on the company's ability to judge the merit and contributions of individual executives and to match them with promotions and higher pay.

But individual merit and contribution can be hard things to judge. And a group of people with high individual performance ratings may not generate high levels of business results. The system would work better if it specifically encouraged these powerful individuals and teams to take those actions most productive to value creation—irrespective of whether they count toward individual performance, bring individual accolades, or secure the next job or the current one. Performance is not something to be hoped for, as some byproduct of a tournament for individual promotions. It should be encouraged and paid for directly. For that to happen, incentive gains must move up or down based on outcomes that people feel they influence. That is a path toward better business decisions, results, and value.

After all, you and your senior management team are in the *decision* business. You commit investor resources to business activities and see them through to success or failure, often over a period of many years.[1] Like any company, if you somehow could have avoided some past mistakes and made more successful decisions, your business performance would have been better. The future will be no different in this regard. Value creation in your business—and the role of your senior management group—is very much about choosing. It is about coming up with a range of real choices, accentuating the positive ones and eliminating the negative. If you could improve business decision making in a broad and systemic way, you could get a materially better yield from the opportunities surrounding your businesses.

Performance outcomes are a bit like the kids' game "Chutes and Ladders." Most of the time, you are moving along a few squares at a time toward your goal. But, once in awhile, you have a big opportunity. You can move far ahead with one good move by landing on one of the ladders and advancing a bunch of squares at once. Or you can hit a chute and fall far back. You may think this setback can be "made up" on later turns. But odds-makers would disagree, noting that falling down the chute actually is a permanent setback, since it does not improve your chances on future turns.

Business is not purely a game of chance, though—instead, you get to chose. If you make better decisions, you can avoid the chutes and land on more of the ladders. Incentives can help by standing vigil at every at the time of every decision—whether the stakes are high or low. Using better incentives, you can improve the quality of many business decisions made at your company and their results for shareholders. You can encourage your senior management team to take better account of first-line value drivers—how their decisions use investor resources, balance risks, and trade off short-term income effects against the more important long-term ones. By using incentive policy more actively in business governance, you can get a better yield for your shareholders from the collection of business traits and market opportunities that underlies the value of your enterprise. Your incentive structure can be a proactive instrument of governance.

WELL-DESIGNED INCENTIVES ARE GOVERNANCE DEFINED

For years, companies have been responding to a wide range of heightened governance concerns. Board deliberations about pay are influenced by regulatory matters including Sarbanes-Oxley, listing requirements, option expensing, 8K reporting, vote disclosure, and new proxy rules. Shareholder activism and corporate guidance is promulgated by a wide range of outside parties, including The Council of Institutional Investors, the Business Roundtable, governance scorekeepers, pension funds, unions, rating agencies, and individual shareholders.

Companies are responding directly to these influences in a range of ways. They also continue to pursue good practice in the administration of pay and performance through the following:

- Competitive benchmarking, to avoid paying more than necessary
- Evaluating incentive practices in the market and pursuing good-quality choices
- Complying with relevant regulations (e.g., accounting, legal)
- Focusing on high-quality implementation of programs

Among these matters, incentive design is especially pertinent to governance subject matter. Well-designed plans can be proactive governance tools. Instead, incentives often are costly arrangements that are of little help to governance.

Consider the arrangements in place among the main figures in the governance tableau shown in Exhibit 1.1. Corporations separate power between shareholders and hired managers. Boards have fiduciary duties to shareholders, overseeing management on their behalf. Managers are meant to act in the best interests of shareholders—as their "agents."

The Corporate Library defines governance as:

> The relationship between the shareholders, directors, and management of a company, as defined by the corporate charter, bylaws, formal policy, and rule of law.[2]

Senior management's incentive programs define the relationship between management and shareholders expressly in money terms. These programs number among the company's formal policies, and arguably constitute one of the higher-impact ones. Implications are set out further in Monks & Minow, *Corporate Governance*.

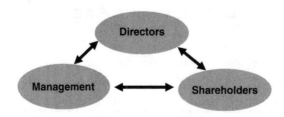

EXHIBIT 1.1   **Corporate Governance Actors**

. . . the structure that is intended to make sure that the right questions get asked and that the *checks and balances* are in place to make sure that the answers reflect what is best for the *creation of long-term, sustainable value* [emphasis added].[3]

Well-designed incentive opportunities—issued in prudent amounts—constitute one set of thorough and formal checks and balances on management decision making. They can be used to create explicit balance among the main drivers of value, consistently favoring long-term, sustainable value creation. Effects on decisions and performance can go far beyond the CEO and a few top officers. They can extend to a much larger group of material decision makers at the corporate and business–unit levels. When well designed, incentives can define the connections between business decisions, value creation for owners, and executive rewards. Incentives are governance, defined.

Management, inescapably, has wide latitude and control. Boards do not run operations, judge prospects expertly, or initiate business decisions. In this setting, proactive agency arrangements are very important. Unfortunately, however, many traditional governance responses are reactive, taking effect too late—after the company and its shareholders have borne performance losses from poor decisions.

Current mechanisms of governance for executive pay itself are limited and reactive. Responses often are test- or checklist-centered. Activists and regulators often express mixed and underdeveloped ideas about what constitutes effective incentive design on the ground—it takes some work to identify their common, actionable themes. Also, current pay governance processes are focused mainly on cost rather than performance. Performance metrics are not evaluated for use in encouraging good performance prospectively. Instead, they are used merely as a scale to evaluate pay costs after the fact.

Sound incentives, by contrast, can take on a proactive role in business governance generally. They can do the following:

- Encourage value-creating decisions in clear and direct terms.
- Do so prospectively, for every year of the near-, medium-, and long-term.
- Put real "skin in the game" by creating clear stakes and accountabilities.

Incentives do not meet on a quarterly basis. They are on the job all the time, pressing for shareholders when the big business decisions are being made. Shareholders normally pay a lot for this sort of protection. Governance and agency costs are high. Outlays add up for things like boards, advisors, stock administration and staff, and executive effort on these time-consuming matters. There are agency costs, too, like the gap between what incentive grants are worth and what participants think they are worth. And there are potentially costly risks from ineffective agency arrangements—the moral hazards of flawed incentive design.

What shareholders are hoping to buy with these costs is prudence and efficacy in the handling of their capital. One might borrow the song title *Dear Prudence*, since prudence in these matters seems to come at a dear price. Well-designed incentives, by contrast, do not require companies to pay dearly. They do not cost any more than typical incentive pay. They take the range of payouts promised now, for the most part, and line them up much more closely with high-quality business results.

Companies can take the lead in addressing the governance concerns pressing on executive pay. They can move the discussion well beyond a compliance activity. Incentive design can be made into a strategically pivotal process, one driving real results.

OLD SCHOOL

Monetary arrangements between investors and hired managers—between principals and agents—have been around for a while. Here is one clause recorded on the Stele of Hammurabi—a monument dating to the reign of King Hammurabi of Babylon. He took the throne in 1792 B.C.:

> If a merchant should give silver to a trading agent for an investment and he incurs a loss on his journeys, he shall return silver to the merchant in the amount of the capital sum.[4]

That quote is nearly 4,000 years old but it sets out some principles that are quite applicable today. It is, in fact, a good idea to take account of capital usage when determining the procedures for distributing rewards between principal and agent. The idea of capital recourse is no less familiar to modern merchant bankers than to Hammurabi's merchant. Some principles are worth carving in stone. Principal-agent arrangements apparently were in Hammurabi's era and, today, they still are.

Incentives lie at the heart of the business, connecting senior management's actions with rewards. Like Adam Smith's *invisible hand*, your system of executive rewards affects many important actions by people throughout your company. Incentive plans may imbue a wide range of senior management decision making with bias, and bias is the boll weevil of value creation.

If you have biased decision-making processes at the senior management level, your company is a mistake-making machine. Consider the biggest mistakes your business has made over the years. Or, if you prefer, consider the biggest ones made by other companies around town. When companies recount such errors, they do not always describe good business decisions that simply did not work out. Rather, they often point out standing problems with decision making—

things like short-term bias, organizational inertia, indifference, either in-sensitivity to risk or disproportionate fear of it, or an unconditional growth man-date driving everything the company does. They often describe problems that contributed to their business mistakes in the past and that might well create more of them in the future. Consider whether it would have been helpful to have incentives that do the following:

- Directly encourage every person in senior management to take a long view.
- Create a predictable and direct stake for them in the results of their business decisions.
- Establish reasonable accountabilities when management uses new investor capital, and fair credit when it gets sent back to investors.
- Balance business prospects and risks as an investor would.
- Attach first-dollar financial stake and unbroken accountability to the money the company budgets, spends, and earns each year.
- Put the bulk of incentive pay, rather than some fraction of it, directly within executives' line of sight.
- Rebalance the system to favor business performance decisively over nar-rower individual interests.
- Make clear that performance gains always are worth pursuing, even if things are going much better or worse than planned.
- Create peer pressure, overcome bureaucratic inertia, and start up a real contest for performance.

How do your incentive policies stack up against these criteria? Would all of the mistakes you envisioned have been made, under these circumstances? And would your business success stories have been impeded by such a system?

Act Now

Most companies simply have not yet looked deeply enough at their incentive policies or considered the full range of available solutions. The situation is chang-ing, however. The proverbial *burning platform* is by now fully ablaze. Option expensing, now in place for a few years, has spurred companies to reverse their heavy reliance on stock options and to consider other alternatives. In the past, zero-expense treatment lead to near-100 percent market reliance on stock options with little serious thought to alternatives. There was a kind of morato-rium on thinking, where the bulk of public company incentive policy was concerned.

Now, everything is on the table. Option expensing has brought far heavier use of other kinds of long-term incentive pay, denominated in cash or shares and often based on attainment of preset performance goals. Long-term incentive design now is much more complex, with far higher stakes placed on matters like metrics, targets, ranges, and leverage. And, for most companies, there is no going back. Companies know they can get better retention, efficacy, and "line of sight" if they improve their mix of long-term incentives as well as the details of delivery. But they continue to face challenges and to make ongoing changes in their efforts to get it right.

Annual incentives have always been a big, big deal at most companies. Dollars promised in these plans tend to be watched very closely. They can drive management decision making very strongly in both positive and negative ways. Decision makers normally understand pretty well what they can do to affect bonus payouts, and payouts occur within a few months. Long-term incentive gains, in contrast, used to hinge on the distant and deferred matter of exercise-date stock prices. That apparently did not redirect executive thinking to the long-term in every case. For example, 78 percent of more than 400 executives interviewed said they had smoothed earnings *at the expense of value creation*.[5] This testifies to the pressures often concentrated on short-term performance.

Annual incentive pay targets climbed rapidly in recent years. The rise is due in part to demands of I.R.C. section 162(m) for explicitly performance-based pay. The higher size of awards—coupled with the new tax-compliance concerns about the goals themselves—has placed increased stakes on how performance targets are specified. And again, not just bonuses move around based on preset goals, but much of LTI pay as well.

Risk concerns are part of the new situation as well. In an earlier book, I predicted that "Risk is the next big thing."[6] That is out of date. Risk is the big thing *now*, when talking about incentives and decision making. Governance experts are weighing in much more heavily on how problems with risk and incentive pay might subvert the interests of shareholders. Government, too, has weighed in, in part with risk-related proxy disclosure rules from the SEC.

The executive pay commentariat is focused on much more than risk, of course. Later, we will review what the governance voices have to say about incentives at the top. We will find that most hold activist views on executive incentive policy. They differ in their details, certainly, and also in terms of how much meat they put on the bone. But, at a high level, many of them are setting out similar general preferences for incentive architecture. Some of their more unanimous preferences overlap with the key themes of this book—not to over-rely on exclusively stock-based LTI pay, to emphasize business goals heavily, and to focus on both the financial quantity and quality of business performance. This last item includes being sure that performance parameters are set properly, focused on the long-term, cognizant of risk effects, and pledged by senior executives with an ongoing commitment to stock ownership.

Overall, companies are operating in an era of new standards. The old ways will not do, but there are not any magic bullets. There are performance gains to be had through improving the efficacy of incentive pay. Companies have been in hot pursuit for years, particularly since the onset of option expensing. You should expect your competitors to pursue those advantages and to use them against you, not only in labor markets but in markets for commerce and capital.

Standards continue to ratchet up in a macro sense, as well. In highly competitive global markets, human capital is decisive, since it is one of the few remaining sources of competitive edge. To an increasing extent, it is the whole game. More and more companies are saying things like, "Our assets walk out the door at the end of the day." This once was a human resource platitude. It is now a genuine business reality just about everywhere. And it is never truer than at the senior management level, where very disproportionate decision-making power resides. Companies should be using the explicit terms of incentives at top levels of the organization to encourage high performance.

YOU DO NOT RUN YOUR COMPANY

The people in your senior management team make the bulk of business decisions on the part of shareholders. Together they hold much more information than you about the truest, best sources of business advantage and gain within your company. They are in a position to decide which ideas get advanced to you and which do not. Their scope of authority means they take many actions without needing to consult you at all. In many other matters, you properly defer to them based on their expertise. They decide which business initiatives are executed faithfully and which are not.

You do not always know what they are thinking. They do not always do what you say. *Liar's Poker* author Michael Lewis provided a lively example after his 2008 conversation with John Gutfreund, former CEO of Solomon Brothers:

> We agreed that the Wall Street CEO had no real ability to keep track of the frantic innovation occurring inside his firm. ("I didn't understand all the product lines, and they don't either," he said.) We agreed, further, that the chief of the Wall Street investment bank had little control over his subordinates. ("They're buttering you up and then doing whatever the f---they want to do.")[7]

Things are not this extreme in your business, no doubt, but your senior managers as a group may well have greater effective decision rights than you. And your position vis-à-vis them is replicated in their own ties to successive tiers of subordinates, in a process cascading throughout the enterprise.

Incentives are present at every level in that cascading process. To an extent that may or may not surprise you, your company is run by its system of incentives. An example, albeit again extreme, involves the CEO of AIG, Robert Benmosche, and the treasury's "pay czar," Kenneth Feinberg. It shows in unusually frank terms that setting pay for one's subordinates is one of the more important powers of the CEO:

> "Benmosche understood that he had lost control. 'It's Feinberg's company. That's what he learned,' one director in the board meeting later told me. 'We all thought there was an ability to run this company. We were wrong.'"[8]

In this example, losing control over executive pay was seen as losing the ability to run the company. Your company may not be at all like AIG, but executive pay no doubt has important effects on who gets into your senior management team, how long they stay, and what they do while they are there. Incentive pay is the centerpiece of your system of executive rewards.

Incentives, of course, are not the only driver of management performance at companies. There are many. Here is a big one—figuring out how to find, develop, and hang onto the best people. To do this, the simple *amount* of incentive pay offered can be more important than the particulars of its design. Nonetheless, problems with the structure of incentives and its effects on decision making are ones that arise frequently, have significant effects, and merit our attention.

The New Standards

I am not quite as old as Hammurabi, but I can recall a quaint era when the term *unprincipled* was an insult. A problem with executive pay is that it often appears unprincipled. Incentive policy at companies often does not follow a consistent, coherent philosophy. We strive to help remedy that problem in this book. In the early part, we examine a range of perspectives that can inform incentive policy:

- Basic principles of finance and valuation—the links from decisions to business results to value creation

- Evident aspects of how decision rights are held in the organization and how financial incentives can affect motivation and decision making

- Fundamental guidance offered by standard setters in the marketplace (e.g., the National Association of Corporate Directors [NACD], shareholder activists)

We then compile them into a set of principles and methods that can be used to set incentive policy for senior management and to design incentive plans. These are basic facts of business governance, performance measurement, and valuation that should shape incentive pay at the senior management level. They are derived and set out in the next three chapters. Here are some of the most salient points:

- Management's job is to run the enterprise in such a way as to maximize the wealth of shareholders.[9] Incentive plans must support this goal by creating a high degree of line of sight from actions to results to rewards. The stakes are high in terms of cost and business impact. They demand that incentives be specific and proactive, encouraging business decisions that create value and discouraging those that do not. Vague and distant incentives waste shareholder money.

- The structure of incentives, like the structure of investor interests, should be unlimited, long-term, concrete, and continuous. It should take account of the capital market criteria and performance expectations that determine the valuation of a business initiative and its results.

- Three basic financial variables describe the value of a business enterprise: long-run operating income, capital usage, and the risk-adjusted cost of capital. For a current or prospective business event to have an impact on the stock price, it must pass through one or more of these doors. These drivers must be represented in proper proportion in incentive pay.

- Pay outcomes should reflect sustained financial results and how those results drive value creation. Executives should have significant, persistent exposure to company performance and share price across a wide range of outcomes.

- Companies must make sure executives, whether found at the corporate level or in business units, have a decisive stake in the business activities they lead. Achieving this kind of "line of sight" includes focusing more on results of operations and less on nonoperational matters like capital structure and share repurchases.

- Incentive plans should be kept clear and simple, creating a direct, enduring stake in value creation that needs limited adjustment or revision over time.

- Executive incentive policy should be deployed as an active instrument of business governance.

These principles are straightforward and obvious. They jump out rather quickly when you link incentive policy with performance and valuation. At the same time, they demand big changes to correct problems with the incentive structures used in the marketplace now:

- Bonus plans whose targets are based on annual, one-off episodes of internally focused study and negotiation, with accountability for pivotal decisions written in disappearing ink

- Payout schedules that enable value destruction, are skewed by financing decisions, and reflect inadequate forethought about how to deal with events like acquisitions, one-time gains, or big variances from target

- Long-term incentives that create low levels of line of sight, engagement, and efficacy along with high levels of economic cost

- An overall structure based almost entirely on corporate-level performance, oriented heavily toward the short term, and constantly being renegotiated, adjusted, or redesigned

Incentives aren't stage props meant for a run of a few months. They shouldn't need constant rework. They should anticipate a range of pressures and events rather than constantly reacting to them.

And incentive principles do not have to be turned upside down in response to the shrillest of critics. Companies should not get rid of annual bonus plans nor make people wait for years to get payouts. Having a long-term pay structure does not mean glacial rates of vesting. Commitment does not require jitter-inducing stock-sale restrictions. Applying proper performance standards does not mean disqualifying most contenders. And lasting accountability does not require a standing threat of capricious pauperization.

Companies can take the overall incentive structure and orient it toward longer-term performance using any of a range of reasonable tools and tactics. Incentives should reflect the enduring connections between business decisions, results, and value. Those rules are never repealed. And incentives work better when the ground rules are stable and well understood. This book will set out a range of specific actions and techniques that many companies ought to pursue. Here is an overview of some of the key recommendations:

- *Feature goal-based pay more heavily in the long-term incentive structure.* Goal-based long-term incentives—with proper standards and metrics—can concentrate payouts on actions that create real long-run value from operations. Stock performance drives most of long-term incentive pay today, via gains from stock options and other stock-denominated grants. However, stock-based incentives create a very weak agency structure for most decision makers in the company. Only the CEO and a short list of others at the very top have a strong impact on the stock price. Stock and option grants create very limited line of sight for almost all who receive them. And options gains occur mainly after the four- or five-year mark—well beyond their freshness date.

Although it is appropriate for the broader senior management group to have a significant portion of their long-term incentives tied to the performance of company stock, basing some of everyone's pay on proper goals is also important. *Stock and option grants do not come with instructions* on how to create value. Properly specified goals, in contrast, can act as instructions on which decisions create value over time and which do not. An apparatus of long-term goals, tied over time to cash, shares, or both, is one of the best opportunities a company has to address some pivotal matters in incentive efficacy—line of sight, targeting, accountability, and controls on decision bias and risk.

- *Pushing long-term financial stakes to the business-unit level, where appropriate.* Basing long-term incentive pay on unit results, with payouts in cash or corporate shares, can increase line of sight enormously for executives below the top tier. Bonuses are the only aspect of pay that creates much line of sight for many executives, since few people can affect the stock price and, thus, influence their LTI gains under stock-based programs. This is particularly true at the business-unit level, where large parts of the company's value, executive workforce, and consequential decision making are found. And, at this level, corporate-level control and knowledge are most distant and diffuse, so the stakes placed on governance and agency arrangements arguably are highest.

- *Upgrading bonus plan design.* Bonus plans are often flawed as agency arrangements. Metrics and award schedules often permit bad decisions to be rewarded. Budget-based targets encourage decision makers to manage goals and results into a modest, narrow range. A very short-term orientation can discourage many of the longer-focused decisions that weigh heavily in value creation. Bonus plans can use metrics and payout schedules that better align with economic success, ensuring that pay is awarded for real performance and that pay costs are not incurred for failure. And they can do this without resorting to unfamiliar metrics or strange incentive plan formats.

- *Escaping the budget trap.* Common approaches to incentive target-setting can bias and thwart the intended effects of key governance processes— budgeting, planning, acquisition review, and capital budgeting. To address this pitfall, companies should make better use of external standards. They can consult peer and analyst data, shareholder expectations, and value-based frameworks to calibrate goals and payouts. These approaches to target-setting can supplement or replace existing methods, improving agency effects in both annual- and long-term incentive plans at the corporate and business unit levels. Companies do not have to rely entirely on centralized governance and control. Incentives can be quite helpful by encouraging more effective, truer planning and enhanced long-run results.

- *Better bang for the buck*. Incentive plan participants often see their stock-based incentives and much of their bonus as matters over which they have little influence. This risks heavy discounting of incentive opportunity. The solution is to re-center pay on compelling and achievable goals and pay them out in cash and whole shares. This can help convert what is often a costly results-sharing apparatus into a proactive governance tool.

- *Keeping costs in line with competitive norms and proper standards*. Executive incentives represent a large cost for many companies. Proper benchmarking of pay—and proper standard-setting—can help ensure that the money is earned and funded in economic terms. Plan calibration and scenario testing can help ensure that this is the case, not just at the targeted award level but in the many other scenarios that may emerge over time.

Although the movement for improved corporate governance continues to gain ground rapidly, let us not forget what really governs much of business decision making much of the time, in many parts of the business—management incentive plans. These agency arrangements can have a very strong impact on business success.

It Is Not about You

When turning incentives into proactive governance tools, the changes to incentive structure for the CEO may be the least consequential ones. In the pay package for the top few corporate officers:

- The long-term incentive component is very large within the pay mix and will remain that way.

- Stock-based pay in one form or another will continue to make up the bulk of top officer long-term incentive granting in public companies.

- Trailing, unvested grants of options and stock, coupled with mandated stock holdings, will continue to give top officers a very high level of exposure to the stock price.

The very top officers *can* affect the stock price over time, and they have huge equity stakes. This means they have a huge stake in high-quality financial results, so their incentives will work in a directionally correct way over time. What the incentive structure says to them, basically, is to do everything they can to maximize value and returns over a sustained period of time. The stock price isn't persistently wrong, after all, as an arbiter of a company's results and outlook. It is hard to read and hard for most people to affect, and sometimes it makes you wait until your performance story is proven. But top officers can affect it more than other executives can. And they can be asked to wait for gains to pile up.

The stock price game can be a tough one, to be sure. A company may offer really superb products and services, sell them at good prices and margins, and beat tough rivals for market share. They may run the most efficient operations in their industries or grow to be the dominant player in each of them. They may beat all their peers in the race for earnings growth. None of these things assures high stock market performance. Why? These business scenarios may not create value for shareholders. The longer-term income outlook, capital requirements, or risks of any of these scenarios may be unprofitable in an economic sense. Also, shareholders may have expected more. The price of their stock is based on the hopes investors hold about future performance. To them, current disappointments may portend bad news that plays out over the longer term.

You may already be a winner. Your company may have won this game every year for years, reaching the top deciles of stock performance rankings. Unfortunately, future stock performance is subject to the same caveat as an investment manager's—past returns are not a guarantee of future results. If a company has had outsized expansion in its stock price, it surely implies outsized expectations for future business results. You have to beat those to regain the pole position.

The stock market ratchets up performance expectations a bit like a golf handicap, but it adjusts more quickly and cannot be fudged for long. Overall, stock markets are efficient, updating expectations and prices so thoroughly that the pattern of future stock price movements is predicted best as a statistical *random walk* rather than any function of past business results.[10] The constant demand of such markets is not merely "what have you done for me lately" but "what will you do for me next?" At the same time, it is quite possible to generate above-market returns with little or no growth in enterprise size or income, depending on the shape of investor expectations and the charges they assess for the risks and capital involved.

One thing is certain, though. All of the strategies, prospects, and results of the business will be distilled by the cruel, reductive math of business valuation into the stock price. And that determines how you get paid. You get paid mainly with stock-denominated grants, and then you are asked to hold large blocks of those shares indefinitely.

So, for those at the top of the pyramid, share price movement has dominant incentive effects. It may not be comfortable to sit atop a pyramid, but the view up there does make certain matters clear enough. The performance standards could be made clearer, though. The view of how to achieve high shareholder returns is often a bit cloudy. And the need for clarity becomes even more compelling as you move farther and farther down the pyramid.

You should not see the system of senior management rewards as the system that pays you. The stock market, for the most part, makes the big decisions about your pay. You should see rewards policy as a business governance tool that you possess. Working with your board, you can use rewards policy to drive better performance and increase the stock price. You should be focusing on the decision rights and performance rewards of the broader senior management group—those dozens or hundreds of top managers who are out making consequential decisions all the time. You can use incentive policy to encourage the best decision making throughout management and at the many places and times where shareholder wealth is at stake.

Incentive effects for the balance of senior management are not like yours. Theirs may or may not align with shareholders. Sure, their equity stakes might encourage them to take decisions that might bring about a little share price bump at some point, if they believe in that sort of thing. However, the message they may be hearing is that they are better off avoiding risk and managing their expectations and results. That, after all, may be how they keep their high-paying jobs and keep themselves in the hunt for bigger ones.

LAST THINGS FIRST

So, how do you get started on solutions? The best incentive design process for top officers is to ignore their incentives during the bulk of the design process. Instead, I recommend focusing on the balance of senior management. Companies should design the system of incentives up to the much higher standards of efficacy and line of sight needed to work well across the broader, more dispersed senior management group.

Along the way, they will have done most of the design work needed for top officers. Once you reach this point, you will probably decide that the top few officers should be paid using the same general set of instruments and premises that applies in the broader senior management group. You may do this for reasons of alignment, but you may also find by then that you have the right system for your company and that it obviously should apply at the very top. At that point, top officer pay is a matter that can be extrapolated up a step or two from the balance of senior management. It might be distinguished by a higher exposure to stock performance and complete focus on corporate results rather than those of business units.

This approach is backward, in relation to the usual process. The usual process focuses far too much on the top few officers and particularly upon the CEO. One of the reasons we have such a heavily stock-centered system now is because it *is* sensible to use stock as the core of the pay structure for the very top officers. Extending that prescription much deeper into the ranks is a mistake, but it is one easily made if you're only paying close attention to the top of the house. Making the system work for the broader senior management group—a group that is, again, pivotally important, yet subject to a highly ineffective incentive system— is the much bigger deal.

Proper incentives broaden and energize the stakeholder group for any materially sized business initiative. This may affect how the whole business is run and change how you approach your job as CEO. You'll be using incentives to ask your key decision makers to put their money where their mouth is. You'll be using incentives—and their effects on the many aspects of the decision-making process that you cannot read or direct—as a supplement to your own business judgment, persuasive powers, and authority.

And let us remember that the big business decisions all bear your *imprimatur*. If you put in place an incentive system meant to engage the senior management workforce more strongly, that means the matters they will be minding more actively are, to a certain extent, yours. You will be inviting a broad group of senior managers to get involved in some productive way and to express what they know when the big decisions are being made, rather than waiting to second-guess the results in private.

These policy changes do not change your decision rights or anyone else's. They do recognize the decision rights already in place at the company and the asymmetric information flows that surround them. Better incentives may change your dialogue with the senior management group. You will be dealing with co-investors rather than functionaries. This will encourage good information to come to the forefront as big choices are being made by the company, potentially improving the process of business decision making and many of its outcomes. And, once a decision is made, these changes encourage everyone to get on board and get it executed.

BOTTOM LINES

Money helps all this to happen, and this is the way to use it. Companies should use senior management incentives purposefully; to help them prosper. Instead, this tool often is left in the shed. This book is about how to employ the company's structure of incentives in an active way to get better business decisions and better results from senior management. This is the best way to use incentives—to encourage high business performance proactively rather than acknowledging it in a distanced and vague manner after the fact.

It is not easy to get better performance out of a business. The virtue of this performance initiative is that it does not involve turning the whole business upside down. Rather, it concerns a limited group of people over whom you hold much sway. It does not depend on actions of your competitors or on market conditions you cannot affect. Rather, it is about getting better economic yield from business opportunities under all market conditions. It is comparatively easy. Getting it done is completely within your control. And it cannot really happen without you.

Incentive policy is important to business success. It also is important in a broader sense. Actions of those at the top of enterprise affect resource allocation in the economy. Ultimately, the material wealth of a nation relies on a few intangibles. These are things like the industriousness of its people, the degree of freedom individuals have in commerce, and the general trust and confidence they hold in markets and laws. Among these key intangibles is a properly functioning system of rewards for top management. The system should use the self-interest of executives as a way to get the best performance for owners. A proper system of management rewards is one of the drivers of the wealth of nations.

NOTES

1. Consulting firm Strategic Decisions Group coined the saying, "Management is in the decision business."
2. thecorporatelibrary.com
3. Robert A.G. Monks and Neil Minow, *Corporate Governance*, 3rd ed. (Hoboken, NJ: John Wiley & Sons, 2002).
4. Text cited from exhibit placard, "Beyond Babylon: Art, Trade and Diplomacy: the Second Millenium B.C." Metropolitan Museum of Art, New York, November 18, 2008—March 15, 2009.
5. David Bogoslaw, "Shareholder Value: Time for a Longer View?" *BusinessWeek,* (March 17, 2009).
6. Richard N. Ericson, *Pay to Prosper* (Scottsdale, AZ: World at Work, 2004).
7. Michael Lewis, "The End," Portfolio.com, November 11, 2008.
8. Gabriel Sherman, "An Inside Look at the Tug-of-War Over Pay at AIG," *New York Magazine,* November 2009.
9. This is a general tenet of the area of economics called *agency theory.*
10. For descriptions of the statistical behavior of equity prices, see Nobel Prize winner Eugene Fama's book, *Foundations of Finance* (New York: Basic Books, 1976), as well as Burton G. Malkiel's *A Random Walk Down Wall Street* (New York: W. W. Norton & Company, 1981).

CHAPTER 2

Business Valuation and Incentive Policy

There are some common conflicts between management decision making and shareholder value creation:

- For many reasons, both business and personal, managers tend to avoid risk. And, in some cases, they gamble too freely with shareholder fortunes.

- Managers tend to focus on short-term results.

- In many settings, they do not pay much attention to how much of other people's money is being used in their business.

These shortcomings have unfavorable effects in some important areas: how risk is balanced against return, how short- and long-run results of operations figure into value creation, and how capital usage affects economic performance. These three matters are, in fact, the three first-line drivers of value. That is, if you have a good sense of these three aspects of a business's prospects, you have enough information to figure out things like what the business is worth and whether a particular decision is likely to add value. Unfortunately, all three criteria can be distorted by the systems that companies use to track business performance and reward their biggest-ticket decision makers.

This chapter opens a broad discussion about how to align incentives with the specifics of value creation. We will look at a commonly used and powerful valuation method, one that will allow us to evaluate in economic terms how management ordinarily gets paid in the marketplace. It can also be used to show instances in which incentive payouts can go in one direction while shareholder value is headed in the other. Linking results and value is important when considering what principles ought to guide incentive policy. So are matters like the following:

- The general effects incentives can have on executive behavior
- Senior management's span of control, individually and within teams
- The agency role of management, and their general charge in the governance structure

We will look closely at all of these things. Our first step will be to derive some insights about business results and value. Then, we will review the rudiments of business governance and how management's scope of authority ought to affect incentive choices. We will take a close look at market norms for incentive pay. Along the way, we will see how governance and executive pay watchdogs are creating a new environment of more exacting standards. By Chapter 4, we will combine our findings into a set of flexible, broadly adaptable guidelines for incentive policy. The rest of the book then shows how to design and implement suitable incentives.

THE ROSETTA STONE

People in senior management are in the "decision" business. Their decisions drive the company's business results and its market value. So, the financial linkages between results and value provide some rather close direction for incentive design. We will look particularly closely at those valuation linkages right up front, then make direct and intensive use of them throughout this book. Our process starts with basic findings in corporate finance and valuation. It ends with specific techniques used in the design and calibration of pay structures, applying our basic findings at every step along the way. Specifically, we will use these techniques to do the following:

- Demonstrate how capital markets, public or private, translate business performance into current valuations and how a range of events may affect value.
- Translate financial results into going-forward estimates of investor return—the valuation gains and cash returns from operations that drive stock price changes, dividends, and gains on stock-based incentives.
- Evaluate market practices in the area of incentive design, specifying what it is that companies are in the habit of paying for in an economic sense.
- Evaluate financial, nonfinancial, and value-based performance metrics, noting their pros and cons and overall efficacy.
- Set up and calibrate specific payout schedules for goal-based incentive plans.
- Specify valuation formulas for phantom stock plans.

- Set specific targets and ranges for financial performance of a company and its business units.
- Examine how new initiatives, investments, or business plans may affect value, establishing how each may affect management incentive pay at the margin.
- Benchmark performance against peer norms (or among business units, or over time) in an economically complete and consistent way.
- Evaluate earnings quality from a value-creation perspective.
- Assess the proper time frame for measurement of performance and distribution of rewards—the *term structure* of incentive pay.
- Compile a set of adaptable standards to be used in making decisions about the design of the executive incentive structure.

That sounds like a lot of complicated stuff to keep straight. Keep this in mind—we have already listed the three moving parts of value creation—income, capital usage, and risk. Each of the techniques we will review in this book can be described by those three drivers. If you know them and you have a sense of how they work together to affect valuation and investor returns—and you will, shortly—you can apply them to the full range of design and calibration methods used here. For example:

- Performance comparisons against peers can be made more consistent and more conclusive if they go beyond income growth and take some account of comparative levels of capital usage and risk.
- Financial metrics can be tested by analyzing cases in which their outcomes differ from what the three value drivers would indicate. This can help in the tasks of choosing metrics, combining them into payout schedules, and administering them in an incentive context.

The three basic valuation linkages together form a key to the Rosetta Stone of executive incentive policy. This key can be used to address many of the complex, high-stakes matters involved when striving to get executive incentives properly aligned.

STEALING THE PLAYBOOK OF BUSINESS VALUATION

Step one is linking results and value. As it turns out, we are rather fortunate in this endeavor. There is a well-developed field of inquiry within financial economics dedicated to this exact issue. It is called *business valuation*. Business valuation—in particular, the financial models used in this area—is about how to convert a given set of future business results into an estimate of shareholder value. The subject is worth a look, as we will find the very simplest prescriptions of business valuation can be used to overcome the problems common in incentive plans at many companies today.[1] This chapter looks at a basic, but broadly applicable and powerful valuation model called the discounted cash flow (DCF) model. It has a lot to say about the specific financial underpinnings of valuation and executive incentives, so we will mine it thoroughly for those insights.

DCF analysis is not the only method that can be used to value a business. Later on, we demonstrate that it provides results consistent with other valuation methods so it stands as a proxy for them. We focus on the DCF model because it allows us to make direct inferences about results, value, and investor returns that are particularly suited to our purposes.

To keep the exposition straightforward, we have adopted basic concepts and methods in valuation and corporate finance mostly as "givens." Despite many areas of ongoing debate in this field, its basic premises are widely accepted by companies. They already apply these methods in areas like investment evaluation, performance measurement, business planning, and financing. Our task concerns *how well* companies apply them, when their incentive systems are throwing off inconsistent signals much of the time. Problems with incentive plans number among the main reasons companies fail to exploit financial tools more effectively.[2]

We use a basic DCF model example based on the three value drivers cited earlier: operating income after taxes, capital usage, and the cost of capital (see Exhibit 2.1).

The DCF method is based on the idea that the value of a business equals the present value of the cash flows that it can distribute to its owners over time. These cash flows are called free cash flows (FCFs). They consist of the funds produced by the company's operations, less the reinvestment requirements of the business (i.e., the money the business needs to fund growth and to replace assets as they wear out).

What remains, net, is the cash flow available to satisfy the claims of all the investors in the business—the holders of its debt and equity. "Free," in the

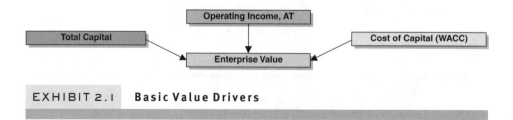

EXHIBIT 2.1   **Basic Value Drivers**

context of FCF, means freely available for distribution to investors. FCF is all that investors as a group get from the business over the long run, and its present value determines the value of all of the capital they have invested in the company.

DCF analysis consists of two general steps: making a forecast of FCFs for a very long period of time, then figuring out their present value. The FCF forecast timeline normally is divided into two parts:

1. *A specific forecast of company financial performance, including FCF, for a finite period of time, often ten years:* Strictly speaking, the company's present collection of competitive advantages—the business attributes that may enable it to earn above-market returns—are assumed to play out within the course of the forecast term.

2. *A residual valuation of the company, representing its value as of the end of the forecast term:* This means translating the company's ongoing earning capacity, measured at the end of the forecast term, into an estimate of its value at that date. In a ten-year DCF model, residual value is the value of all FCF expected in years 11 through infinity.

The DCF model determines the present value of all the FCFs expected during the forecast term. To this, it adds the present value of the residual value. The sum of these present values is equal to *enterprise value*—the value of all the debt and equity capital invested in the enterprise.[3] Exhibit 2.2 demonstrates the basic mechanics of DCF valuation in a three-year format.

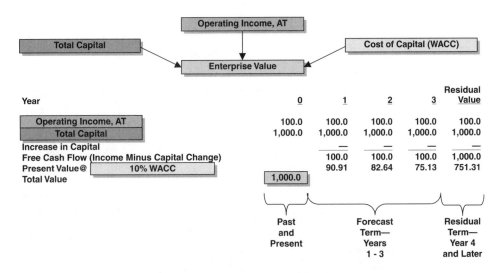

Year		0	1	2	3	Residual Value
Operating Income, AT		100.0	100.0	100.0	100.0	100.0
Total Capital		1,000.0	1,000.0	1,000.0	1,000.0	1,000.0
Increase in Capital			—	—	—	—
Free Cash Flow (Income Minus Capital Change)			100.0	100.0	100.0	1,000.0
Present Value @ 10% WACC			90.91	82.64	75.13	751.31
Total Value		1,000.0				

Past and Present — Forecast Term—Years 1 - 3 — Residual Term—Year 4 and Later

EXHIBIT 2.2   **Basic Value Drivers and Discounted Cash Flow Valuation**

Key concepts are summarized briefly:

- *Basic drivers.* This fundamental, abbreviated version of the DCF model reduces the model to the three first-line drivers of enterprise value and return: after-tax operating profit, capital usage, and the cost of capital. Profit and capital are specified for each period. Capital is the amount of debt and equity capital invested in net assets of the business. FCF is equal to after-tax operating profit minus the change in capital. The cost of capital is the discount rate used to convert projected FCFs to present value.

- *Free cash flow.* The forecast does not involve any new capital needs; rather, capital used in the business remains fixed at $1,000. FCF is equal to $100 each year, or $100 in income minus $0 in new capital requirements.

- *Time segments of forecast.* The simple example just given has a three-year forecast term, so FCFs are forecast for each of three years. The residual value in this case represents the value, as of the beginning of Year 4, of all the cash flows expected in Year 4 and all later years.

- *Cost of capital.* The cost of capital for this company is 10 percent. This means that this company needs to provide overall rates of return to investors equal to 10 percent in order to compensate them fairly for the risks they bear by having their capital tied up in this business. This rate is meant to reflect prevailing returns on similar investments in capital markets. Higher risk would increase the cost of capital and reduce value. Lower risk would reduce the cost of capital and increase value.

- *FCF forecast.* FCF for the first year is equal to $100. The basic model assumes that each year's FCF is received on the last day of the year. To determine the present value of the first year's FCF—its value as of the beginning of the forecast period—we must discount it for one year. Its present value is computed as $100/(1 + 10 percent), or $90.91. The $100 FCFs expected at the end of each of Years 2 and 3 are discounted for two and three full years, respectively.[4]

- *Residual value.* This is the value of the FCFs expected in years 4 through infinity. It is determined in a two-step process. This DCF model assumes that FCFs remain at $100 per year, basically forever (or, that the company's performance scenario involves no additional value creation beyond Year 3—the valuation equivalent of this "zero-growth perpetuity.") Either way, valuation at this date is a matter of converting the company's ongoing earning power into an estimate of value.

  The value of a perpetual stream of free cash flows is equal to the annual amount ($100) divided by the cost of capital (10 percent), or $1,000 in this case. This value, which is stated as of the end of Year 3, is further discounted at 10 percent for three years to convert it into year-zero present value terms at $751.31.

The result of these computations is the present value of all the FCF expected to be generated by the business over a very long period of time: $1,000, consisting of $248.69 of forecast term FCF and $751.31 of residual value. If the company had total interest-bearing debt of $400, then the value of equity would be equal to $600. If equity consisted only of 60 outstanding common shares, the common shares would be worth $10 each.

INCENTIVES AND VALUE CREATION

We can use the DCF model to provide a preview of what is good and bad about typical management incentive plans and how, specifically, to fix them. Consider this example:

- Management makes an investment of $100 in the business in forecast Year 1. This move by itself reduces the value of the business by $100—undiscounted, since it occurs right at the outset of Year 1 (it is presented at the end of base year 0).

- The investment yields operating profit after taxes of $10 at the end of Year 1 and every subsequent year. There are no additional capital requirements since noncash depreciation charges are sufficient to fund asset replacement over time, and zero growth means no new net working capital needs. So, the annual NOPAT gain brings a $10 gain in annual FCF. This is a perpetuity, like the "residual value" we computed a moment ago. It is worth $100 in present value terms ($10 divided by 10 percent).

The $100 valuation gain from the investment is offset exactly by the valuation reduction of $100 due to its cost. So, we know this decision has no effect on value. Exhibit 2.3 is the earlier DCF model, updated to reflect this decision. The company's valuation is unchanged at $1,000.

Year	0	1	2	3	Residual Value
Operating Income, AT	100.0	110.0	110.0	110.0	110.0
Total Capital	1,000.0	1,000.0	1,000.0	1,000.0	1,000.0
Increase in Capital	100.0	—	—	—	—
Free Cash Flow (Income Minus Capital Change)	(100.0)	110.0	110.0	110.0	1,100.0
Present Value@ 10% WACC	(100.0)	100.0	90.9	82.6	826.4
Total Value	1,000.0				

EXHIBIT 2.3   Valuation Effects of an Investment Scenario

Will this decision increase management's bonus for the year? It should not, certainly. But will it? At this point, we do not know. And we cannot assume much, either. Sadly, there is no assurance that the parameters used in a typical company's bonus plans (or long-term performance plans, for that matter) have been set with enough attention to how financial results might drive value creation. Here are some things that could happen, though:

- If the plan were based mostly on operating income, this literally worthless decision probably would boost bonus payouts.

- Whether it increases net income could depend on how it is financed. Equity financing carries no ongoing book expense, so effects on operating income would flow through net income and payouts would rise. After-tax borrowing costs normally are below the 10 percent after-tax investment yield, so net income would rise and so would payouts in a debt scenario.

- If payouts are based mainly on a metric like return on invested capital (ROIC) or return on equity (ROE), we do not know what will happen. If ROIC for the year were on course to come in below 10 percent, then the 10 percent yield on this deal would be ROIC-accretive and bonus payouts likely would rise. If ROIC were coming in at 20 percent for the year, then adding this investment would reduce payouts. The investment itself adds zero value in every case, so we can say the metric ROIC will not by itself connect payouts with value conclusively.

- Some plans use operating income and ROIC together as metrics, hoping to balance the growth-versus-return effects. However, unless such plans are set up deliberately to align payouts with value creation at the margin—and few are—then they risk distortions as well. Such plans have the positive effect of applying implicit ROIC hurdles rates to investment decision making, simply because payouts are affected by joint changes in income and capital. But ROIC hurdles can be troublesome, as we saw earlier. Moreover, in this particular kind of plan they often are inadvertent byproducts of other design decisions, ones often having very inconsistent impacts. As implicit results of the payout schedule, they are often hidden from view. This is probably just as well, until the plan design is upgraded.

- What if the plan is based on earnings per share (EPS) or return on equity? Payouts can be warped, just as in the earlier examples. ROE might rise as well, presuming it was not unusually high, pre-investment. ROE or EPS might rise or fall if the investment were financed with equity, depending on effects on things such as share issuances and interest income. The problem here, again, is that the investment does not create value. Under a strict value creation standard, it should not increase payouts. Matters like whether the company happens to use debt, and whether ROE was high before the deal, are mostly irrelevant when judging economic performance at the margin. But they can be highly consequential in terms of management payouts.

- How about incentives driven by cash flow? If defined gross of capital additions, as pretax operating cash flow metrics are, payouts probably would rise. If stated net of all capital additions, like FCF, payouts probably would fall since FCF is negative. If based on any of the definitions from the funds flow statement, or if used in combination with other metrics, it would depend on a mixed bag of situational factors.

And, in every case, the setting of targets and ranges affects whether anyone gets paid. A perfectly good investment might pay nothing if it causes income to bust the top end of the performance range. It might make it harder to get paid next year if it raises going-forward income targets. And even a miserable investment might bring in enough income to cross the payout threshold in an income-driven incentive plan, very often causing pay to rise from 0 to 50 percent of target. Payouts could also be affected, variously, by the extent to which the investment was contemplated when the year's targets were set.

What drives shareholder outcomes, in contrast? Exactly none of these factors. We already know everything we need to know about this investment. It creates no value. But, as it turns out, that fact tells us very little about how it might drive executive bonuses. We could have examined a value-destroying investment or a value-creating one, trying to affirm that we are paying management to create value. In those cases as well, we would have been stumped by the fact that bonus plans are chock full of terms that can cause value creation and management incentive payouts to diverge. So we certainly cannot presume that bonus plans consistently encourage executives to create value.

Will the decision cause higher payouts on long-term incentives? Again, we do not know. There are goal-based incentives such as performance shares, performance units (and some formula-based phantom stock plans). How this decision affects progress against the financial parameters in those plans is just as much of a crapshoot as in the bonus situation we just reviewed. It is, that is, unless things are set up in advance to track outlays with value-creating results.

How about stock-based incentive plans such as stock options and restricted stock, or share-based aspect of performance shares? Will it cause our investment to increase pay? The stock market works pretty well over time as an arbiter of the quality of financial results and what they are worth. As a rule, you would not expect the stock price to rise from this investment since it does not create value. The problem with stock-based pay, of course, is that few of the people receiving it have much impact on the stock price and many, in candor, profess little comprehension when it rises or falls. The stock price could, in fact, oscillate in a wide range at the time of this deal, for many reasons, making it difficult to discern whether the investment was seen as a positive.

Other holes in the pay administration process could cause pay to escalate in response to bad or indifferent deals like these. The company could start benchmarking itself against larger companies after it does a few such deals, garnering much higher pay packages without ever having increased the scale of shareholder returns.

We noted the stock price element of the incentive structure should reliably link management performance with shareholder returns over time. However, few people are close enough to the stock price for it to act as a real incentive. That means you have to set and administer business goals if you want to use incentives at any close range. And, to do that right, you need to line them up deliberately with value creation. As just seen, traditional metrics and design can lead to payouts that are all over the map. That just will not do. Stakeholders are insisting on new, higher standards for prudence and efficacy in these important matters.

VALUE IS A FUNCTION OF THE QUALITY AND QUANTITY OF EARNINGS

Many companies, analysts, and commentators cite earnings quality when evaluating business results. Governance commentators would like to see it reflected more thoroughly when paying management. So would many members of corporate compensation committees.

The trouble with "quality" as a yardstick is that it is in the eye of the beholder. A lot of other nonfinancial yardsticks can be subjective, too, and they can be troublesome and ill-fitting in a senior management pay context. Later chapters will cover those issues, examining pros and cons of a wide range of metrics. For now, let us go ahead and focus in on the important theme of earnings quality. We can evaluate it in terms of the three first-line drivers of value creation:

1. *Capital usage.* A dollar of earnings is worth more, all else equal, if it is more heavily distributable as free cash flow. So a high FCF ratio or high ROIC would be examples of earnings quality indicators.

2. *Risk.* All else equal, less-risky earnings are worth more. A dollar of earnings (all distributable as free cash flow) capitalized at the low-risk cost of capital of 8 percent is worth $12.50. The higher-risk 10 percent rate would attach a value of only $10.00. Companies are right to regard more stable, persistent earnings as being higher quality.

3. *After-tax operating profit.* A better-quality profile of forecast income carries a higher value. It is worth more, all else being equal, if it calls for steady growth in operational results. Persistence is valuable as well. A one-time, one-dollar income gain is worth a dollar. A permanent increase is worth $10, at a 10 percent cost of capital. And a dollar in EPS growth might not be worth anything if accompanied by zero gain in income from operations (e.g., if achieved through rising debt levels and aggressive share repurchases). Earnings gains from higher-growth sources tend to elevate the whole scale of the future earnings forecast. At the same time, a given amount of income is worth more in a present-value sense if it is expected to be received sooner.

Corporate income is not a "gift horse." You should go right ahead and look it in the mouth. And when you do, these three value drivers are what you should look for. Companies, for their part, cite a range of different factors when they describe earnings quality. Examples include:

- Brand-building activities leading to consumer preference and higher share and margins
- Thorough credit and underwriting procedures that result in fewer charge-offs and lower risk-adjusted capital needs
- Earnings gains from core operations rather than from one-time sources
- Astute high-risk trading activity resulting in gains that are large, albeit one-time, in relation to the capital placed at risk
- Operational gains that occurred while employee engagement was stable or rising

I have heard a lot of earnings quality metrics cited over the years. What I find is that just about all of them are like the previous examples—they affect one or more of the main value drivers favorably, on balance, and tend to do so within a reasonably near-term time frame. That creates value. So, a working definition of earnings quality is that it brings about higher investor returns. It also tends to create lots of intangible value—enterprise value in excess of the historical cost of net assets. That is an indicator of cumulative management success called *Tobin's Q*, one that has been used widely in economic research contexts. A variant called *Market Value Added* has appeared in corporate rankings in the business press.

Earlier, we looked at an example of an investment that increased earnings by $10—a 10 percent yield on the new capital involved—and we looked into whether it would have increased incentive pay. The valuation perspective can be used to judge earnings quality in such cases:

- What if the investment had been expected to produce yields for only five years, chewing up all the capital investment along the way so that none is returned to investors? In that case, the income has a present value of only $38 or so, indicating a loss of 62 percent on the $100 investment.

- What if the investment had big capital needs—requiring outlays of $100 more, at the end of the first five years? That is the same thing as a $100 investment with returns lasting only five years, as we just considered—a loss of 62 percent.

- The investment might have yielded 12 percent rather than 10 percent, making it look like a more genuine success. But, if the income gain had come from a particularly risky source then a higher cost of capital at, say, 15 percent might have been applicable. In that case, the income is worth $67 or so ($10/15 percent) rather than $100 in present value terms, and the investment posts a 33 percent economic loss.

Or the company could have had a growing earnings stream, lower risk, and a more favorable FCF profile, and in any of those cases it would have been worth more. Either way, incentives that are set up to track reasonably well over time with the first-line drivers of value creation will tend to recognize and reward real earnings quality. A key aspect of this is that such effects be assessed *over time*. Whether a particular decision adds value or not has to do not just with how the value drivers are aligned at the outset but how it is expected to perform over time.

COST OF CAPITAL AND EXPECTED RETURNS

We used a cost of capital of 10 percent in the earlier example—a simple, rounded figure normally connoting somewhat above-average enterprise risk in a large U.S. company. A company's cost of capital is driven by its risk level and by prevailing yields for investments with similar risk. In Chapter 5, we will look closely at how costs of capital are computed and other ways in which risk interacts with company incentive structures.

For now, we will review some specific implications that the cost of capital makes when judging business performance. One of the characteristics of the DCF model that is useful to incentive design is the way that it links the cost of capital with future performance. The DCF model can take a forecast of financial results and tell you what the future stock price is implied to be. That is helpful to know when calibrating incentive payouts.

If business results turn out as forecast (and capital market criteria and expectations do not change), the DCF model predicts total returns for investors at a level equal to the cost of capital. Consider the zero-growth example at the beginning of this chapter:

- The company's cost of capital is 10 percent. If performance goes as forecast, it will generate $100 in FCF that is paid out at the end of Year 1. The value of the company remains at $1,000 since, at that date, it is a zero-growth $100 perpetuity ($100 per year, valued in infinity at a 10 percent cost of capital, is equal to $100/10 percent, or $1,000).

- Total investor return (TIR) for a particular period of time consists of the FCFs received by investors, plus any increase in the value of the enterprise they own. Investors get $100 in FCF in this scenario. There is no increase in value, so their TIR is $100. The value at the beginning of Year 1 is $1,000, so TIR amounts to 10 percent, equal to the cost of capital.

If debt is $200 and interest costs are 6 percent after tax, then interest takes $12 out of the $100 in returns. The other $88 is a return to equity holders on the $800 in value they owned at the outset, so their return is 11 percent. The company's cost of capital of 10 percent typically is seen as a weighted average of the returns expected by debt and equity holders—the levels of return predicted, if things go as planned. In this case, 20 percent of the value of the business is debt with an after-tax cost of 6 percent, so debt has 1.2 percentage points of impact on the weighted-average cost of capital. The rate of expected return on equity is 11 percent, or 8.8 points of impact with a weighting of 80 percent. The overall weighted-average cost of capital is 10 percent (1.2 points plus 8.8 points).

The 11 percent return going to equity holders is their projected level of total shareholder return (TSR). TSR equals capital gains (valuation gains) plus dividends. That figure is also known as the cost of equity capital. If this stable, zero-growth company pays a 5 percent dividend and overall returns are 11 percent, then the other roughly 6 percent of TSR must be expected in the form of capital gains. Even though the company's ongoing enterprise value does not rise, gains in the stock price could come about from debt reduction, share repurchases, or from the company just accumulating more cash or other valuable non-core assets over time on behalf of shareholders.

These figures can be helpful when evaluating how the pay structure works. If this company issues stock options, it should predict that annual gains would occur in a range centering around 6 percent per year (the range is, of course, potentially very wide). If it issues restricted stock or performance share grants that allow dividends to accumulate or to be paid currently, forecasts of executive gains should center on 11 percent. The forecast for this company has zero income growth yet it can generate equity returns of 11 percent. If it did not pay a dividend, it would have 11 percent per year as the expected rate of option gains, too. Is that good or bad, for shareholders or management? At this point, we do not know. But we have so far shown that the DCF model allows us to link business decisions, business results, and value, so we can see how they flow through incentive plans.

Year	—	1	2	3	Residual Value
Operating Income	100	150	170	200	200
Total Capital	1,000	1,200	1,400	1,600	1,600
Increase in Capital		200	200	200	—
Free Cash Flow (Income Minus Capital Change)		(50)	(30)	—	2,000
WACC 10%					
Present Value as of End of Year:					
FCF for Remaining Forecast Term	(70)	(27)	—		
Residual Value	1,503	1,653	1,818	2,000	
Enterprise Value	1,432	1,626	1,818	2,000	
Valuation at Beginning of Year		1,432	1,626	1,818	
Value Gain		193	193	182	
Free Cash Flow		(50)	(30)	—	
Total Investor Return		143	163	182	
Return as a Percent of Beginning Value		10.0%	10.0%	10.0%	

EXHIBIT 2.4   Expected Performance and Total Investor Return

Our first example was a zero-growth one, but the same identities hold true under many different performance scenarios. See Exhibit 2.4 for an example of a company with growing income and capital levels.

The company is valued at the end of each year based on the present value of FCFs remaining in the forecast. This company's performance was equal to targeted levels. Other valuation conditions—later year's FCF forecasts and the cost of capital—remained the same:

- This company is worth $1,432 as of the beginning of Year 1 based on its forecast FCFs and residual value. Its valuation at the end of Year 1 is $1,626 so the increase in value during Year 1 is $193.

- Free cash flows are negative at $50.

- Total return is $143, or 10 percent of beginning value.

Again, if performance is at expected levels, investor returns are predicted to equal the cost of capital. Later years work out the same way, as FCFs are collected each year, and the present value discounting unwinds at the same pace. Equity and debt holders each get their share of these targeted returns.

As Long as We're at It

We can apply these DCF-based inferences to tasks and determinations required in incentive design:

- The performance/return linkage specified by the DCF model can be applied to the task of setting targets for company performance. Let us say, for example, that the earlier valuation at $1,432 is a market enterprise value (computed by taking the company's stock price, multiplying by the number of outstanding shares and adding any debt or preferred stock value). The forecast shown earlier is one that squares with the observed market value. It is an estimate of the future performance forecast that investors are using when valuing company shares, an estimate that can be used as a basis for setting incentive goals. This sort of analysis—looking at the stock price as a source of information about future performance expectancies—can be used to supplement or replace traditional budget-based target setting.

- The DCF model can also be used to define business scenarios in which TIR is higher or lower than targeted levels, or when shareholder returns or capital gains are higher or lower. This enables companies to specify not only performance targets, but performance ranges. A typical award schedule would link pay with TIR across a broad range of outcomes. If 2 percent income growth and 8 percent ROIC imply TIR of 0 percent, for example, that might be set as the incentive plan's threshold performance level.

  This approach—basing incentive payouts on the valuation implications of financial performance—is not an unusual or novel one. On the contrary, it is the basic arrangement underlying stock-based incentive plans already. Those plans deliver higher or lower gains over time, based on stock price movement, itself a function of expected business results. As we will see in Chapter 8, value-based target setting allows this basic connection between results and investor returns to be extended into goal-based incentive plans—ones that offer greater line of sight and efficacy than stock-based pay. This approach brings the best of both worlds. It conveys the high degree of line of sight and well-crafted performance metrics possible in an incentive plan based on operational results. And it reflects the expected performance levels, valuation criteria, and shareholder-focused outcomes featured by stock-based pay.

Capital market conditions are not constant, though we assumed they were when we were making inferences about how the stock price reacts to performance. Valuation criteria and expectations shift constantly. We have already seen how changes in the weighted average cost of capital can cause the company's stock price to go up and down. Long-run expectations for performance of the company and its sector might shift as well, affecting FCF forecasts for many more years than the three used in our simplified example.

Uncertainties will affect any forecasting method. Changes in the baseline are a normal part of any business planning process, whether the results happen to be used for incentive pay, capital allocation, financing, or anything else. There are many ways to address them within an incentive structure. One good technique is to take them into account when initiating new grants each year. If the cost of capital changes materially, for example, or if expectations for company results do, these factors can be taken into account when setting targets for future bonuses and long-term incentive grants.

WHAT ARE WE PAYING FOR?

In a field riddled with concerns about inappropriate payouts and a lack of principles and standards, this is not a trivial question. And we can begin to answer it now using valuation-based inferences about how results drive value. This lets us examine the normal economic delivery system for incentive pay and use this understanding to make proper choices.

Companies often say that their incentives are meant to reward value creation. Let us consider an example in which payouts have indeed been calibrated based on the quantity and quality of earnings, so they avoid the kinds of misspecifications and risks we have been citing. When incentives meet those high standards, do executive gains indeed halt when value creation is negative, accruing only when value creation is positive?

But first—what is value creation, exactly? That is, what is value creation, as opposed to some of the other yardsticks we have been throwing around, like valuation, or gains in value, or returns earned by shareholders or by investors as a group?

Here is a strict standard of value creation from a management performance standpoint—achieving business results in excess of applicable standards. Finding an unplanned new investment with returns in excess of the cost of capital is an example. Also, simply achieving profits in excess of expected levels creates value. Performance above standards warrants a higher-than-expected market valuation, so value-creating business results should be expected to drive stock returns that are higher than the cost of equity. This kind of performance also tends to cause a company's market value to exceed by far the amount of capital that has been invested in the company, evidenced by the Tobin's Q ratio we examined earlier.

Here is an example of value creation. The company we examined earlier makes a $100 investment that is expected to generate $15 in after-tax operating income in its first year and $20 in every subsequent year. The applicable performance standard is a cost of capital of 10 percent, so this investment beats that hurdle. And it is a better economic performance scenario than the one that investors had baked into the stock valuation. Exhibit 2.5 shows how we would predict it would affect financial results, valuation, and returns.

Year	0	1	2	3	Residual Value
Operating Income, AT, Base Case		150	170	200	
Total Capital, Base Case	1,000	1,200	1,400	1,600	
Operating Income, AT, With Investment		165	190	220	220
Total Capital with investment	1,000	1,300	1,500	1,700	1,700
Increase in Capital		300	200	200	—
Free Cash Flow (Income Minus Capital Change)		(135)	(10)	20	2,200
WACC 10%					
Present Value as of End of Year, With Investment:					
FCF for Remaining Forecast Term	(116)	7	18		
Residual Value	1,653	1,818	2,000	2,200	
Enterprise Value	1,537	1,826	2,018	2,200	
Valuation at Beginning of Year		1,537	1,826	2,018	
Value Gain		289	193	182	
Free Cash Flow		(135)	(10)	20	
Total Investor Return		154	183	202	
Return as a Percent of Beginning Value		10.0%	10.0%	10.0%	

EXHIBIT 2.5   Expected Performance and Total Investor Return with New Investment

The company was valued formerly at $1,432. Now it is worth $1,537, so the investment adds $105, or about 7 percent, to the value of the company. Do executives' incentive gains rise or fall? We should expect them to rise:

- Stock-denominated grants like restricted shares and performance shares pay for gains in stock price, and sometimes for dividends, too. To the extent the TSR levels involved are higher than the cost of capital, the company has posted "excess performance" and these grants are paying out for value creation. But, even without excess returns, they often permit at least modest gains. So stock grants encourage value creation directionally, simply because management's gains rise when TSR rises.

- Options work in a mostly similar way by paying for that subset of TSR that comes in the form of capital gains. So they encourage TSR and its role in value creation, directionally.

- How goal-based annual or long-term incentives pay out is a matter of how they are set up in terms of metrics, goals, and payout calibration. But even those explicitly correlated with value may permit participants to get into the black before returns outpace applicable standards.

So the stock-based elements of the incentive structure should be expected to show some gains for value creation. Goal-based arrangements might pay out at any level—most such plans were enacted without much testing of their economic basis. But, when results are high enough to support value creation in the strict sense, goal-based plans normally are paying out well.

Incentives do not, as a rule, ask for positive value creation before paying dollar one of participant gain. Stock is an investment security, like a bond. Its holders receive dividends and, if things work out, substantial capital gains over time. Getting average returns on a stock does not require unusual management performance, at levels exceeding a strict value creation threshold. It requires average performance—around the middle of the range of relevant standards and expectancies.

When stock-based incentive grants are issued, they can be regarded as *present values*. Later, at payment or exercise dates, they are denominated in *future value*—higher, over time, as financial results accumulate and are converted into investment yield. If companies issued bonds rather than stock as incentive devices, we would expect them to work the same way, delivering predicted yields over time. Stock returns were 11 percent per year, in an earlier example, without any value creation.

So, a *value creation* standard typically is not a *threshold* for incentive gains. Rather, a value creation rule is more readily applied to the *targeted* level of performance. A target tends to be a mid-range performance level having a roughly 50 percent chance of achievement. The average company can be expected to earn TSR at about the cost of capital for its shareholders over time. A typical company has around a 50 percent chance of posting TSR at or above the cost of capital. Over the past 20 years, for example, median TSR per year is in the 10 to 11 percent range for companies in the S&P 500; right around the range for the equity cost of capital (covered in Chapters 3 and 5). Middling TSR tends to mean moderate equity returns each year, bringing typical appreciation on stock options and other equity-based incentives.

The typical company also earns incremental ROIC that is not much higher than the normal range of overall costs of capital. And this average company, having little or no value creation in the precise sense, pays out at target for goal-based incentive plans. Incentive targets tend to be set at middling-to-stretch performance levels having, again, about a 50 percent chance of being met.

So value creation is not the tipping point for incentive funding. It would be easy to demand that it should be, though. At first blush, it seems like a pretty good threshold criterion for performance of a management team. Some companies have approached it that way, using performance standards like earning ROIC or TSR in excess of relevant peer-based or cost of capital standards:

- British companies have been asked for years to consider a kind of strict value creation standard—TSR or other metrics in relation to peer performance—to underpin their long-term incentive granting.[5]

- Companies adopting *value-based* metrics sometimes apply strict value creation demands within their incentive plans. They might pay only for positive readings in terms of economic value added, or for gains.

- Private equity investees sometimes trigger the highest gain levels on their equity-based incentive pay only after top-of-scale rates of return are achieved.

Most of the time, the more strict approach creates an unusually high chance of nonpayment that leads to uncompetitive rewards. That may force increases in grant sizes or other types of pay. Sometimes it creates the moral hazards of a pay system that pays out only for triples and homers (risk-taking, income manipulation).

What companies pay for, much more consistently, is not value creation but *investor return*. Gains on equity-based pay have an explicit connection to stock price, and they tend to start accruing at dollar one of stock price gain or TSR. Value creation, in an economically strict but common connotation, actually is not the prevailing standard. It is a valid capital market construct. But it is not a workable performance threshold for most companies, in their efforts to hire, retain and motivate the best. The more competitive tactic is to align payouts with the degree of return that a company's operations generate for investors.

The financial performance levels underpinning bonus pay can be calibrated to line up with positive investor return. The threshold can be set at a level indicating zero return, with targets around the cusp of value creation. If this arrangement results in incentive funding that creates a *sharing rate* of, say, 3 percent of investor returns, that same ratio can be used to establish the upside range.

Alternatively, leverage can be made higher or lower, or made to differ above or below target. We will get to that in Chapter 8. For now, let us agree that the task is to tighten up the linkages between incentive pay and value creation. We can do this without imposing payout jeopardy at a dysfunctional level.

At this point, we can go back to defining the term *value creation* loosely. After all, that is the approach that clears executive labor markets.

TOTAL BUSINESS RETURN

We just discussed what we are paying for, and found that, on a good day, the market-clearing standard is to pay management to generate returns earned for investors. To make incentive plans do that, we also need to address *when* we are recognizing such returns and paying for them. Valuation is anticipatory, as the DCF model clearly shows. It means to include in its present value computations all gains that are expected in the company's future fortunes.

So, do we need to be making forecasts of future performance all the time, to figure out what results to pay for? If we think the company is on track for high income growth three or four years from now, should we calculate its present value and cut a check to management now? We will not know what returns have been earned until several years down the road, and valuation at that time will pivot on expected performance for the far longer term. So, do we need to see how all of that works out for shareholders before we can pay anything? Under that approach, we would not pull out the checkbook until five or ten years down the road.

Neither is a good choice. Here are more practicable approaches for the overall incentive structure:

- *Let the stock market do some of the hard work.* Corporate long-term incentives are mostly denominated in shares, and share prices are highly anticipatory and heavily risk-discounted present values. You can rely on them to judge how management's performance has driven longer-term expectations and value. Phantom share plans in business units and private companies—ones based on market valuation—can be put to work in the same way when needed. The market valuation mechanism can be used to ensure that overall executive gains are held close enough in scale to shareholder gains. This prudent mechanism should be operating to at least some extent even for executives who do not affect the stock price much.

- *Pay as you go.* Set targets and payouts based on actual results and the value they warrant. A South American utility used a *warranted value* concept in its incentive plans alongside actual stock market performance as a way of placing some weight on the notion of value evidenced by performance and not just market value (which it felt was unrepresentative due to market illiquidity). Some companies have incentives that pay out, in effect, for calculated present values of forecast results. Phantom plans that are valued based on an internal process are an example. So, often, are incentive plans for large project sales. Those are special circumstance cases, though, and they have their own pros and cons. The near-unanimous choice in the marketplace, certainly, is to base incentive payouts on actual rather than forecast financial results.

- *Take one step at a time.* Goal-based incentive plans can be made to track well, over time, with investor returns. That is true for both annual incentives and those long-term incentives that are based on explicit financial metrics (performance units or shares, formula-based phantom stock). Goal setting tends to occur each year in these plans. That means the plan can be recalibrated each year, to the extent needed. This is the opportunity to introduce updated forecasts into the process, so that executives have a financial interest in relevant long-term results at all times.

So, we would like to pay based on actual results, which are historical. And we would like to pay based on valuation and how it drives investor returns, which are forward-looking. We will see lots of ways to do this later on, including several based on the idea of warranted value. These approaches involve value-based metrics. Value-based metrics can be used to take a set of actual financial results, estimate their impact on value creation, and assign the results to time periods for purposes of measurement and rewards.

This last feature is quite helpful when running an incentive structure for senior management. *Total business return* (TBR) is an example of a method that can be used in this area. It is a value-based metric that is especially similar to the DCF model. It takes the valuation gains and investor returns indicated by the DCF model and apportions them among years, on a forecast or actual basis.

In Exhibit 2.6 we consider a company whose income starts out at $100 as in earlier examples. This company makes a $250 investment in Year 2 that increases income by $50 per year. Absent the investment, the company would generate $100 in income and cash flow per year. It would have a present value of $1,000. The DCF model shows that the investment increases value to $1,248. This anticipated gain is accelerated into enterprise value at the outset.

TBR computations are shown at the bottom of the exhibit. TBR is equal to the gain in the value of the business each year, plus its FCF. TBR values the

Year	0	1	2	3	Residual
Forecast of Business Results:					
Operating Inc. After Tax	100	100	150	150	150
Capital	500	500	750	750	
Free Cash Flow		100	(100)	150	1,500
DCF-Based Computation of Valuation and Investor Returns:					
Present Value of FCF 10% *Cost of Capital*		91	(83)	113	1,127
Enterprise Value	1,248	1,273	1,500	1,500	
Investor Return (Value Gain Plus FCF)		125	127	150	
Inv. Return % of Beginning Value		10.0%	10.0%	10.0%	
TBR-Based Computations:					
Value of Capitalized Earnings	1,000	1,000	1,500	1,500	
Value Gain		—	500	—	
Free Cash Flow		100	(100)	150	
TBR, Annual		100	400	150	
TBR, Annual		10.0%	40.0%	10.0%	
Present Value of TBR:					
PV of Annual FCF and Resid. Value Gain		91	(83)	113	376
PV of Residual, at Beginning Income Level	751				
Total Present Value	1,248				

EXHIBIT 2.6   **TBR Example**

business as a fixed multiple of income each year—as a perpetuity, which is the technique our DCF model used when determining residual value. In this example in which the cost of capital is 10 percent, value is equal to ten times income (1/10 percent = 10). In the TBR approach, the $50 income gain in Year 2 cause a $500 increase in value, but not until the year when the actual results occur. In TBR-based incentive plans, management does not get credit for the value of financial performance gains until those gains are in the books.

This is a value-based approach to measurement, in the sense that it reflects the major drivers of value creation and reconciles in present value terms with the DCF model. Such metrics are examined in more detail in Chapter 7. We can use this approach in a range of ways to link goals and metrics with value creation and pay. TBR itself can be used as a performance metric in a goal-based plan or as a valuation formula in a phantom stock plan.

Also, payouts in plans using traditional metrics can be set in scale to TBR, thereby aligning the overall plan with value creation effects. That is, payouts for various performance levels, stated in common metrics such as ROIC and operating income growth, can be set based on their implications for TBR. Average ROIC in the earlier TBR scenario, for example, was 20 percent while operating income growth was 14 percent. If that TBR scenario was suitable for use as a target, then these ROIC and income growth equivalents could be used. A scenario with twice as much TBR could constitute the basis for a 200 percent payout. The forecast can be translated into other metrics as well. This approach will give credit to management for generating returns, paced by their achievement of the financial goals that drive them. So, management gets paid for value creation but is subject to a "show me the money" standard of proof.

THE DCF MODEL SERVES AS A PROXY FOR OTHER VALUATION METHODS

We have relied on one valuation method—the DCF model—to describe the general connection between business results and shareholder value. And we have started using it to compile a specific set of methods and mandates for executive incentive design. We should be sure this method is valid because we are putting a lot of weight on it.

For most companies, the total value of capital invested in the enterprise can be reconciled, using the DCF model, to reasonable assumptions about its future income, capital usage, and comparative investment risk. And if you want to figure out how stock prices will react to a range of business events, academic studies have found consistently that the best predictions are based on the discounted value of an event's projected FCF effects.[6] For our part, when we run simulations using our simple DCF model along with forecast norms like those set forth in this chapter, we get stock price behavior over time that approximates market norms.[7]

I have been using the DCF model in valuation and analytical contexts for nearly 30 years. My experience is that, when you find a big gap between what a reasonable DCF model says about the value of a business, and what the stock market says about it, something has got to give. Japanese equity values in the late 1980s provided a good example of what happens and so did technology share values in the late 1990s. In each case, financial analysts and commentators called into question DCF and other common, consistent valuation indicators. A crash followed each of these bubbles, just as in the South Sea bubble and Dutch tulip bulb crazes occurring hundreds of years before. The general rule is that valuations do not diverge very often from what a reasonable DCF model would indicate, and when they do, it is not for long. In case you want to trade on this basis, let me add John Maynard Keynes' proviso, "Markets can stay irrational for longer than you or I can stay solvent."

The financial crisis of 2008 had big effects on equity valuations but not anomalous ones. Instead, effects were mostly reconcilable to DCF parameters. When equity markets fell to levels around 50 percent of their year-earlier peaks, it did not mean that market believed that all expected future corporate performance had been halved. Capital markets were suddenly made cognizant of a heightened scale of financial market risks and their frightening systemic nature. They demanded higher risk premiums for investments in risky securities of all types, and equities were not exempt. The drop in stock prices was a combination of contraction in the performance outlook and heavier discounting of all hopes about future performance. Prices were not necessarily irreconcilable. Rather, they appeared to be adjusting to continual changes in a very uncertain outlook.

It is true that many acquisition prices are hard to explain using a traditional DCF model. However, acquisitions often are overpriced in relation to realistic performance expectations. The synergies driving many high deal prices appear particularly elusive. Business headlines and studies have made clear for years that most big acquisitions fail. The fact that the DCF model has to be "stretched" to make a bad deal look good is evidence of the model's validity.

The stock market, for its part, appears to keep its eye on the ball when evaluating likely acquisition success, undistracted by terms like *strategic* and *synergy*. In fact, the market appears to be using a DCF model—its anticipatory nature, particularly, and its demand for future free cash flows—to figure out the current valuation consequences of deals. Just as a DCF model would predict, the market regularly offsets acquisition overpayments and risks by subtracting them from the buyer's stock price as soon as it gets wind of the deal. And it does this irrespective of how the deal might end up being presented on the books. For example, it saw through the "pooling" methods that greatly affected deal accounting under former rules.[8]

The DCF model is based on a long-term forecast of FCF but it does not require that investors stay around for the long run. New buyers can be expected to value their investment consistent with the DCF model, and so can all their successors. As a group, all they will ever get from the enterprise is FCF, so expectations for income and capital performance will drive its value now and at every time in the future.

Among legitimate valuation methods, the *market comparison approach* is paired with DCF as the two most typical. Under the market comparison approach, companies often are valued based on various multiples of earnings, volume, or capital. These are drawn from study of public company peers or of acquisitions of comparable companies. Results of these valuations tend to reconcile to the DCF model.

Using industry peers as valuation indicators works well because it reduces valuation assessments to matters of relative performance and value. Peer companies are in the same industry and have important things in common with the company being valued. Making sound calculations does not require coming up with isolated, independent assumptions about expected performance and risk. Sector norms for those drivers are built into the peer share prices and their valuation multiples. If you simply apply those, you are already in the ballpark. The difficult thing is deciding what multiples your company warrants. To do that, you are obliged to figure out where you ought to be in the range of multiples, and why. The answers to those questions tend to boil down to comparative earnings quality, as we defined it earlier:

- The companies' relative prospects for income growth from the "base" year.
- The extent to which income is more or less "free" from re-investment demands.
- Comparative risk and the price investors charge for bearing it.

That means that having a sound market comparison approach is a matter of applying properly the same criteria used by the DCF. For its part, the DCF model also should exploit the information contained in peer multiples, in its search for reasonable forecast parameters and discount rates.

Holding all else equal, a DCF valuation of a company with higher earnings growth, more highly distributable income or lower risk will be higher as a multiple of current income. Market comparison methods pick up on this. For example, some companies have safe, profitable growth profiles that are not offset heavily by capital requirements. That is why they attract higher-valuation multiples in the marketplace, just as they would in a DCF valuation. "Asset build-up" and "adjusted equity" approaches also tend to reconcile to results of a DCF analysis. The income streams underlying individual assets values ought to add up to the consolidated DCF forecast, for example. And using book equity value as a starting point is like imputing a market rate of return to book equity, in a DCF context.

FREE CASH FLOW

The idea of FCF merits a bit more of our attention. How FCF is treated in an incentive context is a big deal when trying to figure out whether plans are functioning properly, fairly, flexibly, and in service of shareholder interests.

You do not actually have to use FCF itself as a metric in any plan, although some companies do incorporate it as an incentive goal. It is complex. And it is affected strongly by big investments, so it can be low in years of high investing activity and vice versa. Perhaps most important, though, it may end up imposing a very high cost on new capital. New capital outlays reduce FCF dollar for dollar. Unless accompanied by equal dollars of income—which would amount to a 100% hurdle rate of return—FCF will fall.

By itself, FCF is not a good incentive metric. But that does not mean you can ignore FCF. If you do not know what is happening with capital usage and FCF over time, you do not know what is happening with valuation and returns. That is a nonstarter, if you mean to use incentives to encourage value creation consistently. So we will be obligated to return to the subject of FCF and its contribution to value creation several times in coming chapters.

Earlier, we reduced FCF to two simple moving parts, computing it as after-tax operating profit minus the change in capital. This was to make FCF comprehensible and to facilitate its application in incentive plans. A more familiar formula to compute FCF is:

> Operating income
> − Taxes on operating income
> = After-tax operating income
> + Depreciation (a noncash expense)
> = Operating cash flow
> − Additions to net working capital and other (operating) assets
> − Capital expenditures (net of disposals)
> = FCF

The shorter version of FCF reconciles to this one because the terms following income in the computation—depreciation, net capital expenditures, and net working capital additions—add up to the net increase in capital. This increase can reflect higher investment levels and also merger and acquisition activity.

The more detailed way to get at FCF from operations would be to look at the details of the company's cash flow statement, ignoring changes that have to do with financing (e.g., effects of interest expense). In an uncomplicated company (e.g., one without material mark-to-market effects), these three definitions of FCF are equivalent. From here on, we will define FCF in the simplest way based on its main drivers: FCF equals income net of capital usage.

In any given year of a DCF forecast, FCF can be positive or negative. Many high-growth companies experience negative FCFs as they make large investments and even incur current losses in the hope of achieving future profitability. Expectations about FCF have to turn positive eventually, though, for its present value to be positive and, therefore, for the company to be valuable at all. Exhibit 2.7 outlines the various possible fates of FCF.

Debt holders get interest payments and return of debt principal. Stockholders get dividends. FCFs also might be used for share repurchases, perhaps increasing earnings per share. It might be accumulated in investments and held there on behalf of shareholders. In these cases, the value of the business will reflect not only FCF from operations but also these extra assets.

In the general, simplified examples used throughout this book, companies are assumed to distribute any FCF to investors in one way or another, not to let it pile up inside the enterprise. This means the capital levels used in each DCF forecast represent the amount of capital necessary to support business operations and forecast growth. They do not include any "excess" or *nonoperating* capital. This is like defining capital as the sum of *net debt*, meaning debt stated net of any excess cash and other nonoperational assets, plus equity.

We saw that FCF has a few possible destinies. The DCF model values them all equally. One dollar of future FCF, irrespective of whether it is meant for debt repayment, share buy-back, or something else, contributes the present value of

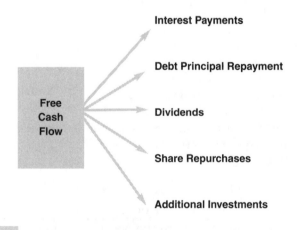

EXHIBIT 2.7   **Uses of Free Cash Flow**

one dollar to the value of the enterprise. However, all FCF may not be of equal value to owners. Depending on tax laws, share repurchases may be seen as a lower-tax way to distribute FCF than paying taxable dividends. Repurchases also often permit shareholders to defer recognition of income for tax purposes. We will take these matters up shortly, when we turn to effects of financing decisions.

FCF AND THE IRRELEVANCE OF ACCOUNTING CHOICES

One of the key findings of financial economics is that accounting choices are not important when determining business value. Our event study regarding option expensing announcements, covered in Chapter 3, contributes to the evidence in this area. The key driver of value, instead, is long-run FCF. Consider the accounting choice made when capitalizing expenses. If a company capitalizes and amortizes $100 in current expenses over two years, it attaches $50 of that expense to Year 1 and $50 to Year 2. Under this approach, Year 1 income falls by only $50 rather than by the full $100 amount of the expense. This might increase Year 1 financial performance, and payouts, in a traditional incentive plan.

However, this accounting choice does not affect FCF or DCF valuation. The $50 that did not run through expense must go somewhere in the company's financial statements, and FCF tracks it when it does. If the outlay does not run through the income statement, it generally is posted (or "capitalized") to a balance sheet account. That means the $50 income gain from the expense deferral is offset by a $50 increase in capital. FCF is equal to income minus the increase in capital, so it reflects the full $100 outlay $50 as expense and $50 as capital increase.

The next year, the $50 that was capitalized is taken back into income, reducing it by $50. But, when computing FCF, this income reduction is offset by the $50 capital reduction that occurs when the $50 deferred balance is taken off the balance sheet. So FCF in Year 2 is zero. FCF places the cash impact of the expense into the year in which it was incurred. Capitalization has only temporary effects upon income, so it does not affect the longer-run earning power that drives the ongoing valuation. Overall, this expense deferral tactic is like most accounting maneuvers—it has no impact on real value drivers or company value.

The details of the DCF model make clear the more general maxim of financial economics: what matters when valuing an enterprise is not how results are portrayed in the financial statements; what matters are the economic effects of results and their impact on risk-adjusted free cash flow over time. Accounting, in short, does not matter. Incentive plans should reward management only for economically meaningful results over time, not for choices about their accounting portrayal in the short run.

Many metric adjustments, especially done with value-based metrics such as economic value added, are meant to convert accrual accounting to cash. This is mainly unnecessary since the timing differences involved have little impact on longer-term performance and they get reversed out by FCF or balance sheet effects, anyway. Incentive metrics do need adjustment from time to time for issues that arise, including some that concern bookkeeping. Effects of large capital expenditures, for example, are often spread out over time. Some expenses may be capitalized and spread out as well, like big research and development investments. This is to be sure the incentive plan does not discourage good investments. But these adjustments need not cloud or dilute the plan.[9]

INCOME AND CAPITAL: FCF'S DRIVERS SHOULD BE THE MAIN INCENTIVE DRIVERS

Within the DCF model, operating income after tax and any changes in invested capital are netted against each other, and the cash that is left is FCF. The other big value driver, the cost of capital, is based mainly on external variables like business risk and on market norms for expected return. So, as far as pre-set incentive performance metrics are concerned, FCF and its two main ingredients are the entire game. They take you all the way from business decisions to results to valuation. They should also drive incentive payouts in most cases.[10]

Are income and capital really complete enough to capture the company's entire contribution to value creation? After all, stock prices move all over the place, generating big capital gains or losses. TSR can be very large or small. The FCF part of the valuation story, one of modest dividends, share repurchases, perhaps some debt pay-down, does not seem large enough or variable enough to drive all of a company's stock price action.

So what happens if a stock price just goes way up without any movement in FCF? Businesses are valued based on future FCF, so a jump in price normally is linked to rising hopes about future FCF (or perhaps to a lowered cost of capital, but that is a separate matter from business results). Exhibit 2.8 provides an example in which a company's income is expected to jump by 20 percent.

Compared to the base case presented in Exhibit 2.2, expectations for company income jump by 20 percent in the first year and remain at that level. This expands FCF, increasing valuation in scale to $1,200.[11] The DCF model provides proportionally reasonable results in many other cases as well. FCFs main drivers explain all performance-driven stock price movements we need to capture in incentive metrics.

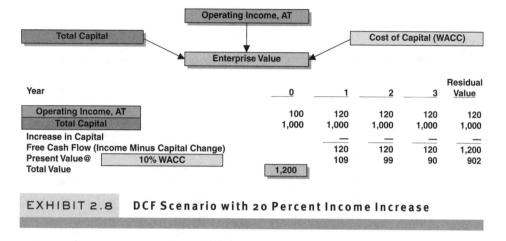

EXHIBIT 2.8   DCF Scenario with 20 Percent Income Increase

Overall, when we use FCF's moving parts to judge business performance over time, we are capturing how performance drives value and merits reward. A payout schedule based on operating income and ROIC, for example, or operating income and FCF, covers the main drivers in a great number of cases.

THE SHAPE OF THINGS TO COME

It is fine to say that value is a function of future performance, but that does not tell us much about the size or shape of the forecast. Stock prices and DCF valuation conventions do have a lot of say about the shape of things to come, however. For one thing, the forecast driving stock prices tends to be very long. Value is based on very long-run expectations. That is why a company's stock price tends to be a multiple—often large—of the current year's earnings or dividends. Our initial DCF scenario is an example: Investors would be willing to pay ten times one year's returns to own this particular zero-growth business.

Higher multiples than that are common for growing businesses. Most companies do not fit the zero-growth profile, and they normally are worth more than the perpetuity value of their current results from operations. This means that investors expect they will create value in the future. At the same time, DCF forecasts typically assume that the competitive advantages enabling value creation will diminish over time due to competition. A company may well beat such expectations, outdistancing competitors for an unusually long time. But the typical company's stock price suggests that investors are not willing to pay for such distant hopes when pricing shares today.

This "forecast pattern" question is an element of how markets translate business results into valuation, so it affects our thinking on how to pay management for performance. It may affect target setting as well. In Chapter 8, we will start using stock prices as evidence of future performance expectations. In each case it is helpful to identify forecast conventions that explain market stock prices:

- Normally, a company's most compelling advantages and strategies are expected to provide their greatest performance gains in the next three to five years. When stock analysts develop forecasts for companies, this is the time frame in which they tend to assert any specific sources of income growth and returns on new investments. Companies do the same thing with acquisition *pro formas* and long-range business plans.[12] For most companies, performance through this key mid-range period sets the level and trajectory of financial results in the balance of the typical ten-year forecast term. Overall, a company's value and the returns it earns based upon performance center heavily upon specific hopes attached to the next few years.

- After this first three- to five-year period, the effect of the company's individual performance picture on its valuation becomes more vague. The longer-term end of the forecast tends to be based upon more generalized assessments about the strength of the business franchise. This end of the forecast is often based on assumed growth over prior years, so it hinges on having nearer-term forecasts that play out as planned. Forecasts in the longer time frame also reflect the industry's growth prospects. During this time, a reasonable forecast convention is to assume that any performance advantages will diminish as a result of competition.[13] Overall, DCF analyses of established companies rarely involve an acceleration of performance in late projection years, and their stock prices normally do not square with such a forecast. Indeed, a common marking of an inflated forecast is the assertion that high near-term income growth will persist for 10 or 15 years. This has the same effect as applying a high residual value at the end of a short DCF forecast term. It dilutes near-term performance standards and any linked accountabilities.

- The residual term, typically beginning after Year 10, most often is governed by an assumption that the company's current set of competitive advantages by then will have run its course. The business at that date is valued assuming zero growth (or, equivalently, zero value creation) or upon a very low growth assumption equal to the level of long-run inflationary expectations impounded in the cost of capital.

Most company stock prices can be explained with this general pattern of assumptions. Individual companies with valuations differing greatly from this pattern tend not to stay that way. That means this pattern of results is very relevant to setting incentive targets. An example of such a DCF valuation appears, in a target-setting context, in Chapter 8.

QUANDO, QUANDO, QUANDO

Some observers say that performance, vesting, and holding terms of incentives need to be lengthened in an effort to better align executive payouts with results they produce. But longer vesting tends to put rewards at a great distance. This wastes money by diluting the perceived value of incentive investments. Waiting a long time does not sit any better with executives than it did with Englebert Humperdinck, who posed the musical demand, "Tell me when you will be mine. Tell me *quando, quando, quando*."

A better approach, to get executives' attention, is to concentrate incentives into the far more appealing near-to-medium term. But does this create a structure that is indeed too short in overall focus, ones that risks emphasizing nearer pursuits over value creation? Valuation methods have something to say about this. They make clear that, at every measurement date, it is the next few years that are the most critical. Performance during this period allows management to prove or disprove the viability of current strategies, skills and actions. Nearer-term results matter greatly to the stock market, as many companies find when they release disappointing earnings news. But it is a mistake to conclude that all the stock market cares about is near-term earnings. Quite the contrary, the stock market bases value on very long-term hopes about performance, a fact made clear, again, by the large multiples of current earnings, dividends, and returns customarily paid.

When a company's valuation falls due to bad earnings news, it typically falls by far more than the amount of the earnings disappointment itself. This is the long-run valuation mechanism in action. The stock market uses near-term results to update its pivotal three- to five-year scenario and to set the level and trajectory of FCF for all the years to follow. After the first few years, the forecast is set heavily by industry performance norms, with the individual company's results expected to converge toward them at some pace.

This is convenient. We do not have to wait 10 or 15 years to judge the success of a given management team and strategy. Rather, the usual time conventions of business planning—three- to five-year projection cycles updated periodically—will suffice as a benchmark against which to judge management's actual results and their contribution to value creation. Bonuses normally are measured on an annual cycle, and grants under long-term incentive plans tend to last three to five years. Three-year grant vesting is most common. And options are exercised, on average, around five years after grant.

Lengthening the term structure of executive pay would be costly since its perceived value and efficacy would fall. The thing that needs to be turned to the longer-term is the focus and calibration of the incentive structure, not its maturity or vesting terms. Well-structured goals, administered within three-year cycles, continually extend the focus of incentives and bridge the gap between short-term and enduring results.

This bridges an important information gap as well. Management knows more about the business than its owners. This is an "informational asymmetry" of the general type meant to be targeted by agency arrangements. A proper incentive structure encourages management to deliver the best possible results over the long term, not to posture and position for the biggest rewards in the current year. This means paying management to bring to bear whatever advantages they have on behalf of investors, including any informational edge they hold, whenever and to whatever extent they can. Parceling incentives into a series of limited-time offers and crapshoots—as is often done, in effect—is of little help here. The same principle applies to business-unit executives and how they might share information with the home office and run their businesses.

THE PAST IS RELEVANT ONLY AS PROLOGUE

The present value of an enterprise is based on expected future cash flows. This has some very specific implications for what does and does not matter when valuing a business. The DCF model exposes these crisply.

Past income levels, strictly speaking, do not matter. They literally do not enter into the computation of value. They are only relevant to the extent they provide evidence of what the company's future earning power might be.

The same is true for historical capital levels. By themselves, they are irrelevant to the value of a business. What matters—and what affects FCF—is the future change in capital. Historical capital simply is another input of potential use in assessing future performance. For example, they may provide evidence of the level of investment needed to support operations as they grow, or of the scale of income needed to support expected returns on investment.[14]

Exhibit 2.2 showed a valuation of a company with $1,000 in beginning capital (Company A). Exhibit 2.9 shows company B, which is identical except it has an initial level of capital of only $500.

Despite different beginning capital levels, the companies have the same value. That is because income remains at a level of $100 per year and capital, though lower at $500, does not change. FCF remains at $100 per year. Company A might be thought of as a business unit that was just acquired for a price equal to its value of $1,000. Using the purchase method to account for the acquisition, it appears in the acquiring company's financial statements at its cost of $1,000,

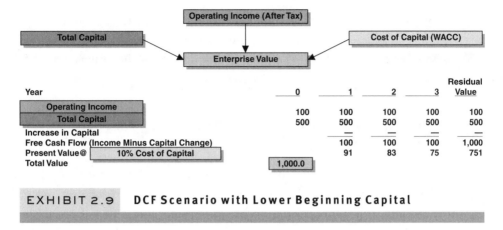

Year		0	1	2	3	Residual Value
Operating Income		100	100	100	100	100
Total Capital		500	500	500	500	500
Increase in Capital			—	—	—	—
Free Cash Flow (Income Minus Capital Change)			100	100	100	1,000
Present Value@	10% Cost of Capital		91	83	75	751
Total Value		1,000.0				

EXHIBIT 2.9   DCF Scenario with Lower Beginning Capital

which consists of fixed assets and net working capital valued at $500 plus non-amortizable intangibles valued at $500.

Company B can be thought of as the same company on the day before its acquisition caused $500 in purchased intangibles to be recognized on a balance sheet. It is the same company, with the same future risks and prospects, so its value is the same. If historical income of either company had been $50 rather than $100, the company still would be valued at $1,000. That is because prospective earnings and FCF at $100 are what determines value. If past income had been $50, then forecast results simply would be higher than historical levels. In that case, historical earnings would have underrepresented future earning power and would have been less helpful in predicting future results.

Here are the implications for incentive design:

- *Historical capital levels by themselves are irrelevant to valuation, but they can have a huge impact on incentive plan design and target setting.* The biggest problem with the treatment of capital in incentive plans is the vague, incomplete way in which this key value driver and its opportunity cost affect pay. The second biggest problem arises when companies try to fix the first one. They often attach a more prominent role to capital by, say, using a metric like ROIC, ROE, or economic value added. This often leads to distortions and unintended consequences. The general solution is better calibration. The general role of capital within an incentive plan should be to reward high returns on new capital usage, not to penalize investment.

- *Many techniques used in value-based incentives focus heavily on a company's long-run earning power.* Often, they look at current income as a source of information about the company's ongoing earning power, valuation, and future performance requirements. The economics of traditional incentives also rest on the presumption that a given increase in income will be persistent enough to warrant reward. Material, nonrecurring income sources may warrant adjustment. Reviewing the quality of earnings is prudent regular maintenance for any incentive plan involving metrics and targets, whether earnings quality is a formal plan adjustment or not.

VALUATION PERSPECTIVE: OPERATIONAL RESULTS, DEBT, AND CAPITAL STRUCTURE

Archimedes said, "Give me a place to stand and with a lever I will move the whole world."[15] The basic version of the DCF model does not pay a lot of attention to Archimedes and his lever, irrespective of the big impact it might have. Instead, the model assesses economic results as a separate matter from financial leverage. It starts with operating income after taxes. Operating income is stated before subtraction of interest expense, so it is a measure of income that is earned on behalf of both debt and equity capital investors. In this regard, operating income is constructed from a "total capital" perspective. Correspondingly, capital in the DCF model is defined as the sum of the values of the debt and equity capital invested in the business. That is the way the DCF model happens to be structured. But it is also the way that many incentive plans should be structured—focusing on overall results of operations and overall capital usage.

Capital is the sum of debt and equity capital invested in the business, and is generally equal to net assets. In Exhibit 2.10, both capital and net assets equal $40. The capital accounts show where the money came from. Asset accounts

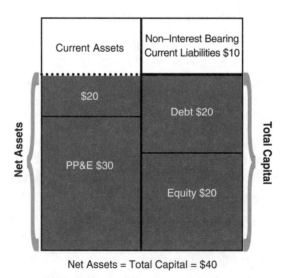

EXHIBIT 2.10   Measuring Capital

show where it was invested: net working capital, fixed assets, and other assets. Net working capital consists of the most liquid of the assets used in operations—mainly cash, receivables, and inventories—net of the most liquid operating liabilities—mainly accrued expenses and payables. The items in these accounts tend to come due within a year, but they are nonetheless a long-term commitment of capital since the business can't function in any future year without them. Blood is liquid, too, but that does not mean you can withdraw it all at once.

Current assets equal $20 while nondebt current liabilities total $10, so net working capital is $10. Fixed assets consist of the land, building, and equipment used in business operations (plant, property, and equipment (PP&E)). Other assets often consist of intangibles like patents, brand names, or goodwill recognized in a merger or acquisition. This company has $30 in fixed assets, no intangibles, and net working capital of $10, so net assets total $40. Debt and equity also total $40 at book value. This capital definition is used not only in the DCF model but also in the basic version of lots of capital-conscious metrics like ROIC (which is basically the same thing as return on net assets, or RONA) and TBR.

The DCF model determines market value from a total capital perspective: the present value of FCFs is equal to enterprise value, or the total value of the debt and equity capital invested in the business. To get at equity value, net debt is subtracted from the total.

The model tells us everything we need to know about the connection between business results and business value without paying much attention to capital structure.[16] The "total capital" basis of measuring both income and capital reflects a basic principle of corporate finance: the separation of operational and financing decisions. Changes in capital structure—in the debt/equity composition of enterprise capital—can distort many performance measures. Exhibit 2.11 demonstrates how financial leverage affects measured performance. A venture with return on equity of 20 percent (equal to return on invested capital in the zero-debt scenario) can be converted into one with 26 percent return on equity if financed 30 percent by debt. In that case, after-tax interest costs of $1 reduce income to $9, but equity capital falls to $35, so ROE rises to 26 percent.

Interest expense tends to be a tax-deductible expense to the corporation while dividends and capital gains are not, so corporate tax laws in many countries favor at least some debt financing. Nonetheless, companies should separate incentive policy from financing policy generally. Here is why:

- Not many people in the organization can affect the company's financing policy. When incentive plan metrics are affected by capital structure, a broad group of managers are made free riders or victims of such policies.

	Return on Invested Capital (ROIC)	Leverage Effects	Return on Equity (ROE)
Operating Income After Tax (OI)	$10		$10
− Interest (After Tax)		− $1 in interest	− 1
Net Income (NI)			$9
Capital	$50		$50
− Debt		− $15 in debt	− 15
Equity			$35

ROE (NI/Equity)   26%

ROIC (OI/Capital)   20%

EXHIBIT 2.11   **The Leverage Effects of Debt on Return on Equity (ROE)**

- Allowing plans to be affected by capital structure poses some risks of manipulation. The gain-only structure of most stock options encourages share repurchases rather than dividend increases. EPS-based bonuses can do the same thing (unless repurchases are adjusted out). Using debt to fund growth or to repurchase shares often makes measures like ROE and EPS overtly "game-able" in company incentive plans. We have seen some of those issues already and will take a closer look in Chapter 6.

- Differences in capital structure can confound performance benchmarks. A company with superior economic results can have lower EPS growth and ROE than peers, for example, simply because they chose to use less debt. This throws off basic but important questions in incentive policy, like "How are we doing against sector peers," and "What is a fair performance objective?"

- To encourage executives to maximize shareholder returns, companies need not isolate the shareholder perspective in metrics and plan structure. Maximizing the overall returns of the enterprise for its owners is the same thing, practically speaking, as maximizing returns for shareholders. Shareholders are residual claimants on returns, after satisfying largely fixed debt claims.

Financial executives and chief executive officers ought to be encouraged to use capital structure to create value for shareholders to the extent they can. We noted that stock-based incentives surely will remain a big part of how these few are paid, so they will have a strong incentive to pursue such gains. That alone should be sufficient. Other incentive plans need not be driven, or warped, by capital structure effects.

There are some instances in which financing policy has a pivotal impact on business results. In leveraged buyouts and other private-equity financed businesses, the amount of debt in the capital structure can take investor returns equal to 10 or 12 percent and turn them into equity returns that are two or three times as high. In pre-IPO technology ventures, the timing and terms of financing rounds often has more impact on founder returns than the overall extent of venture success. And in each case, the eventual public offering or sale is a necessity, being either the deal's *raison d'être* or the means of getting the business to proper scale. Still, even in these extreme cases, operational results actually are in the driver's seat:

- In the leveraged buyout case, if high leverage were felt to be desirable for incentive purposes, it could be calibrated directly into the incentive payout structure. No debt needed, no LBO transaction needed (Chapter 9).

- Management of an eventually successful tech venture might dawdle and overspend along the way, or it might just get things wrong for awhile. If this compels the company to seek more equity funding than planned, it will pay a price in terms of dilution. In each case, though, it is the operational results and prospects that drive the available financing terms at each juncture. They also determine how hard-pressed the company is to take those terms (Chapter 10).

Overall, the DCF model is complete and resilient enough to be well-suited to almost all of the tasks at hand in setting executive pay. The most important finding of this chapter, however, is the most basic assertion of the DCF model—value is a function of expected performance over the long run. One of the most troubling aspects of the executive incentive structure at companies today is the outsized concern with short-term results.

▪ NOTES

1. A more detailed approach is not helpful to our task. Trying to engineer an incentive plan to address all of the complex economic and business issues facing an individual organization is not worthwhile, as a general matter. That approach attaches a governance mandate to the incentive structure that is at once too broad and too detailed, making it hard to communicate and administer. It is one of the main reasons why value-based incentive plans, including many based on the metric "economic value added," have failed in the past. Instead, we will take the basic principles that link results to value and apply them consistently and broadly.

2. Chapter 11 outlines how proper incentives can help the company implement financial principles more effectively through effects on budgeting, long-range planning, financial training, and other activities.

3. Details of the DCF model, its underpinnings in areas like the theory of the firm, its application to many business decisions, and the many academic contributors in this area are set out in many graduate textbooks on corporate finance.

4. Here is a quick refresher on the basic math of present value discounting of single cash flows. If $90.91 were invested today at a 10 percent expected rate of return and this return were realized, it would be worth $100 one year from now. That is computed as the $90.91 we begin with plus a 10 percent return equal to $9.09, for $100.00 in total. The present value of $90.91 and the future value of $100 are, in a sense, the same thing. They each are representations of the expected future FCF of $100, but the $100 is stated at a time one year from now and the $90.91 is stated in present terms. The equation involved in compounding the $90.91 investment to future value is $90.91 × (1 + 10%) = $100. To determine the present value of $100 to be received one year from now, we rearrange the equation and solve for present value: $100/(1 + 10%) = $90.91. A sum to be received two years from now involves two years of compounding. $82.62 invested now will be worth $90.91 at the end of one year and $100 at the end of two years. The compounded future value of the investment is computed as $82.62 × (1 + 10%)^2 = $100. We can rearrange these terms to get the corresponding equation for discounting the second-period cash flow: $100/(1 + 10%)^2 = $82.62. Computations at Year 3 involve three years of discounting and so on.

5. Directors' Remuneration, Report of a Study Group chaired by Sir Richard Greenbury, July 17, 1995.

6. Seminal studies of LIFO conversions made this point starkly clear many years ago, as has much empirical research since. Regarding LIFO conversions, see the Sunder article in the 1973 *Empirical Research in Accounting*, and Biddle and Lindahl in the *Journal of Accounting Research*, Autumn 1982. The more general point about the stock market's preference for the economic portrayal of events (cash flow) over their accounting characterization is one upheld broadly for decades and a finding made clear in any review of relevant financial research. Examples include Hong, Mandelker, and Kaplan on purchases versus poolings in *Accounting Review* in 1978, an SEC study on R&D announcements published by the Office of the Chief Economist in 1985, Copeland and Lee on exchange offers, stock swaps, and their EPS effects, published in *Financial Management* in 1991, and Kaplan and Ruback on the importance of cash flow in driving business value, "The Valuation of Cash Flow Forecasts: An Empirical Analysis," NBER working paper 4274.

7. The version of the basic DCF model used in the simulations is the one described in earlier in this chapter. Simulations yield a statistical distribution of results that resembles that of a typical company's stock price; the natural logarithm of annual returns follows a generally normal distribution with a mean around 10 percent and a standard deviation of about 30 percent.

8. Ibid.

9. A limited, reasonable set of adjustments is described in Chapter 7.

10. Management has some influence over the riskiness of business activities it pursues and therefore on the company's cost of capital. Relevant risk effects are addressed in Chapter 5.

11. Changes to the cost of capital might have similar effects.

12. In low-accountability situations, they have a tendency simply to inflate such forecasts. Another tactic sometimes observed is to continually defer business gains into the out years, creating the classic "hockey stick" projection.

13. Economic theory and empirical research indicate that securities are priced as if business advantages are expected to wear away over time. Michael Porter's book *Competitive Advantage* addresses this phenomenon. New York, The Free Press, 1985. Other illustrations of the assumption of finite competitive advantage appear in several books on valuation by Al Rappaport and in the "fade" forecast construct applied in mass stock valuation analysis done by HOLT Value Associates.

14. Even when applied to businesses in which capital is highly relevant (e.g., ones with regulatory capital requirements like banks and insurance companies) the change in capital is more important. For example, the DCF model deals with any capital deficiency or excess based on its prospective impact on capital needs and cash flow.

15. John Tzetzes (12th century AD), *Book of Histories (Chiliades)* 2, 129-130, Translated by Francis R. Walton.

16. The company's capital structure may have a strong impact on its estimate of the cost of capital and therefore on a given valuation scenario. It is argued in Chapter 5 that costs of capital do not actually vary that much, in practice, based on company decisions about capital structure. Overall, it is recommended that company incentive plans consider costs of capital explicitly, but only in rough, reasonable terms and without allowing changes in the cost of capital to affect very strongly the payouts on outstanding incentive cycles.

CHAPTER 3

Market Practices in Incentive Pay

In this chapter, we examine pay levels and incentive composition for jobs at top levels in U.S. companies. We analyze these data from a range of perspectives, including looking closely at how executive incentives work. We will also get a good sense of what incentives cost, and how incentive design choices can take into account matters of affordability and financial prudence.

Executive pay has undergone a major restructuring in recent years. The most valuable part of pay for a typical top officer used to be their annual stock option grant. That is no longer true. There is now much more incentive pay delivered based on preset performance goals due to larger amounts of bonus pay and a greatly expanded weighting on goal-based long-term incentives.

First, let us look at the general composition of pay. Exhibit 3.1 shows how CEO and top manufacturing jobs get paid based on a sample of companies, mostly public ones, drawn from general industry. Management pay is connected strongly with company size, and data reflect a wide range of different company

| EXHIBIT 3.1 | MARKET COMPENSATION DATA FOR SELECTED TOP OFFICERS | | | | |

Position	50th Percentile				75th Percentile	
	Top Mfg.	CEO	Top Mfg.	CEO	Top Mfg.	CEO
Organization Size	1875	1875	7500	7500	7500	7500
Organization Level	Division		Corporate		Division	Corporate
Salary	$205	$295	$295	$1,050	$350	$1,245
Target Bonus	$85	$155	$180	$1,295	$250	$1,695
Target Total Cash Compensation	$290	$450	$475	$2,345	$600	$2,940
Long-term Incentive Value	$95	$310	$295	$4,215	$480	$6,505
Target Total Direct Compensation	$385	$760	$770	$6,560	$1,080	$9,445

sizes. These figures are "regression-based" estimates at two revenue levels—$7.5 billion and one-fourth that level, $1.875 billion. What this means is that the data are statistical estimates of what market median pay would be, if all the companies in the sample had revenue equal to $7.5 or $1.875 billion.[1]

Three components of pay are shown:

1. Annual base salary

2. Annual incentive (bonus) compensation, at target (the amount paid if the targeted level of performance is achieved)

3. Long-term incentive pay. This is the value, as of the date of grant, of long-term incentive vehicles like stock options, restricted stock, performance units, and shares (Options are valued using pricing models, and other grants are shown at target or face value as presented for accounting purposes.)

Base salary plus bonus is often called *total cash compensation*. Total cash plus long-term incentive pay is called *total direct compensation*. Benefits can be valuable elements of pay as well. CEO benefits often are worth 30 to 40 percent of salary. Perquisites might only be 2 percent of the value of someone's pay but, as a colleague once put it, they are "the 2 percent that really matters." We focus on incentives here, though, and benefits and perquisites are not measured or addressed.

The first thing one notices about data like these is that there is a ton of money at the top. The CEO gets paid a lot more than other top officers, who, in turn, are large margins ahead of their subordinates. High and accelerating pay at the top creates a kind of grand tournament for top posts. It draws in lots of contenders to compete intensively for the top spots. The stakes in this competition are very high from a shareholder perspective as well. When a company selects top management, it typically puts them in charge of billions of investor capital. The risks can be high, too, for both tournament participants and sponsors. Few managers attain the upper ranks in medium- to large-sized companies, and the ones that do have pivotal effects on what happens to those billions in capital.

Demand is not terribly elastic in the corporate CEO market, so you would expect to see high pay for the few who can compete at this level. Similarly, ringside seats for the heavyweight main event are worth a fortune, but they sit empty for a third-tier welterweight.

Over time, top officer pay has become much more variable. Exhibits 3.2 and 3.3 make long-term comparisons for the composition of CEO pay in medium-to-large companies, compiled in 1994 and 2008.

In 1994, 38 percent of top officer pay, on average, consisted of base salary, with 19 percent in bonus and the remaining 43 percent in long-term incentive grants. Exhibit 3.3 shows similar data drawn in 2008.

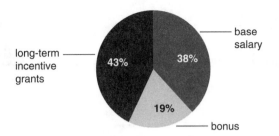

EXHIBIT 3.2   CEO Pay Composition: 1994

Now, base salary accounts for only 15 percent of the mix, while bonuses are 20 percent and long-term incentives are 65 percent. Top officer pay always had a large variable component, but now that slice of the pie, at 85 percent, is nearly six times as large as salary. Nowadays, a lot more of executive pay is based on explicit incentive programs and the many design choices that underlie them. And the dollar stakes placed on incentive design have grown far more, since the increased incentive percentage applies to a greatly expanded overall pie.

The mix of incentives has undergone large changes over time as well. Big changes in recent years were driven by the onset of option expensing—stock option usage fell off sharply. The data in Exhibit 3.4 are for named Fortune 500 executive officers other than the CEO (median revenue $12.4 billion). The data make clear how option granting fell off, once it no longer appeared in the profit and loss statement to be a costless matter.

Exhibit 3.5 sets forth proxy data just for the CEO for a more recent period from 2004 to 2008 and 2009.

Performance plans have stepped in where option granting left off, increasing their role in the pay mix by about the amount of the decline in option granting. Performance share and unit plans are grants of shares and cash, respectively, earned based on the attainment of multiyear performance goals.

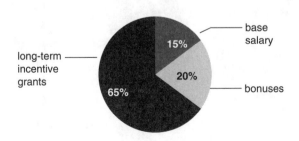

EXHIBIT 3.3   CEO Pay Composition: 2008

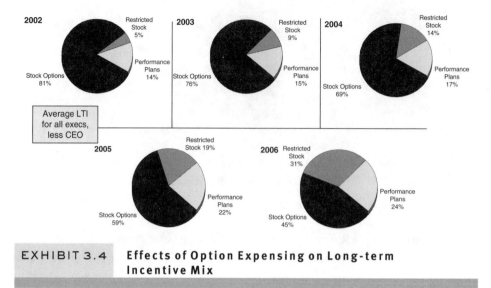

EXHIBIT 3.4   Effects of Option Expensing on Long-term Incentive Mix

You used to hear a lot of reasons for the overwhelming levels of option usage in the marketplace. Advocates would claim options were a nearly perfect incentive, one whose high usage was explained by their own merits rather than by the fact that they were the only expense-free form of pay. Then, option expensing arrived on the scene. Option usage fell substantially, and fast.

Options are off by a third to a half or more, in this sample and many others, but they continue to carry significant weight in the pay structure. Years after losing their bookkeeping advantages options merit a much–reduced but still significant part in incentive pay delivery.

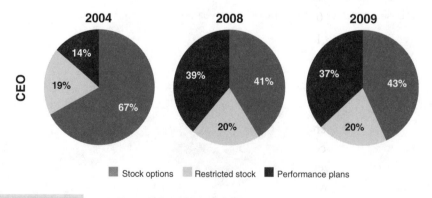

EXHIBIT 3.5   Composition of CEO Pay

Restricted shares, in contrast, have held a stable share. Ordinary restricted stock grants are shares of stock (or stock units) that vest over time. Many critics cite an important disadvantage of such grants—they can allow executives to accumulate a valuable equity stake even when share price performance has been poor. One of the board's top functions, however, if not the most important one, is to attract and retain a well-chosen CEO for the company. Restricted stock can be effective for this purpose since its value and retention effects tend to be comparatively durable.

Increasingly, the amounts of restricted stock grants are made contingent on attaining performance criteria. Those criteria are not always very rigorous, however. They are sometimes set at low thresholds meant simply to enable tax deductibility (under IRC section 162(m)). Companies should take trouble to secure tax deductibility, of course; failing to do so usually increases after-tax grant costs by more than 50 percent.

A general backdrop to these compositional data is that senior management pay has risen strongly over time, with much of that growth coming from big expansions in the amount of incentive opportunity. Bonus pay has risen greatly as percentage of salary. And, of the overall long-term incentive pie, much more is delivered based on formal, multiyear goals. A few years ago, multiyear performance expectations had little money riding on them—only 14 percent of the long-term incentive mix was in the form of performance units and shares. Now, such grants are 37 percent of a greatly expanded pie. This has important implications for how companies specify, set, and administer their performance criteria:

- Short-term goals—budgeted earnings per share (EPS), for example—always were very consequential for senior management because they drove bonus funding.

- Now, the bulk of goal-based incentive pay is long-term. In CEO pay mix examples, 65 percent of pay is long-term incentives and, of that, 37 percent is in performance shares and units. That means formal, long-term goals drive 24 percent of total direct pay (65 percent times 37 percent). That is more than bonus pay, which is 20 percent of total direct pay at target.

The rising prominence of long-term goals is a positive development, on balance. It is one of the company's best opportunities to ensure that payouts to top management have been earned based on sustained, high-quality performance. At the same time, however, it makes incentive design and administration a more intensive and complex process.

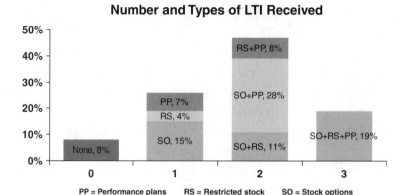

Number and Types of LTI Received

PP = Performance plans   RS = Restricted stock   SO = Stock options

EXHIBIT 3.6   Number and Types of Long-Term Incentives Received

For performance unit and share plans, having proper goals is the key to effi-cacy. This raises some questions for many companies. Has your long-term goal-setting process improved to deal with the greatly heightened incentive stakes placed on it? Are your metric choices and plan designs set up to maintain proper incentive effects in regard to risk and return, even when the outlook is un-certain? If not, you have overloaded a weak vehicle and you could end up in the ditch. This book provides an extensive set of target-setting, measurement and design solutions meant to enable companies to use goal-based pay more effectively.

The long-term incentive mix has changed greatly, but the general menu of choices has not. It remains the case that many companies use combinations of different types of long-term incentives, as shown in Exhibit 3.6.

2009 data indicate that executive pay levels fell and became more irregular following the crisis of 2008. This is not surprising—actual bonuses fell due to performance, and long-term incentive grant levels fell along with market capi-talization in many cases.

How Much Are We Paying for Management Incentives?

Public companies disclose stock-based incentive costs in their annual reports. That normally is most of their long-term incentive cost. Non–share-based plan costs are not included. Exhibit 3.7 provides a summary of the stock-based pay costs reported by S&P 500 index companies in annual reports for the three years ending in 2008 (current year).[2]

EXHIBIT 3.7	STOCK COMPENSATION EXPENSE AS A PERCENTAGE OF NET INCOME

	Stock Comp. Exp. % of Net Income		
	2 Years Ago	1 Year Ago	Current Year
Median	6.0%	6.2%	**5.7%**
75th Percentile	11.5%	10.5%	10.7%
25th Percentile	3.0%	3.2%	2.3%
	Stock Comp Exp. % of Sales		
	2 Years Ago	1 Year Ago	Current Year
Median	0.6%	0.6%	**0.6%**
75th Percentile	1.2%	1.2%	1.2%
25th Percentile	0.3%	0.3%	0.3%
	Stock Comp. Exp. % of EBIT		
	2 Years Ago	1 Year Ago	Current Year
Median	3.7%	3.9%	**3.8%**
75th Percentile	7.1%	6.4%	6.4%
25th Percentile	2.0%	2.4%	2.2%

So stock-based compensation expense represented a median of 5.7 percent of net income for S&P 500 companies for 2008 (or fiscal years ending early 2009). It was six-tenths of a percent of sales and 3.8 percent of earnings before interest and taxes (EBIT). Costs varied a great deal, reaching 10.7 percent of net income at the 75th percentile.

Exhibit 3.8 shows results for the reporting companies in total. That is, they compare the sum of costs of stock compensation for all companies in the sample to cumulative income of the sample. From this viewpoint, midrange costs are higher. Some of the S&P 500 companies lost money or posted far lower earnings in 2008, but almost all were obliged to continue expensing past option and restricted stock grants, and most made more grants. Costs became much more concentrated in the low-earnings year of 2008.

Such costs do vary by organization size. Exhibit 3.9 shows that median expenses are smaller in relation to net income for larger companies.

Results are shown for many industry groups in Exhibit 3.10.

EXHIBIT 3.8	STOCK COMPENSATION EXPENSE AS A PERCENTAGE OF EBIT

	Stock Comp. Exp. % of EBIT		
	2 Years Ago	**1 Year Ago**	**Current Year**
Total Sample	7.6%	9.3%	20.3%

EXHIBIT 3.9   **STOCK COMPENSATION EXPENSE PERCENTAGES BY REVENUE CLASS**

	Stock Comp. Exp. % of Net Income		
Revenue Class	2 Years Ago	1 Year Ago	Current Year
Over $20 billion	5.4%	5.6%	4.8%
$10 billion to $20 billion	4.7%	5.1%	5.0%
$5 billion to $10 billion	5.6%	6.0%	5.8%
$2.5 billion to $5 billion	6.6%	7.2%	7.4%
Under $2.5 billion	8.5%	9.1%	8.4%
Full Sample	6.0%	6.2%	5.7%

People-intensive businesses and those with higher margins, valuable brands, and technological content top the list, as has often been the case with statistics on share usage as well.

These are annualized costs for equity-based pay. As noted, non–share-based LTI costs are not included. Cash bonuses are not, either. One could rough up an

EXHIBIT 3.10   **STOCK COMPENSATION EXPENSE BY INDUSTRY SECTOR**

	Median Stock Comp. Exp. % of Net Income		
	2 Years Ago	1 Year Ago	Current Year
Computer, Communications	12.8%	13.7%	13.5%
Hotels and Restaurants	7.3%	14.9%	13.0%
Inv. Banking, Securities, Inv. Mgt.	11.5%	9.8%	12.1%
Health Care Facilities	9.3%	8.2%	11.6%
Consumer Products	8.6%	8.7%	9.0%
Services	9.5%	10.5%	8.7%
Wholesalers	8.8%	7.2%	7.3%
Surgical and Medical Instruments	8.9%	7.6%	7.2%
Pharmaceuticals	7.1%	9.5%	7.1%
Electric and Electronic	8.3%	8.2%	7.1%
Retailers	6.5%	6.2%	6.7%
Food	6.1%	7.2%	6.4%
Chemicals, Paints, Plastics	6.8%	5.7%	6.1%
Builders (n/a due to net losses)	5.8%	n/a	n/a
Industrial and Gen'l Manufacturing	4.8%	4.8%	5.5%
Transportation Services	8.7%	5.7%	5.2%
Commercial Banking, Thrift	3.5%	5.1%	5.1%
Agric., Logging, Oil & Gas, Mining	4.0%	4.5%	5.1%
Cars, Ships, Aeroplane, Transport. Eqpt.	4.8%	4.7%	4.5%
Wood, Paper, and Printing	6.6%	6.3%	4.3%
Insurance	3.3%	3.2%	3.6%
Real Estate	2.4%	2.7%	3.1%
Electric and Gas Utilities	2.8%	2.5%	2.9%
Metals	2.1%	2.5%	2.2%
Oil Refining	2.0%	2.0%	1.3%

estimate of overall incentive costs by looking at general guidelines. Let us consider a company with consolidated revenue of $7.5 billion. Using midrange margins and valuation multiples, let us say it has income of $500 million and a market equity valuation of $7.5 billion.

Next, add up the cash plans. Management bonus plans typically cost about 5 percent of net income after tax. That figure, be aware, represents the rough central tendency of a wide and situational range. Three percent is a better estimate for plans having very restricted senior management eligibility, while 7 percent is closer for cases of all-employee participation.

Cash-based long-term incentives might cost another 1 percent or 2 percent. Let us call it 1 percent, so 6 percent is the estimated cost of cash-based incentives for management. Our example company has net income of $500 million, so the cash cost of goal-based cash incentives is about $30 million at 6 percent. Stock-based grants cost another 6 percent at the median, so let us call it $60 million in total.

There is no question that the company is spending a lot on management; their incentives alone amount to 12 percent of consolidated net income. It goes higher, too, if you consider that actual payouts may be considerably higher than the annualized present values being expensed. Stock prices themselves are heavily risk-adjusted present values. They are likely to be higher at the time of future vesting, payout or exercise. $30 million in stock-based long-term incentive expense is meant to bring $40 million or more in eventual participant gains. Any way you slice it, this is a big cost to company's owners.

VARIABLE PAY VERSUS INCENTIVE PAY

Let us talk in detail about the typical company and about a typical participant. He is the head of manufacturing for a group that accounts for one-fourth of the value and results of the consolidated enterprise. He is typical of the dozens or hundreds of executives in the senior management group—a step or two removed from affecting the overall stock price but clearly having a big impact on a business unit or key function. So, looking at his pay provides a good test of aspects of incentive line of sight and efficacy.

His total direct compensation is worth $450,000 and consists of:

- A salary of $200,000.
- Annual bonus potential of $100,000. This year, he will get his target bonus if operating income in his group and corporate EPS each grow by 8 percent. His bonus is based 50/50 on these two goals.
- A long-term incentive grant worth $150,000 annually, consisting one-third each in stock options, restricted stock, and performance shares. His

performance shares are designed in a common way, based 100 percent on corporate results.

His pay structure has a typically high level of performance sensitivity, or payout leverage. Exhibit 3.11 shows how his LTI grant sizes are determined and how his incentives can pay out under various circumstances.

Overall LTI value of $150,000 is converted into grant sizes in the exhibit. One-third, or $50,000, is meant to be issued in the form of restricted stock. $50,000 is the face value of the grant, since these grants are valued at face for this purpose.[3] An option grant worth $50,000 means the grant size is $125,000 in terms of the value of option shares at grant, at a 40 percent valuation ratio ($50,000/40 percent = $125,000). The balance is a performance unit or share grant with a $50,000 payout target, again valued at face for this illustration.

The rightmost columns show payout scenarios. Salary is fixed, but bonus scenarios are shown ranging from $100,000 to $200,000 at 100 percent, 150 percent, and 200 percent payout levels. Scenario values for restricted stock grants are shown based on annual rates of gain of 8 percent, 12 percent, and 16 percent over a five-year period (period is used irrespective of vesting terms, and dividends and taxes are ignored). In the 8 percent scenario, for example, gains compound to 46 percent overall, so the $50,000 initial value of the shares becomes $73,000 after five years. Option gains are computed similarly. The block of shares under option increases in value by 46 percent, from

EXHIBIT 3.11   INCENTIVE PAYOUT SCENARIOS

Head of Manufacturing Payout Scenarios—One Year's Granting				Performance Scenario		
Bonus and Perf Plan Payout				100%	150%	200%
5-Year Annual Stock Gains				8%	12%	16%
Salary at 50th	$200			$200	$200	$200
Annual Incentive (AI) Payout	$100			$100	$150	$200
LTI 5-year. Payouts (Mid-Range Grant)	$150					
	Weight	Valuation	Grant Size			
Restricted Stock	1/3	100%	$50	$73	$88	$105
Stock Options	1/3	40%	$125	$59	$95	$138
Performance Units or Shares (3–5 years)	1/3	100%	$50	$73	$132	$210
Total LTI Payout				$206	$316	$453
Total Cash - Actual, Plus LTI Gains				$506	$666	$853
Difference from Target					$160	$347

$125,000 to $184,000, with the difference being a $59,000 option gain. The $50,000 in targeted shares awarded under the performance share plan increase in value to $73,000, like the restricted stock grant. At target, then, the three forms of LTI pay out $206,000 in total.

At the 16 percent growth rate, the performance shares gain 110 percent overall so if the payout were at 100 percent of target they would be worth $105,000. In the 200 percent scenario, twice as many shares are earned so the payout actually is worth $210,000 (Note: A performance cash plan could be set up to convey similar leverage, even though not denominated in shares). Option and stock grants have larger upside in this scenario as well, and LTI gains in total are $453,000.

Over this ordinary performance range, the pay structure shows a substantial amount of variation. Our sample executive has a rather variable pay structure, one strongly connected to the stock price and to financial performance.

But does that mean he has incentive pay, in the cause-and-effect sense? His role has a pretty strong connection to results of his group, so pay based on group results should be reasonably compelling to him. But all of his long-term incentive pay is based on corporate stock and corporate financial results. And half of his bonus is based on corporate EPS. That means these incentive outcomes are driven by many things outside of his control. Before they bring any reward, results of his business unit are diluted by results of other business units, interpreted by the stock market in an opaque process, affected by the overall company's capital structure, and filtered by the specific terms of incentive plans. The process is a roundabout one and Exhibit 3.12 depicts it aptly in this regard.

The black boxes show areas over which the executive and his teammates have reasonably strong control—business-unit-level decision making and business unit results. The team members also have some control (denoted in dark gray) over the risks and prospects of their business unit's activities. They have some influence over target setting in their own business unit and perhaps over other aspects of plan design at that level. The balance of the structure of incentive rewards—the bulk of it—is out of their hands.

Accountabilities are not lacking in this pay system, in a general sense. Pay is responsive to actual and expected business performance. But clarity is lacking, and so is line of sight. Most management types do not have a very clear view of the market's valuation mechanism. If they did, we would see them behave differently when they exercise their options or acquire another company. They have some ability to "time" their option exercises and share sales to their advantage (though such activity is constrained heavily by securities laws). Still, as a group they demonstrate little timing "edge" in these situations. They also routinely make acquisitions that destroy value.[4]

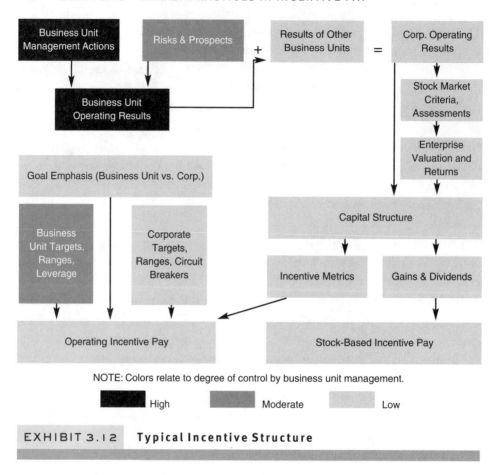

NOTE: Colors relate to degree of control by business unit management.

High   Moderate   Low

EXHIBIT 3.12   Typical Incentive Structure

Let us see how much the executive gets paid for his own performance as opposed to matters outside of his sphere of influence. This is a bit complex to do, but let us do it anyway. We are spending many tens of millions per year on incentive pay, after all. If we were reviewing acquisitions or investments of that scale, we would be willing to review some data and run some spreadsheets.

His group has an operating income target for this year of $200 million. His group represents one-fourth of the overall company's consolidated income of $800 million. Applying a 37.5 percent overall tax rate reduces overall operating profit to $500 million. Since the company has no debt and no other income and expense, the $500 million in after-tax operating profit is the same as net income after tax.

Let us say that the management team come up with some cost reductions that can increase his business unit's operating income to $220 million, or 10 percent above target. These performance improvements, if enacted, are seen by all as permanent. And they do not cost anything to produce. This is hard to do in most businesses, actually, but let's assume they can.

The stock market agrees that this year's income gain is permanent, an enduring increase of $12.5 million in after-tax cash flow every year from now on. In fact, assume the stock market is providing more or less perfect performance feedback, adjusting the stock price by exactly the present value of the performance improvement. That would be the absolute best case in terms of the efficacy of the stock market as a pay delivery system, so it is a good place to start.

Let us say the company's cost of capital is 9 percent. Measured at the end of the year, this performance improvement is worth about $150 million, consisting of $12.5 million in extra cash flows accumulated this year plus the present value of cash flows for many future years ($12.5 million of current cash flow, plus $12.5 million divided by 9 percent: beginning-of-year convention regarding timing of cash receipt). This is a perpetuity valuation method like the ones we used in Chapter 2.

The overall company is worth $7.5 billion. $150 million is a 2 percent gain in value, occurring as soon as the market gets a whiff of it. This should increase payouts on his long-term incentives. This year's grant was worth $150,000, but we saw that it conveys the upside on a block of shares worth $225,000 ($50,000 each in performance shares and restricted stock, and $125,000 under an option grant).

The 2 percent stock price move increases his expected stock gains by $4,500. The income gain would boost LTI by another 4 percent due to additional impacts on performance share grants. The $12.5 million income gain is 2.5 percent of target; a 12.5 percent impact on payouts when payout schedule leverage is 5:1. Those grants are one-third of LTI, so the percentage impact is around 4 percent, for a total impact of 6 percent or so.

He also might make some money on other stock-based LTI grants he has received in the past. But we are not looking at those right now. We are just assessing the impact of the $150,000 in long-term incentives granted to him this year.

So, in a static world with perfect markets and foresight, the executive gets paid $13,500 on this year's LTI grant for actions that created a great deal of value. It still is a small part of his pay, but it is enough to get his attention.

For our incentive scheme to work, however, the executive has to believe that the value of awarded shares will maintain the 6 percent gain at some future time when he cashes out. Should he believe the gain will be there? He is likely to see price changes of 6 percent or more—owing to all kinds of valuation factors—within a typically volatile quarter. Here are some things that could offset his gain:

- An increase of 60 basis points (0.6 percent) in the cost of capital used by the stock market to price company shares. If expected yields on corporate equity move around in a way similar to corporate bonds (standard deviation of one percentage point or so per year), you would expect at least this level of movement almost every year.

- Similar movement in either the price of risk (i.e., the premium in yield that investors demand in order to bear the risks of equity investments) or in very-long-run expectations for expected growth.

- A 10 percent decline in income—one seen as enduring—in the other businesses. If targeted income for other units is $600 million in total and the company came in 10 percent below that, it would offset all of the $60 million in gains.

Smaller movements in each of these factors could combine in such a way as to wipe out the gains. Larger movements could boost the price, making an executive's incremental contribution hard to distinguish as incentive pay as a separate matter from general price variation over time.

Overall, his change in LTI pay for helping boost the company's income is a drop in the bucket. Most people in the senior management organization are like our example executive whether they are found at corporate or in business units. They have big jobs. They have a strong impact on some important part of the company. But they have modest to negligible effects on the stock price and on their LTI gains as a whole.

Our executive will end up with higher bonus pay as a result of this superb performance, even though its impact on the 50 percent corporate part of bonus will be diluted. The $20 million pretax income gain is 10 percent of target, increasing the payout by 50 percent on unit-level operating income if leverage is 5:1. And the $12.5 million after-tax increase is 2.5 percent of target against the corporate net income figure that drives EPS, so the impact is 12.5 percent at 5:1 leverage. The overall bonus gain, at 31 percent or so, is good money. But, the typical bonus plan may not by itself encourage sustained performance and value creation. It might have made the same payout for shorter, riskier, or more capital intensive sources of the $12.5 million income gain, ones not worth nearly $150 million.

It is our LTI programs that are meant to focus directly on sustained results and value. And that is not where most of our investment in incentive pay went. The LTI pay structure is weighted heavily not toward unit results but toward corporate stock price movement. We saw that had the effect of severely diluting rewards. If that part was meant to be *performance incentive* pay in any strict sense, it was largely wasted.

Our executive is likely to get some LTI gains one way or another, though. If it is not related to performance, it is reasonable to ask, what did it go for? I developed a valuation/pay simulation model to answer this question, one that attaches reasonable levels of movement and predictability to three factors that influence the movement of a company's stock price.

1. *Performance of the executive's own business unit and its contribution to shareholder value.* This is measured based on a valuation formula applied to business unit results, a particular variant of the TBR metric introduced in Chapter 2. It is designed to capture the valuation implications of current business results.

2. Performance of other business units based on their measured TBR. We could add effects of corporate actions as a separate item, but instead we will assume that source of uncertainty is reflected in combined results of the other units.

3. Stock market factors that affect valuation. These include interest rates, equity risk premiums, and long-run growth expectations for the economy and its various sectors.[5]

Using the model, I ran a few thousand random scenarios of incentive gains. I addressed an "anticipatory pricing" issue by ascribing perfect foresight to the stock market and allowing near-term performance variation to compound into stock prices for a typical option holding period of five years.[6] So the stock market was assumed to be able to predict future company performance perfectly, an approach that accorded higher efficacy to stock-based incentive pay. Here is what I found:

- Over the five-year holding period, only about 20 percent of the variation in LTI pay can be tied to performance of the group, meaning decisions made by the management team, or to risks and prospects of the industries in which they work.

- The other 80 percent of the range of gains is driven by the performance of the other businesses or corporate actions, or is unrelated to company financial results. It is due to market factors outside the control of management.

- Of the $150,000 devoted to long-term incentive pay for our executive, only $30,000, or 20 percent, is an incentive plan. The other $120,000 is to him a random, uncontrollable pay source like lottery tickets. As far as incentive effects are concerned, he may as well be getting LTI grants 80 percent from some other company.

MISMATCH MAKERS

These observations do not mean there is anything wrong with the stock market. The stock market is doing its job perfectly in all our examples. It is reacting properly to company performance as well as other important factors affecting security prices. The market was assumed to be more than efficient in this simulation. It was assumed to be omniscient.

But the stock market's job does not include managing our particular executive's performance. The stock market does not even know our executive. It should not be put in charge of determining his LTI payouts. If you want line of sight effects, you need to accord a stronger role to relevant long-term goals rather than to stock price movements.

We find there are serious efficacy and line of sight issues for corporate-level management as well. Again, most do not have a driving role on the stock price. In the nearer term, the period of one to three years that is most relevant to incentive design, stock of most companies moves around mainly for reasons unrelated to current financial results.[7] Not all of that unexplained movement is really statistical "noise." Much has to do with efficient performance anticipation, reaction to events, and risk discounting. Nonetheless, to many people in senior management it sounds just like noise.

Stock and option gains tend to take a few years to amount to much. We find nearly half have negligible gains after a year and nearly a third after three years. Most performance plan cycles, in contrast, are paid by then. And, in a reasonable design, they pose only a 10 or 15 percent chance of nonpayment. Performance-based plans can do a better job of centering gain potential into the critical medium-term. Option leverage effects are superb in the top percentiles, but, overall, most option holders have to wait a bit too long for interesting gains to emerge.

The company may have enumerated some business strategies and performance goals at the time of the option grant. But option grants are held by executives most often for around five or six years, and gains look iffy much of the time before then. By exercise, any original performance context is a distant memory. And a good part of option value at grant is based on a distant and unlikely hope. Option values do not center on "target" gains in the manner of a goal-based performance plan. Instead, they are influenced heavily by a few high-gain scenarios that are not very likely.

Option gains have not been shown here to be unfair. Rather, they have been shown to be mismatched with normal objectives and expectations for incentive policy. If a company makes a big incentive commitment today, it should expect it to work strongly now and for the next few years. That is not happening, much of the time, with option grants. Current incentive effects probably stem mostly from grants made years ago. Monetary policy is said to be effective, but with long and variable lags. For incentive policy, that won't work. Incentives, even long-term ones, should be more concentrated, direct and purposeful.

Financial researchers have run a few numbers on purely stock-based incentive pay as well, centering in on the hoped-for performance effects. Generally, they find no statistical linkage between corporate use of stock options at the senior management level and company performance.[8] Actually, stock options by themselves appear to risk some adverse effects on company decision making. Options do not expose executives to downside in the stock price. When top corporate officers have a ton of stock options, they are more inclined to roll the dice on acquisitions. And most acquisitions fail. In contrast, companies influenced by holders of large blocks of shares, particularly when the block holder is the CEO, are significantly less inclined to go down that path.[9]

OTHER MARKET-BASED CONSIDERATIONS OF MARKET-BASED CONSIDERATION

Many companies issue lots of stock options as a means of attracting the best talent and to get the best results. Some of them succeed with this remuneration strategy. But that does not mean they have the design and mix right. It does not by itself address at all the efficacy of stock-based pay as a performance incentive device. Those companies might have succeeded just as well or better by offering boatloads of cash rather than options in their attempts to attract, retain, and motivate the best.

In the past, they overused options as award currency since such grants appeared to be free from a financial accounting standpoint. Back then, trying to get companies to remix LTI away from stock options was rather quixotic mission. But I did it a lot nonetheless. In a January 2002 publication, I contributed to the debate by writing, "Overall, belief in the book advantages of options—in the idea that options accounting keeps stock prices higher than they otherwise would be—appears to be a broadly held financial illusion. This is unfortunate since the focus on bookkeeping skews incentive design greatly and renders it ineffective for most participants."[10]

Later developments provided a perfect opportunity to test this prediction. Hundreds of companies announced they would voluntarily expense options in their income statements. My colleagues and I studied stock market reactions to these announcements. Exhibit 3.13 summarizes our results. It shows announcing companies' stock price performance in typical "event study" format. In this case, it sets forth announcers' stock prices, normalized to a common value of $10 per share at the time of announcement and adjusted for market movements.

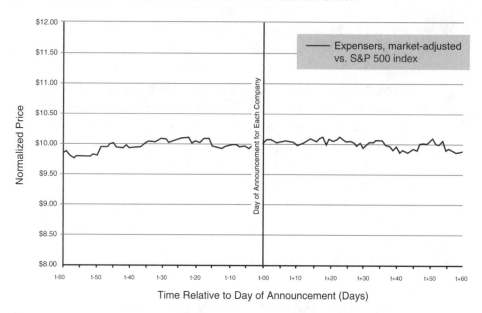

Source: Towers Perrin

Source of financial information: Thomson Financial

Sources of announcement information: Standard & Poors, Dow Jones News Service

EXHIBIT 3.13   **Event Study: Stock Price Performance of Expense Announcers versus S&P 500 Index**

If the market saw option expensing as a bad thing, this line would blip or trend downward as this remarkably bad earnings surprise was received and assimilated into prices. It did not. The stock market shrugged off expensing as a nonevent. Stock prices of expensers did not dip, on average, at the time of announcement nor during the surrounding time periods when the market might have been anticipating or digesting this information. Overall, stock price movements of the expense announcers were indistinguishable from those of the average S&P 500 company.

Why? Because the stock market was already well aware of stock options and their economic cost, so the prospect of a change in accounting to recognize these facts provided no new information. Companies may have believed that the fictitious accounting portrayal of stock options was allowing them to escape the economic consequences of making these grants, but as predicted, this was a broadly held financial illusion.

Companies should worry a lot less about how events are presented in the books. After all, one of the biggest accounting breaks ever devised—outright "no expense" treatment of a really enormous cost—turned out to be literally worthless. Decades of studies find similar results on matters such as accounting for acquisitions, depreciation, and inventories. Stock prices were found to be more strongly related to diluted EPS than to basic EPS as well, making clear the stock market was well aware of the economic costs of dilutive claims like options all along, expense or no expense.[11]

Back to the subject of design, we might find stock-based pay compelling if most executives had a good understanding of how various business decisions are likely to translate into financial results and stock value. But outside of the finance function at a company, not many executives have that kind of specialized training. One of the duties of company financial management is to step into this gap of financial knowledge, helping the organization make business decisions that create stock market value for shareholders. They do this by applying analytical tools such as discounted cash flow (DCF) analysis to matters like acquisitions or major capital expenditures. But that process—its timing, scope, and time frame—is not consistent with the structure of incentive pay. So the expected results on which many big-ticket business decisions are made (e.g., acquisition synergies) may not figure directly into the usual budget-based incentive plan goals. If accountabilities are weak, then the finance department's valuation skills won't have much effect. Chapter 11 lays out a range of ways in which adopting rigorous incentive standards supports strategic priorities of the finance function.

MARKET PRACTICES AND PRESUMPTIONS

Another form of market-based input is the conventional rationales behind common pay choices. Some of these widespread views are flawed:

- *"Our shareholders are very focused on near-term EPS results."* Shareholders want short-term EPS? One of the central findings of financial economics is that shareholders disregard EPS results whenever they conflict with underlying economic performance. Another clear finding is that shareholder criteria are overwhelmingly long term. Lastly, EPS and many other familiar yardsticks can be improved by business actions that do not create shareholder value, and shareholders surely do not want that. A system of rewards that allows payouts for bad management decisions is a triumph of hope over reason.

- *"Our stock-based incentive policy encourages a broad segment of our workforce to focus on shareholder value creation."* Encouraging value creation? Stock-based incentives offer such a poor line of sight for most managers that they have no plausible impact on performance. Studies on stock options, in particular, have found no consistently discernable linkage with performance, though amounts of grants were huge and heavily concentrated on corporate officers. Where we saw connections emerge, actually, is between option usage and risk taking. If stock-based pay is not driving a more effective performance focus at the top, it cannot be expected to do so in the broader workforce. The "ownership" movement is decades-long and viable, but the particular practice of all-employee option granting was knocked out by a one-two punch—the tech crash and option expensing.

- *"Our bonus plan applies a strong emphasis on consolidated results. This encourages organization-wide teamwork."* Corporate bonuses encourage organizationwide teamwork? Teamwork is critical and should be encouraged with incentive pay. But the teamwork that is relevant for most at the senior management level has to do with the people on the executive's immediate team: the group of managers running a group, division, profit center, or other business unit. Corporate performance measures offer plausible incentive effects only for the corporate-level executive cadre. Basing pay of others on corporate performance distances their incentive pay from their own work, discrediting the very idea of an incentive. Conversely, matching rewards more closely with one's scope of responsibility reinforces important notions of accountability and ownership. At the senior management level, after all, you normally can identify where the buck stops.

- *"Our bonus and performance incentive plans use goals from the budget and long-range plan as performance targets. This helps build accountability to the budgeting and business planning processes."* This reinforces the goal-setting process? Perhaps, but companies should be on guard. Incentives can subvert the company's planning processes as often as they reinforce them. Companies should tread more carefully here, particularly with so much more incentive pay riding on preset goals. As one provocative author in the *Harvard Business Review* put it a couple of years ago, when describing the moral hazards here, "The corporate budgeting process is a joke and everyone knows it."[12]

- *"Our pay packages reflect market norms, helping us attract and retain talented people for key jobs."* So, do we need to mimic the market in every regard? Companies used to feel obliged to do so. Options were nearly 100 percent of the game and were expense-free, and bonuses were nearly 100 percent budget-based and delivered by just a few common metrics. It was hard to ignore nearly unanimous market preferences. Pay opportunity should indeed be set with an eye on the market. And important matters like risk and term structure can be read from results of market action. But the market no longer issues mandates on matters like LTI mix or standard-setting. Those should have been company-specific choices all along, anyway.

One can bash market practices in incentive pay, as we have done in this chapter. And one can point out how governance actors and business competition are imposing new standards, as we do in the next chapter. But one cannot ignore market standards. Companies are acting prudently when they take them into account. Trying to keep top management pay below market is a very poor way of saving money, for example. It leads to mediocrity, turnover, or both. Another way to waste money is to make pay notably more risky, confusing, or deferred than market norms. Keeping pay systemically above market is just a waste of corporate assets.

Some assume that the use of pay survey data in and of itself allows pay levels to ratchet up well beyond what market forces would indicate. But that ignores that a functioning executive labor market exists and that pay levels are market prices, driven by supply and demand. Publishing the market trading price of a bushel of corn does not in and of itself make corn prices escalate. Pay is not corn, and this level of market efficiency cannot be expected as strongly in the more administered market for top officer pay. The executive pay market is not a perfect one in either sense of the term—it is neither flawless nor complete. It is, however, a fairly liquid market composed of willing, well-informed buyers and sellers. Its price outcomes should be expected to comport in gross terms with forces of supply and demand.

Companies sometimes cite "cream of the crop" hiring tactics when their pay is high. But these high-performing candidates should, as a group, bring about performance levels that fund their higher rewards. Some companies also say they set high goals for performance so they must set their pay objectives above the market's median. In each case, the company's general performance/award scale may be equivalent to market norms; they may simply have affixed the label "target" to a higher point on the scale.

Much of executive pay data is arrayed based on company revenue. Pay tends to be related to company size, and revenue figures are consistently available. Revenue does not by itself do a good job of measuring the investor capital at stake in a business or its ability to fund incentive pay out of expected financial results. If a company has a poor business outlook and a low market capitalization, paying executives at levels paid by similar-revenue companies may not be affordable. Companies with more value at stake and higher income prospects, by contrast, may sensibly target pay at levels higher than their revenue alone would indicate.

Ideally, such factors can be considered when defining the competitive market. Overall, once a typical company has its competitive market defined well, there are not a lot of valid reasons to depart greatly from its 50th percentile.

Incentives can help with selection dynamics in a market setting. Well-designed plans will appeal to those who are confident they can make a contribution and will discourage those who are not. An incentive plan's terms can be a highly effective way to ask managers to put their money where their mouth is. There is a performance edge to be had with better functioning incentives, and this is another way companies can chase it.

Fairness often is cited alongside market competitiveness as a tenet of pay strategy. But the pursuit of fairness can have mixed effects. That's true even when the incentive plan participants are dogs. Researchers at the University of Vienna trained dogs to shake hands. Then they brought in new dogs and asked them to do the same but gave them a piece of bread as a reward for every handshake. The unrewarded dogs were not happy. "They get so mad that they look at you and just don't give you the paw anymore," said Friederike Range, one of the scientists.[13] When they took away fairness, they found there was not a whole lot of shaking going on.

We are talking about using goals to differentiate pay more strongly, but that does not necessarily endanger fairness. If a handshake normally earns a piece of bread, dogs that shake hands more will end up with more bread. And if handshakes don't pay out any bread to any dog, that is fine, too. Companies don't have to place cash bounties on every line in one's job description. But, if they do, they need to be fair about it.

The pursuit of higher rewards is fine, on a level playing field. Pursuing fairness by equalizing outcomes is not. Incentive plans tend to equalize incentive payouts for peers across wide swaths of the organization. Everyone who is in, say, the 5,000-share granting tier gets the same grant and the same gains through the vesting period. Much of bonus pay is based on corporate results, so the bonus plan has more leveling and distancing effects.

An executive is likely to see the pay system as fair so long as it holds people to reasonably consistent pay and performance standards. To him, income inequality does not mean a bad pay system. Instead, it is what you expect to see when the system encourages performance by linking differential success with higher reward. Other approaches will rub our executive, and his dog, the wrong way.

▆ NOTES

1. Source for this data and other pay data presented in this chapter unless otherwise noted: U.S. CDB Executive Compensation Databank.
2. Current year data are for periods ended in 2008 or early 2009. Data are for the 472 companies whose stock-based compensation expenses were reported by Standard & Poor's for each year. Averages are not shown since they are distorted by outliers (e.g., companies with low or negative earnings).
3. Just as they are in our database, which follows the general presentation methods for LTI grants under U.S. generally accepted accounting principles (GAAP).

4. For example, see Mark Sirower, *The Synergy Trap: How Companies Lose the Acquisition Game* (New York: Free Press, 1997).
5. This variable was simulated by attaching a 1.4 percent standard deviation to the cost of capital; an approximation of the combined effects of independent, random movement in the cost of capital and in long-run growth expectations, each being normally distributed with a standard deviation of one percentage point.
6. Simulation model specifications: Market-based parameters were assigned to incentive plan terms and financial performance. Typical variation was applied to operating income in the near term (15 percent root mean square error around ten-year regression trend line) and this variation drove the 10,000 scenarios examined. Default assumptions about capital usage and capital structure were used to convert each scenario's operating income into the measures used in the annual incentive plan (constant capital structure in market value terms, excess equity cash flows used for share repurchases at ending share price each year). The most common measures were used at the corporate and business unit levels (EPS and operating income). Using this information about financial performance, annual incentive plan payouts were simulated. The annual incentive plan was assumed to comprise modal award ranges and leverage (80 to 120 percent performance range, 50 to 200 percent payout range). A random error of one percentage point from most likely forecast for growth in operating income was used to determine the target used in the annual incentive (this was done in order to simulate uncertainty, but not bias, in the annual incentive target-setting process).

   Stock returns (and option gains) were simulated using a ten-year discounted cash flow (DCF) model with separate assumptions applied to near-, medium-, and longer-term performance. Year 1 financial results in each scenario were the same ones used in simulating the bonus plan. Medium-term results were based on adaptive revision of the DCF forecast based on variation in one-year results. Modest random movement was attached to long-run expectations for business growth and also to the cost of capital (levels of variation resembled the variation in long corporate bond yields). The model's outputs were also validated by market norms; overall, the DCF simulation generated a pattern of stock returns resembling the stock market (continuously compounded share-holder return with a mean around 10 percent, a standard deviation of about 30 percent, and variance driven about one-half by consolidated financial performance over a five-year period). The 50 percent explanatory power attributed to financial performance was higher than typical. This was done in order to give some weight to the stock market's anticipatory nature and to its ability to reward for business decisions based on expected rather than actual results. The corporate performance share plan was based on EPS with performance ranges and payout leverage resembling the corporate element of the bonus plan.

   The simulation of the incentive structure focused in this case on a typical participant: a member of top management of a business unit. Movement in business unit financial results was assumed to be largely within the control of business unit management, or at least to represent a tolerable or customary risk. Variation in results of other businesses was assumed to be outside of the control of business unit management, as were market valuation parameters like the cost of capital and very long-run growth expectations. In this example, the overall "line of sight" figure of roughly 20 percent is the amount of variation in cash and stock-based incentive pay that is explained by variation in business unit results. The other 80 percent of the variation in incentive rewards was driven by variation in the cost of capital, in long-run growth expectations, in performance of other business units or in the outcome of the annual budget process.

7. For a representative example of statistical evidence, the report, "Company Performance and Measures of Value Added," by the Research Foundation of the Institute of Chartered Financial Analysts, examines a wide range of metrics and value creation. Findings make clear that the bulk of nearer-term variation in stock prices is not correlated with differences in measured performance.

8. "There is no relationship whatsoever," said Dan R. Dalton, dean of the business school at the University of Indiana, in his 2002 study examining research on linkages between stock option usage and company performance, quoted by David Leonhardt of *The New York Times* (D. R. Dalton, C. M. Daily, C. S. Trevis, and R. Roengpitya, "Meta-Analyses of Financial Performance and Equity: Fusion or Confusion?" *Academy of Management Journal*, April 2002). Separately, Kevin J. Murphy indicates, "Although there is ample evidence that CEOs (and other employees) respond predictably to dysfunctional compensation arrangements, it is more difficult to document that the increase in stock option incentives has led CEOs to work harder, smarter, and more in the interest of shareholders." (K. J. Murphy, "Executive Compensation." In O. Ashenfelter and D. Card (eds.), *Handbook of Labor Economics* (New York: Elsevier, 1999)).

9. W. G. Sanders, "Behavioral Responses of CEOs to Stock Ownership and Stock Option Pay," *Academy of Management Journal* 44 (2001), 477–492.

10. "Addressing Structural Issues in Executive Incentive Design," *WorldatWork Journal* (First Quarter 2002).

11. Seminal studies of LIFO conversions made this point starkly clear many years ago, as has much empirical research since. Regarding LIFO conversions, see the Sunder article in the 1973 *Empirical Research in Accounting*, and Biddle and Lindahl in the *Journal of Accounting Research* (Autumn 1982). The more general point about the stock market's preference for the economic portrayal of events (cash flow) over their accounting characterization is one upheld broadly for decades and a finding made clear in any review of relevant financial research. Examples include Hong, Mandelker, and Kaplan on purchases versus poolings in *Accounting Review* in 1978, an SEC study on R&D announcements published by the Office of the Chief Economist in 1985, Copeland and Lee on exchange offers, stock swaps and their EPS effects, published in *Financial Management* in 1991, and Kaplan and Ruback on the importance of cash flow in driving business value, "The Valuation of Cash Flow Forecasts: An Empirical Analysis," NBER working paper 4274.

12. Michael C. Jensen, "Corporate Budgeting is Broken. Let's Fix It," *Harvard Business Review,* (November 2001).

13. Gail Collins, "The Dreaded Fairness Doctrine," *New York Times* (December 13, 2008).

CHAPTER 4

The New Standards

Executives control trillions of dollars in business capital, opportunities, and ideas. Their incentive plans affect how they put all of that to use on behalf of many millions of stakeholders. Companies that use their resources effectively are companies that succeed and enrich their owners.

When they do, they enrich society more broadly. Successful companies in a competitive economy are the ones doing the best job of allocating their resources. When many enterprises are pushed by competition toward the highest performance standards, the usual result is a wealthy society. The gains from competition accrue mostly to customers, after all, and not to the competitors themselves. But there is still a big purse for the contenders, one large enough to attract a lot of them into the ring. They compete for capital, labor, and management talent, channeling each toward their highest-yield uses. All of them are being all they can be, in this situation, and they are prospering as a result.

But things can get messy. We all know the competitive process may be creative, destructive, or a lot of each. The outcomes may be winner-take-all.[1] They may entrain externalities like pollution and noise. Dislocations are ongoing and painful. There are critical duties for ethical governments. They maintain the economic platform. They also manage the collateral damage, regulating commerce, imposing taxes, and redistributing results in the manner tolerated by a democratic society.

But in the end, it is the contest for return on resources—precisely, this continual struggle to put business assets to their best use—that results in efficient and wealth-building outcomes for society in sum. And competitive self-interest is at the center of the machine. That is what keeps the economy's gigantic wheels moving. In an affront to both Malthus and Marx, economic activity, spurred by private market incentives, keeps billions of people alive from one year to the next. Government does not create the blessed middle-class lifestyle achievable in large swaths of the developed world. Efficient private market activity does.

To paraphrase Winston Churchill, free-market capitalism is a terrible mess but it works better than all the other systems that have been tried. It is a great force for the promotion of a society's material welfare. Milton Friedman put the prescription succinctly when he said, "The social responsibility of business is to increase its profits."[2] I might quibble with the metric "profits," preferring the phrase "long-run shareholder returns," but that is what economists mean by profit anyway. Society's highest and best use of its business resources is to maximize the financial success of competitive enterprises. This approach creates the most wealth for a society overall and for the bulk of its citizens. We are not making public policy here. But when societal wealth hinges on successful capital deployment, there is an overlap between public policy and corporate governance.

The corporate governance apparatus is necessary for the health of the capitalist system. We have identified some key agency arrangements—well-designed incentives at the senior management level—as one of the more effective governance tools available. They constitute one set of thorough and formal checks and balances on management decision making. They can be used to create explicit balance among the main drivers of value, consistently favoring long-term, sustainable value creation.

When companies address these matters these days, they do so in an environment of new standards. As we noted at the outset, this book is called *The New Standards* because it emphasizes that management incentives should now respond to new, tougher standards. These new standards originate from several sources. Shareholders and their activist representatives demand that executive pay costs be spent in exchange for real performance. They expect incentives to meet high quality standards for prudence in design and administration. They expect incentives to be used actively in governance and effectively as performance devices.

The new market situation obliges companies to do a better job of setting performance standards themselves. Capital markets impose standards, ones that identify conditions for value creation and shareholder returns. In the new environment around executive pay, capital market standards should be examined and implemented explicitly in matters like incentive structure, target setting, metric selection, and payout calibration.

The business world gets tougher and more competitive each year, and standards for business performance ratchet ever upward. All elements of business operations have been under great pressure to improve. Bookkeeping rules for a long time had the effect of stunting the evolution of incentives as critical performance devices. Now, companies feel much freer to choose. They can craft their designs after looking at a broad menu. They can do so fully in pursuit of potential business advantage in their own particular setting. The pace of "catch-up" and change has been rapid and will continue to be so.

To meet the new standards, companies need to look much more closely at their incentive policies and practices. We found helpful input by looking closely at how business results interact with value creation. We have also made an initial review of market norms in this area. Next comes a review of a representative sample of public commentary on executive incentive policy, setting out those elements that are endorsed most often. Then we will review how incentives match up with the scope of influence and accountability for a typical member of senior management. We will confront obstacles to incentive restructuring, highlighting in particular the necessity to set proper business goals. Along this way, we'll have completed our review of the new standards driving incentive design forward. That enables us by chapter end to pull together the full range of insights into a set of incentive design guidelines.

Let us outline some general ideas for strengthening the role of management incentive plans in support of key governance objectives. Top management, inescapably, has wide latitude and control. Boards do not run operations and are not charged with judging expertly all of the company's business initiatives and opportunities. That is management's job. In this setting, proactive agency arrangements are very important. Many traditional governance responses, in contrast, are reactive, taking effect after the company and its shareholders already have borne performance losses from poor decisions.

We are not the only ones talking about this. There are many voices in the governance sphere now and they have more to say about executive pay. New compliance demands have come from quarters like option expensing rules, Sarbanes-Oxley, exchange rules, new proxy rules, and other Securities and Exchange Commission (SEC) reporting and disclosure matters. Shareholder activists and scorekeepers include proxy voting advisory groups, the Council of Institutional Investors, pension funds, unions, Risk Metrics, and bond raters.

In the area of executive pay in particular, current governance mechanisms are limited and reactive in effect. Common approaches are often test- or checklist-centered, focusing incentive review on compliance rather than business efficacy. The role of performance benchmarks here is often to set a scale for evaluation of pay costs rather than to drive better performance itself.

In this book we have set forth arguments in favor not just governance *of* incentives, *but for the use of incentives in business governance.* I have been advocating an activist role for incentive policy in corporate governance for a long time in speeches, articles, and in an earlier book called *Pay to Prosper.*[3] But do not take my word for it. In recent years we have seen pronouncements from the corporate policy sphere becoming a lot more pointed, and a lot more activist, in regard to these very matters. Nowadays much more is said about linking executive pay with performance, where performance is measured in a high-quality way and demonstrated over time. We will take a scan of those pronouncements, culling their insights as input into our own statement of principles.

Here are some of the recent money quotes, pun intended, on incentive structure from the National Association of Corporate Directors (NACD):

- "Compensation committees and boards need to design pay packages that encourage long-term commitment to the organization's well-being."

- "While executives do need to meet short-term targets and should be rewarded for doing so, companies should award additional variable compensation based on achieving key metrics over an extended period of time—using company performance measures, rather than stock price alone, as criteria."

- "Pay must motivate and reward performance."

- "Boards need to set clear performance objectives for senior executives and measure performance against those objectives."

- "54 percent of board members believe that the main cause of inappropriate CEO pay packages is the absence of goal-oriented performance objectives against which performance can be rigorously evaluated."

- "Companies should be free to choose their own metrics in accordance with their own circumstances, but the current system has much room for improvement. Ideally, boards should strive to reward long-term, sustainable performance, as opposed to immediate gains."[4]

These statements provide a rather clear thumbs-up or thumbs-down regarding specific choices in the area of incentive design. Is it acceptable to base long-term incentives purely on the stock price, through grants of stock options and restricted stock? Not to the NACD. It is quite clear with demands for long-term performance against targets, not just stock gains, as a payout contingency. And where is the NACD on the subject of one-size-fits-all incentive schemes? It recognizes that business circumstances vary. Do these folks regard long-term target-setting as a particularly difficult and uncertain exercise? They might, but they apparently consider it to be part of the job.

Would they be content to outsource performance management to the stock market? And would relatively inert, after-the-fact results-sharing devices be acceptable as executive incentives? Hardly. The NACD wants to see pay used as a performance-driving mechanism. Is it okay for many millions of dollars to go out based on goals no one can affect? The NACD is making an implicit demand for strong line of sight, clarity, and efficacy.

It also said that "each corporate board must begin by adopting a compensation philosophy and a set of principles to guide its actions." So, will the NACD be okay with incentive policies that reflect a set of one-off issues and reactions that piled up over time? Or would it rather have incentive terms set deliberately, working as a system for sustained success?

The NACD also asks boards to involve themselves in strategy more heavily by "challenging the underlying assumptions of management" and "establishing high, realistic standards." That is a high expectation for board participation in standard setting, one that requires outside benchmarking and vetting of performance objectives. We set out a range of ways to approach this in Chapter 8.

The CFA (Chartered Financial Analyst) Centre for Financial Market Integrity weighed in on incentive policy in a white paper addressing the more general matter of short-term thinking, titled "Breaking the Short-term Cycle."[5] Some relevant quotes:

- "Align corporate executive compensation with long-term goals and strategies and with long-term shareowner interests. Compensation should be structured to achieve long-term strategic and valuation goals."

- "All three panels identified executive incentives that focus disproportionately on short-term objectives as a key driver of short-termism."

- "Stock ownership guidelines should require all executives and directors to hold a meaningful amount of equity . . ."

Here is another organization that is not content to see performance criteria confined to short-term incentive plans. Rather, it demands a regimen of persistent results. And the results clearly are meant to be high-quality ones, since the "meaningful" amount of required equity holdings stands ready to take a big hit if results do not support the share price. This organization clearly has activist expectations, not doubting incentive impacts on business decision making. In fact, they indict incentives in a culture of short-termism, and not without evidence:

> ". . . in a recent survey of more than 400 financial executives, 80 percent of the respondents indicated that they would decrease discretionary spending on such areas as research and development, advertising, maintenance, and hiring in order to meet short-term earnings targets and 50 percent said they would delay new projects, even if it meant sacrifices in value creation."

The Council of Institutional Investors offers some specific views of incentive policy in its discussion of corporate governance:

- "The Council believes that executive compensation is a critical and visible aspect of a company's governance."

- "Pay decisions are one of the most direct ways for shareowners to assess the performance of the board."

- "The Council endorses reasonable, appropriately structured pay-for-performance programs that reward executives for sustainable, superior

performance over the long-term, considered to be five or more years for
mature companies and at least three years for other companies."

- "Except in unusual and extraordinary circumstances, the compensation
  committee should not lower the bar by changing performance targets in
  the middle of bonus cycles."

- Among many specific design preferences, the council notes that "Stock
  awards should not be payable based solely on the attainment of tenure
  requirements."[6]

This group does not see incentive policy as an exercise in competitive mim-
icry and administrative expediency. Their take is an activist one as well, and they
are looking for incentive policy to improve governance. They want sustained
performance, ruling out purely time-vesting restricted stock in particular. And
they do not concede that goal-setting is just too tough to do. They want it
done, and then they want to see feet held to the fire.

CalPERS is not silent on this matter, either. Here are guidelines from their
Core Principles of Accountable Corporate Governance that go to the question
of incentive design:

- "A significant portion of executive compensation should be comprised of
  at risk pay or tied to . . . achieving performance objectives."

- "Performance objectives should be set before the start of the period. . . .
  (these) include but are not limited to, Return on Invested Capital (ROIC),
  Return on Assets (ROA), and Return on Equity (ROE)."

- "Meaningful performance hurdles that align the interests of management
  with long-term shareowners should be established with incentive compensation being directly tied to the attainment and/or out-performance of
  such hurdles."

- "Equity based compensation plans should incorporate the achievement of
  performance-based components . . . premium-priced options, index-
  based options, and performance targets tied to company-specific metrics
  that are required to achieve vesting."[7]

Goals should be achieved for stock gains to be monetized by management.
Fair enough. And they want to see companies measuring results in comparatively complete terms—using capital-conscious metrics such as ROIC rather
than just income, and requiring that payout mechanisms be set to line up with
shareholder interests.

The Business Roundtable sets out some relevant notes in its white paper
"Executive Compensation—Principles and Commentary":

- "Executive compensation should be closely aligned with the long-term interests of shareholders and with corporate goals and strategies."

- "It should include significant performance-based criteria related to long-term shareholder value and should reflect upside potential and downside risk."

- "The compensation committee should understand all aspects of executive compensation and should review the maximum payout and all benefits under executive compensation arrangements."

- "The compensation committee should require executives to build and maintain significant continuing equity investment in the corporation."

- ". . . the structure and components of an appropriate executive compensation program will vary widely among corporations. . . ."[8]

So, goals are compulsory, calibration and testing are crucial, and executives should stand along with shareholders as the economic consequences of their actions play out over time. I do not know about anyone else, but I am beginning to detect a pattern here.

In their nod to practicability, the Roundtable notes that designs cannot follow a one-size-fits-all pattern, since circumstances differ so much. We near the end of our circuit at the Financial Stability Forum (FSF), reviewing its FSF "Principles for Sound Compensation Practices." These are targeted at large financial institutions:

- The firm's board of directors must actively oversee the compensation system's design and operation.

- The firm's board of directors must monitor and review the compensation system to ensure the system operates as intended.

- Compensation is an incentive system, not simply a market wage.

- Too little attention is given to links between compensation and risk.

- Compensation must be adjusted for all types of risk.

- Compensation outcomes must be symmetric with risk outcomes.

- Compensation schedules must be sensitive to the time horizon of risks.

- Payments should not be finalized over short periods when risks are realized over long periods.

- The mix of cash, equity, and other forms of compensation must be consistent with risk alignment.

- Supervisors must include compensation practices in their risk assessment of firms.[9]

These folks have caught onto the idea of governance and of incentives as a system, and they clearly have high expectations for how actively and competently the board is meant to manage all that. And, focusing on financial services companies, they emphasize risk matters very strongly. Does risk interact with incentive pay design? Yes indeed, and its importance is as great in general industry as it is in the financial services sector. Chapter 5 is devoted wholly to risk and incentive pay.

The FSF report acknowledges that management and compensation committees have to delve into the details to track performance properly in the high-stakes arena of executive pay: "As a practical matter, the compensation system often includes its own accounting system for profit-and-loss (so called "management P&L"), with rules for the treatment of revenue and expense that differ across business units and that depart from accounting standards for financial statements."

The FSF report also sets out a form of the remote-control-governance strategy for incentive pay, in observations that could apply to any company in any industry:

> Major financial institutions are too large to be managed solely by the direct knowledge and action of senior management. Consequently, systems such as accounting systems, budgets, position limits, capital allocations, risk management and control systems and, importantly, compensation systems are designed to encourage employees to accomplish the goals set by senior management and the firm's governing bodies.

Last, but certainly not least, The Conference Board weighed in profoundly on executive pay in late 2009. Some key excerpts on incentive policy and other matters:

- Metric should be chosen "taking into account the potential risks associated with the various metrics."
- "Incentive compensation should not encourage excessive or inappropriate risk taking, nor discourage an appropriate level of risk taking . . ."
- "Payouts for achieving shorter-term goals should support the company's strategy for building long-term shareholder value."
- ". . . a 'one size fits all' or 'rules-based' approach to executive compensation is not workable."
- ". . . require executives to have a meaningful position in the company's stock . . ."[10]

These folks said quite a lot and did so in specific terms. They clearly desire a balanced risk profile, connections to shareholder value, and a focus on the longer term. They do not endorse inflexible limits and formulaic tests, either.

They want executives to earn their money, asking for payouts to be based on matters that executives can influence and for business-unit executives to be paid on business unit results. They would also like to see the role of happenstance reduced in favor of genuinely earned results, and for payout schedules to be calibrated and tested closely for unseen biases and costs (matters covered extensively in several later chapters):

- ". . . take into account an executive's responsibility for and/or ability to affect the achievement of the metric . . ."
- "Compensation committees should consider the extent to which performance has been significantly influenced by external circumstances, rather than by the efforts and skills of executives."
- ". . . business unit executives may have a relatively higher percentage of incentive compensation based on business unit results."

Should incentive targets be an inside game? The Conference Board came down strongly on the other side, pressing a range of external benchmarks of the types covered extensively in Chapter 8:

> Committee should consider appropriate information regarding the company's industry and company growth rates, historical targets and actual performance relative to those targets, investor expectations, and key competitors and their performance levels. External expectations regarding the company, such as analyst reports and models and expectations built into the current stock price can also be useful sources for assessing appropriate targets for incentive compensation.

The Conference Board also takes aim at common but poor policy-making practices like these:

- In regard to having controversial pay practices, "Everyone else does it" or "It is market practice" are not sufficient reasons.
- "Poorly executed benchmarking, particularly when coupled with widespread targeting of above median pay levels, is widely believed to have contributed to the upward spiral in executive pay."

COMMON SENSE

These watchdog groups often differ in the details of their pronouncements, but they are displaying remarkable consistency in the broad strokes. Putting the details aside, they provide a set of common, specific preferences for the structure of executive incentives at the top of the house:

- Executive pay should be linked to proper business goals, not just stock price.

- Top officers should be obliged to hold substantial amounts of company stock, enough to enforce a kind of "economic clawback."

- Compensation committees and boards face high expectations—they are meant to participate actively in pay design and to make prudent and fitting choices.

- Incentives are agency/governance devices, not just elements of competitive wage administration.

- Incentive outcomes should not just reflect near-term earnings but be focused strongly on longer-term results, their quality and sustainability, and the levels of risk and capital usage involved.

- Pay outcomes should be linked to shareholder wealth, be based on incentive plans that encourage value-creating business decisions, and should protect shareowners from unwarranted pay costs.

- Pay decisions should be guided by agreed-to principles or overarching philosophy, and programs should work together as a system.

- There is no one-size-fits-all solution—proper designs depend on each company's circumstances. Judgment and adjustments are not prohibited and goals do not have to be limited to financial results as reported.

- Combinations of metrics can create a favorable balance. Metrics and plans are expected to work effectively as a system.

BIAS IS THE BOLL WEEVIL OF VALUE CREATION

Turning our view back inside the business, you can say the role of incentives in business performance has to do with decision making—with making specific improvements to specific decisions. Many companies know they would look better if they could go back in time and expunge some big mistakes from the economic record. They cite a bad acquisition, an ill-conceived new product, or a failed reorganization. In other instances, complacency can leave even a very successful business franchise vulnerable. As a former CEO of 3M once put it, "Success inoculates against change." When describing bad turns in a business, executives do not always tell of solid business decisions that just went bad. Rather, they often recount the writing that was on the wall for all to read, the trail of management decisions that ignored it, and the persistent decision-making issues that make it a risk the next time around, too.

So, should the enterprise work to avoid mistakes? Sure, but it should not make it Job One. Mistake avoidance can be taken to the point where it outlaws the proper risk taking involved in business success and value creation. Just like scrap reduction, customer satisfaction, and so many other nodes on the causal chain to value creation, an ethic of mistake avoidance has its point of diminishing returns. In the context of executive decision making, bias is the real enemy:

- Risk-related biases can paralyze the company or, on the other hand, encourage it to gamble too freely with other people's money.
- Short-term bias may exclude much of the landscape of business opportunity.
- The system of rewards may bias managers to pursue individual accolades, empires, and advancement over greater team results.
- Growth biases may lead to overinvestment in mediocre businesses, overspending on product and promotion, overpriced acquisitions, and other wastes of corporate assets.
- Biases against investment may starve the business of capital needed for perfectly good growth opportunities.

If you want incentives to work, you have to set them up to work at the *decision* level. But that does not require identifying every decision that might get made and devising incentive terms to address it. Incentives need to be consistently, directionally proper when applied to the wide range of circumstances that may prevail. What we need to do is to chase the biases out of the system. Then we can let the money do the work—the money we already are spending each year on incentive pay.

GET CYNICAL

Does this approach place too much emphasis on money and its influence? Perhaps incentive money does not matter all that much. Instead, perhaps most executives practice a kind of capitalistic altruism, always aiming to do right by shareholders even when it threatens their own rewards. If the world actually looked like that, there still would be good reasons to align incentive pay with the operant parts of value creation:

- As we have said, stock and options do not come with instructions on how to create value. Bonus plans have a more didactic format, but their message is often erroneous since many allow pay to increase when investor returns are falling. Better-designed incentive plans clarify the real path to value creation. Most companies can get better economic yield from business opportunities by evaluating them more consistently in terms of their main value drivers. Linking these concepts to pay is another way to increase their visibility throughout the enterprise and get better business decisions. A well-designed incentive plan is a bully pulpit indeed.

- From a purely fiscal viewpoint, competitive amounts of incentive pay bring a large cost. This cost behaves better if it is funded by value creation close to the source. In that case, measures of business results—ones used to make business decisions—are netted at every level by the substantial pay costs they entrain. A more complete portrayal of the net success of business units allows better judgments about them, better resource allocation and better results over time.

For at least some of the people some of the time, incentives do matter. A certain amount of diligence in these matters is required, just as it is for other commitments made on behalf of owners. Just as companies do when forming legal contracts, they should design incentives under the assumption that the parties will not act exclusively in their mutual interests in the future.

The problem with a broad-based assumption of altruism is that it is very often wrong. Recall the Michael Douglas character in a signature movie of the 1980s, *Wall Street*, and his tagline, "Greed . . . is good." For incentive purposes, self-interest is good. It is reliable as a motive, while altruism is not. Companies can depend on it.

Adam Smith did not hesitate to point out the role of competitive self-interest in the causal chain that builds the wealth of nations. Consider one of Milton Friedman's arguments, as well. Say you are shopping for something for yourself. Clothes, food, a dozen spider monkeys, it does not matter. If you are shopping for yourself, you are diligent in getting the best value for your money and in getting exactly what you want. In a second case, you are shopping for someone you do not know. You might still be careful with your money, but you are not likely to zero in on getting the perfect item for that person to the same extent as you would for yourself. In a third case, you are spending a third party's money to buy something for a stranger. At this point, you are not as careful either with the money spent or the choice that is made. The first case is what we mean by ownership when talking about management incentives. It means you have a direct stake both in the resources used and the benefits they create. The third and worst example is the incentive system in place at most companies (and in government). The source of the capital and its rewards are found only at a distance.

As for investors, they want competitive, money-focused people running their companies. When these people are spending owner money and chasing business opportunities, investors want them to covet gains and fear risks. If they did not have a healthy interest in money, investors would not trust them to apply the proper diligence to the many, many money decisions involved in their jobs. You want first-class executives in those jobs, not first-class philosophy professors.

The assumption of self-interest is proper and prudent to build into the design of incentive plans. And the reality is workable as well, if you want those plans to have an effect on company results. We are going to assume that the people in management have the motive to enrich themselves in whatever way their incentive plans allow. We are going to ensure we do not give them the means to do so, instead concentrating their financial interests to support those of owners. The presumptions of this kind of analysis will appear cynical at times. The details of many legal agreements may seem that way, too, but, in those contracts as well as these, looking for trouble is diligent and proper, while ignoring it is sloppy and hazardous.

INCENTIVIZATION AND ITS DISCONTENTS

Well-designed incentives are not going to discourage anything management should be doing. That is the easy part. All incentive systems accentuate the positive, enabling some reward for high-quality decision making. They may have lots of biases, to be sure, and they often obscure the incentive linkages. But directionally at least, they allow good things to happen to good people.

The issues have to do with the bad stuff. Badly designed incentives allow bad decisions to pay off. If incentives are to be used actively in governance—to stave off biases, as just noted, and to encourage value creation—they will have to be based on things people understand and feel they can control. They will have to employ proper, measurable goals, ones set well enough to hold up to the heavy duties of accountability and reward for senior management.

Bonus pay already is based mainly on goals, but those often can be made to work better—to be more directive, to align more closely with value creation over time and to create a stronger sense of control. The big change in long-term incentive pay in recent years is a heavier reliance on formal goals, and there is room for improvement in corporate practices there. To get to where companies should be, running goal-based incentives effectively is the biggest challenge. That is what most of the balance of this book is about.

Goals always have been challenging to set and administer at companies. The financial crisis of 2008 brought some of these problems into relief. Some executives and compensation members wanted to beat a retreat from the rigors of goal setting. They said, reasonably, "we can't set reliable long-term goals for our business right now, so let's just grant options and stock or maybe use relative TSR."

Hesitancies about goal-based pay always have been around, though. And the events of 2008 exposed the difficulties of stock-based pay at least as strongly as those of goal-based pay. Relative metrics are no picnic, either, as we will see in

Chapter 10. The fact is that goals can be set and administered practically in just about all business conditions. And, post-crisis, we still find high prevalence for goal-based opportunities. Doing so is, by now, *de rigueur*:

- For most companies most of the time, there is plenty of evidence available regarding the central range of performance expectations and how pay programs are meant to share it with management.

- Performance ranges likely should be wider when things are uncertain, but that does not mean they cannot be set. Very risky businesses set up performance/payout schedules all the time. An example is a bonus pool used in a trading business.

- Metrics and goals can be flexible, adaptive, and accommodating to business events. Companies do not have to see their incentives short-circuited by predictable events or even by very unusual ones, but they do.

- Just about everyone runs a bonus plan, every year. It is an exercise that places high stakes on attainment of financial performance at levels sufficient to warrant and fund the bonus. In any year, in the most strange or troubled cases, the bonus plans may operate without formal financial standards. But that does not mean that standards are not meant to apply. Wait until year-end. If core indicators of management's financial contribution have gone in one direction, do not expect bonus funding to go in the other, even if everyone's performance was dazzling against nonfinancial goals.

- Long-term goals are said to be harder to set than short-term ones. But they are easier in a sense because the overlapping set of long-term cycles, each of which involves an averaging of results, is more forgiving of inaccuracy over time. These plans can be high maintenance, but they do provide lots of swings at the piñata. Companies also have a broader set of external indicators to consult when they are setting longer goals and they have more design solutions on the table as well.

- Management works up budgets for the board every year, along with long-range plans and specific forecasts related to deal or investment approvals. In the ordinary course of business, lots of big-ticket decision making hinges on guesses about the future. Running goal-based incentives is a lot easier than that. You do not have to predict the future. Instead you have to devise a reasonable performance/payout schedule that applies only *once the future performance outcome is known*. As bets go, incentive promises can be designed as rather hedged ones.

Not using long-term goals also means forgoing one of the most effective ways to use incentive policy to address risk management in the enterprise. For most companies most of the time, long-term goals should be on the menu.

A large, diversified manufacturing client indicated it would not set consolidated goals for long-term incentive (LTI) purposes in 2009, indicating uncertainties were too great. Another large client in the medical products industry, not particularly diversified and also facing uncertainties, went ahead and committed to paying out for long-term goals as it had in the past. Since past results were not a useful guide to prospective targeting, it consulted analyst forecasts and other forward-looking indicators. It acknowledged the uncertainties of the goals by using somewhat wider performance ranges than it had in the past (each technique is noted in Chapter 8).

This is an area where most companies should address and solve the problems rather than capitulating. In any activist incentive approach, you are obliged to place more emphasis on business goals in order to get greater efficacy from the huge amount of money spent on incentives. Absent this rigor, you cannot really link payouts with management's contribution to value creation, at the corporate or business-unit level.

Senior management cannot escape the general idea that they are accountable to concrete standards of performance. To assert otherwise is self-discrediting from someone in such a role. And it is a nonstarter in any governance discussion. If a board wants to be more engaged, expect financial standards and accountabilities to be the first tools they reach for. Governance groups clearly expect boards to make a close review of business strategy and plans, challenging assumptions and forecasts. Incentives can be helpful to this process as well, consistently encouraging plans that create value for owners and doing so in direct and specific terms.

Avoiding the setting of long-term business goals does not mean evading standards of performance. It just means using exclusively stock-based long-term incentive vehicles and metrics. This tactic punts the most important performance determinations to the stock market. The company has a generalized kind of accountability, in that case. It just does not have effective incentive pay. That means it is wasting corporate resources. Also, it is abandoning a performance tool that governance bodies consider to be important.

LEADING CHARACTER

We have heard a lot from the stock market, from the pay market, and from the lively market of corporate punditry. Before we move on to finalize our standards, let us examine a last constituency—the sell-side actors in the executive labor market, also known as senior management.

Let us return to the example executive from Chapter 3, the one who heads up manufacturing in a large business unit. He is like many senior management members. They have big, well-paid jobs, ones in which they have a material impact on long-term performance, either for the overall company or a good-sized profit center or function. His influence plays out either through his own scope of authority or his contributions within the management team.

Designing incentives for senior managers should be easy. Their roles and characteristics pose no serious problems with measurement or accountability:

- *His actions affect results, so we can judge his performance or that of his team based on actual business performance.* It may take a few years for some of the things the team does to show up in measured results, but they will, one way or another.

- *He knows his business.* He and his fellow group executives understand the cause-and-effect and timing dimensions of most business decisions they make. We can tie his pay to simple measures of business success and not have to write him a script for how he is going to get there. Remember, when we are talking with an executive, we are on the wrong side of an asymmetric information divide. If we try to micromanage his actions through complex schemes of performance objectives, we may simply put him in a position to exploit the inevitable loopholes.

- *He is a fairly good judge of risk.* You do not see many executives playing Three Card Monte or buying an extended warranty on a new toaster. On the contrary, they are pretty good intuitive statisticians. That means they will make better business decisions. So we need to set up pay structures that pose a reasonable chance of paying off. Otherwise, they will discount what we give them. Also, just to be careful, we should not put them in a position where they can gamble with shareholder money without bearing associated losses.

- *Our example executive is relatively entrepreneurial.* He is comfortable being held accountable for his actions and for business results, and he does not find the normal uncertainties inherent in his own business to be unnerving. He will sign up for lots of typical incentive pay risk as long as he has reasonable influence and upside.

- *He is not comfortable with risks that are way out of his control or that do not have anything to do with his business, like results of other business units or the parent company's stock price.* If we subject him to a lot of risks that are far beyond his control, one way or another he will make us pay for it.

- *He has a reasonably long-term perspective.* And most of the things he does are things that, if effective, show up in measured results within a reasonable period of time (one to five years). We do not have to try to bridge any time span with nonfinancial "value drivers" or "leading indicators" of success to incentivize him on a reasonably timely basis.

- *He likes money.* He uses it in the traditional way—as scorecard points in an ongoing competition with his college buddies. If his pay is mostly unrelated to his performance, or if it actively discourages him from taking the kinds of difficult and uncertain actions that are often involved in improving business performance, his performance probably will not be as good.

- *He is not a perp.* We do not have to use the precise terms of incentive plans to police all of his actions. If we simply draw a bold line from good business results to high personal wealth, then we will not have to worry too much about him spending all his time trying to game the system.

- *Senior managers are found at too great a distance from the CEO, board, or shareholders to be monitored directly by them or for stock-based incentives to be particularly effective as agency tools.* That means corporate leadership has to lean heavily on other governance tools (e.g., performance management, reward systems, and financial controls) to be sure these folks are consistently serving shareholders.

- *Lastly, for someone at this level, incentive plans are the biggest part of how he gets paid.* So, when we design incentive arrangements, we probably have his attention.

This is the ideal situation in which to be designing incentive plans and hoping they'll work. We do not need to draw a picture for our participant. All we need to do is set up something that tracks good business results in a reasonably clear and complete way, then tie pay to that over a period of years. He knows his business, and he likes money, so he can take it from there.

GUIDELINES FOR INCENTIVE DESIGN

Companies are in an era of new, higher and more specific standards for the use of incentives in business governance. Following are guidelines for executive incentive design, compiled based on inputs from the wide range of sources we reviewed:

- *Management's job is to govern the enterprise in such a way as to maximize the wealth of shareholders. Incentives should support this charge directly.* All of the enterprise's other stated pursuits are signposts along the path to value creation. Management serves as the agent of the company's owners—its shareholders. People in senior management are in the "decision" business and their product is value creation. Their unique charge is to make long-term commitments of the company's resources and to manage its ongoing operations in the hope of earning returns for shareholders. Stock price changes plus dividends equal the "total return" earned by shareholders. To serve shareholders, incentives must directly encourage management to maximize long-run total shareholder return.

- *Companies must use incentives as a proactive instrument of corporate governance, one that stands a continuous vigil in pursuit of high performance.* Within the corporate governance structure, senior management is the group that holds the bulk of the important information and prerogatives. Shareholder influence on business matters is comparatively fractional, anonymous, and distant. The board does not run the company and therefore cannot act in an intensive and timely way on business problems or opportunities. The general governance structure of business—board and shareholder oversight, relevant laws—cannot by itself encourage high performance consistently in the many actions that management can take. People in management can be counted on to act in their own financial self-interest, so companies must be sure that maximizing shareholder wealth is in the interest of management. Management incentives are that part of the rewards system that is meant to link executive pay and performance in a particularly explicit and compelling way.

- *To be effective, incentive plans must create a high degree of line of sight from actions to results to rewards.* They must be clear and specific, encouraging business decisions that create value and discouraging those that do not. Effective incentives must focus on matters that management can control, and most cannot affect the stock price much. This means *company stock cannot be used effectively as the centerpiece of the incentive structure for many executives.* For most companies, it also means using goal-based pay more heavily and more effectively, in annual- and long-term incentive plans. This is the key to having a proactive, compelling incentive structure and also one that creates a structure of accountability to fair standards of business performance.

- *Incentive mechanisms must take account of how performance is valued by capital markets.* The stock market judges business performance in relation to its own valuation criteria and expectations—expected levels of cash flow that can be distributed from business operations in the future and the risk of those cash flows. These external benchmarks determine whether a given set of business results is likely to create value. That is how the market judges what is and is not good performance, and how it determines whether earnings are high quality or not. Incentives must take account of these investor valuation criteria. Incentive goals also must take clear account of the level of performance expectations held by investors. To the market, a company's budgets and financial plans are just one potential source of information to use in forming expectations. That is true whether the company is listed on an exchange, is privately held, or is a business unit or venture interest of a larger company.

- *Investors hold financial claims on business performance that are unlimited, long-term, concrete and continuous. A company's incentive structure should be similar in each regard.* Investors enjoy the full range of upside in business performance, as well as the downside. Their claims are long-term in nature and contractually strong, so they are concerned not only with the near term, but with the long run. Even if they sell their interests and do not stay for the long term, they know the price they receive will be driven by the long-run performance expectations prevailing at the time of sale. Their claims are unbroken, so every dollar the company uses, every bit of income it generates, and any resulting change in value will support or reduce their returns over time.

- *Executives in relatively separable business units must have a decisive stake in the businesses they run.* A glance at a typical company's annual report shows enterprise income, capital, and risks dispersed into reasonably separable business units. Substantial opportunities for value creation are found at the business unit level, along with a large part of the senior management workforce and important degrees of decision-making authority. To match stake and accountability properly with authority, companies must create a substantial stake in success of entities like groups, divisions, profit centers, and joint ventures.

- *The effective time horizon of incentive pay must be long term, to align it with share-holder interests.* The incentive structure should create a continuously forward-looking reward mechanism, one with high concern for results each year. Enterprise value is based on long-run performance. Nearer-term results account only for a small part of a typical company's value, although they often are used by the stock market to revise longer-term performance expectations. Most of what differentiates one stock price from the next, particularly among industry peers, stems from differences in the expectations about performance over the next few years. Most of the things management does will produce measurable success or failure within a few years. Long-term incentive grants spanning three- to five-year periods will align management's perspective on business results with that of an investor. Annual incentive parameters can be improved and stabilized as well, working to create an effectively longer-term stake for management.

- *Three basic financial variables drive value: long-run operating income, capital usage and risk. Incentive structure must take proper account of each.* Most methods for business valuation boil down to these three drivers. They are the financial doors through which all business results, prospects, or other factors must pass if they are to have an effect on value.

- *Incentives must be calibrated to align closely with value creation.* The traditional metrics used in most incentive plans—yardsticks such as earnings per share (EPS), net income, revenue, operating income, and ROE—do not drive value creation consistently at all. They do not reflect the three basic value drivers in proper proportion, so they can allow many kinds of value-destroying business decisions to be rewarded. They also can discourage many value-creating decisions. This is a serious flaw in many plans. Remedies can be pursued in a range of ways involving plan targets and ranges, traditional and value-based metrics, the calibration of performance/payout schedules, and the specifics of plan administration, communication, and training.

- *Companies should deliver goal-based pay based on sustained results of operations with little effect from nonoperational matters like financing policy.* Capital structure decisions like debt or repurchase policy may have some impact on company value and returns, but any such effects are uncertain, modest, and outside the control of most people in senior management. Much of top officer pay is stock-based, so any gains from financing policy are felt there. Companies should not undertake financing transactions like an initial public offering (IPO), the full or partial sale of a subsidiary, or a leveraged buyout (LBO) primarily in pursuit of incentive effects. Such effects can be created without the transaction.

- *On the particular matter of metrics, market valuation principles are agnostic about which to use for incentive purposes.* Valuation methods identify specific linkages between performance and value, but they do not prescribe which measures to use in management incentive plans. They simply encourage any approach that supports value creation, just as they encourage any other business initiative that is likely to create value for investors. The task of value-focused incentive design is not to implement any particular metrics. It is, instead, to ensure that the principles of valuation are reflected consistently within the more general structure of incentive pay.

- *To be fair and complete, incentives must take account of the "total return" that an enterprise delivers to its owners—cash flows and gains in valuation.* There is no single combination of value drivers that maximizes value creation, as a general rule. Many different kinds of companies with different performance profiles can generate a given amount of value creation for investors. Low-growth companies may generate more cash flows for distribution to investors, while higher-growth ones build more value. Incentives often are biased in favor of businesses with higher growth. This is a common source of unfairness in company incentive plans, one that often encourages the pursuit of economically unprofitable growth.

- *Business conditions often are volatile or difficult to foresee. For incentives to be consistently effective, they must be adaptable.* Inflexible incentives may bias decision making, shorten time frames, and encourage income manipulation. Incentive terms should include methods for addressing business events like acquisitions, divestitures, large investments, and nonrecurring income or loss. They should also accommodate a wide range of potential business outcomes, properly scaling rewards to results in each situation. Here again, many tools and approaches are available.

- *Value is a function of anticipated results. Incentives should not fall prey to biases that stem from irrelevant historical results.* In business valuation, the past is relevant only as prologue. Value is driven by expectations about the future. The metrics and standard-setting procedures companies employ in incentive plans, in contrast, can be distorted by legacy effects. This affects assessments of performance against industry standards, over time, or among business units of a company or after acquisitions. Instead, they should encourage growth, risk management, and capital accountability at the margin.

- *Accounting does not matter.* Business value is based on economic results, not on the accounting portrayal of those results. Performance metrics should be based on economic performance. And accounting rules should not affect the choices companies make about how to structure incentive pay. Companies should design their incentive plans in pursuit of business efficacy, not bookkeeping expediency.

- *Risk is a major concern, affecting incentive choices in many ways.* Incentive design is chock full of risk-related subject matter, and risk is a top driver of business value. Risk management is an important aspect of corporate governance more generally. Incentive plans can encourage inappropriate risk-taking or a culture of risk aversion. Many specific choices—metrics, the term structure of incentive pay, targeting for ROIC, and other metrics—connect explicitly with risk effects. Incentive policy should take explicit account of risk. It should specifically encourage executives to balance risk against return as an investor would and to be on guard for ways in which plans might encourage inappropriate risk taking or risk aversion.

- *Executives should be required to hold meaningful amounts of stock.* Shared ownership has a range of benefits, even if the holders do not always feel much influence on the share price. One purpose is to impose a kind of "economic clawback," devaluing the general results of past incentives if the stock price does not hold up. This is a reasonable linkage between shareholders and senior management as a group. Ownership may be helpful in an incentive sense, strictly speaking, for the very top officers. It also creates shared stakeholders for every business initiative, with the heightened level of vigilance that buy-in transactions are meant to create.

- *There is no one-size-fits-all solution for incentive design.* Design advice from governance and watchdog groups is consistent in its broad strokes. However, company circumstances differ greatly, and so do their structures and strategies. A given set of principles can be implemented, much of the time, in a range of different ways. Companies should strive to pursue what will work best for them in their own unique set of circumstances.

- *Companies should not attempt to use incentives as a substitute for business strategy or as a tool of micromanagement.* Incentive plans are comparatively blunt instruments. The basic value drivers, time intervals, and organizational levels involved in a company's incentive structure do not allow it to track all of the dynamics of market value. To be effective, incentive plans must focus on the basics. They must create a clear, enduring stake in value creation and not be adjusted or revised heavily. Even in basic form, however, proper incentives can be remarkably resilient in the way they address the details of business decision making. They are not a substitute for business strategy but they can support high-quality strategy formulation and execution in specific and decisive terms.

- *Well-functioning incentives are important to companies and to society more generally.* Companies can get better business results through better incentive design. This subject matter warrants the best efforts and attention of senior executives and board members. Speaking more generally, a business environment that does a good job of encouraging competitive success, particularly for those in key decision-making roles in the economy, contributes importantly to national welfare. The design of senior management incentives is an essential component of this system. It is worth doing well.

These guidelines challenge current practices in the area of executive incentives, but this is good news for companies. A typical company is not getting strong differential performance from most of the money it spends on incentive pay. Companies can change what they do and get substantial returns on these outlays. The balance of this book shows how to address the new standards for incentive pay, using these design guidelines to create better executive incentive programs.

■ NOTES

1. Robert H. Frank and Philip J. Cook, *The Winner-Take-All Society* (1995 Simon & Schuster). The notion of creative destruction was introduced in Joseph A. Schumpeter, *Capitalism, Socialism and Democracy* (New York: Harper, 1975) [orig. pub. 1942], pp. 82–85.

2. *New York Times Magazine*, September 13, 1970.

3. WorldatWork, 2004.

4. National Association of Corporate Directors: NACD White Papers: Series 1, "Key Agreed Principles to Strengthen Governance Risk Oversight/Transparency/Strategy/ Executive Compensation."

5. CFA Centre for Financial Market Integrity, "Breaking the Short-Term Cycle," copyright© 2006 CFA Institute, Business Roundtable Institute for Corporate Ethics.

6. The Council of Institutional Investors Corporate Governance Policies, October, 2008.

7. California Public Employees' Retirement System, "Core Principles of Accountable Corporate Governance," 2007.

8. The Business Roundtable, "Executive Compensation—Principles and Commentary," 2007.

9. Financial Stability Forum, "FSF Principles for Sound Compensation Practices," 2009.

10. The Conference Board, "The Conference Board Task Force on Executive Compensation," 2009.

CHAPTER 5

Risk and Executive Incentive Pay

In a book I wrote a few years ago, I referred to risk as "the next big thing."[1] That is not true anymore. Risk is the big thing *now*. The financial crisis of 2008 pushed risk to the forefront, raising concerns that corporate incentives encouraged inappropriate risk-taking up and down the corporate ladder. This did not require a crisis, though. Business risks of all kinds were becoming a more prominent concern for senior management, company boards, and a range of regulators and advocates.

Whether widely known or not, the fact is that risk is an increasingly explicit part of common business decision making. Many products and services involve risk transfers. The leasing and mortgage sectors changed the basic risk profile of many durable goods purchases, for example—and some of those risk changes were intentional. Risk transfers go far beyond financial industry products like insurance, swaps, and hedges. Bundled outsourcing arrangements, for example —from staff functions to energy management—are replete with risk-shifting implications. Restructuring of corporate retirement benefit policies has moved an enormous amount of net risk from the business sector to households.

It is a big world full of risky opportunities. *Astute management teams understand that many business decisions require them to buy and sell risk.* Balancing and managing risks is now widely seen as a key governance charge. Those who have done it well have a serious performance advantage. Less astute players have self-immolated. Some have taken big risks and gotten by unscathed, but that experience does not endorse a *habit* of excessive risk taking. Christopher Walken's character in the movie *The Deerhunter* survived his initial, forced round of Russian roulette. So, was he a winner?

It makes sense to think through the ways in which executive incentives connect with the risk dimensions of business decision making. So far, we have identified risk as a primary driver of the cost of capital. It is one of the three primary drivers of business valuation. It sets the valuation scale of the other two drivers, income and capital usage:

- It translates income into value. A $100 level income stream is worth $1,000 at a 10 percent cost of capital but $1,250 at an 8 percent cost of capital.

- It determines whether capital deployed in a business creates value or not. An investment yielding 10 percent in total returns will create value if the cost of capital is 8 percent and destroy it if the cost of capital is 12 percent.

The cost of capital is the rate of return that investors need to compensate them for the risks they bear. And, as seen in Chapter 2, expected business performance, if achieved, creates results for investors equal to the cost of capital (holding all else equal).

When companies make risk and its costs a visible element of their incentive plans, they do it most often by incorporating a cost of capital into the measurement or benchmarking apparatus. In Chapter 7 we will see how value-based metrics do this explicitly. They attach a formal risk-based capital charge to business performance, perform a valuation of business results based on the company's cost of capital, or attach notional risk-based capital requirements to the business when computing its level of return. Companies using the traditional financial metrics set forth in Chapter 6 may address risk by benchmarking measures of return on investor capital against standards that reflect risk in one way or another. Risk can have an explicit role in incentive target setting as well. As we will see in Chapter 8, generally, companies with higher risk need to generate higher business results to satisfy investor demands.

Those concepts are all about risk from an investor viewpoint and risk as an explicit element of the incentive pay structure. When assessing risk and its important effects on incentives, it would be a mistake to stop there. Risk has a range of implicit effects, permeating many aspects of the incentive rewards structure. And looking at risk effects from the personal viewpoint of executives is at least as important as from the more predictable viewpoint of diversified, liquid investors.

This chapter deals with a range of risk-related matters affecting how senior management incentives work, including the central, big-ticket risk issue of the cost of capital.

Risk Management Policy and Incentives

These are subjects of high concern to investors and boards, particularly in financial services companies. President Obama called on companies to place greater weight on prudent risk management practices when determining executive pay, appointing a pay czar to see it through. Administrators of the Troubled Asset

Relief Program (TARP) have a large stake in the subject. So does the Securities and Exchange Commission (SEC), as it requires companies to comment on risk as part of their executive pay disclosures. Policy guidance is coming from all directions, including companies in the most affected industry sector. For example, Goldman Sachs' chairman indicated that compensation policies at financial companies should be recrafted to discourage excessive risk taking.

Incentives for corporate officers of public companies do create very substantial risk exposure for participants. Imbalanced risk taking often brings short- and long-term incentive losses and hits to stock holdings. Profit reductions from bad risks hit the income statement sooner or later, and risk-based hits to the stock price arrive soonest. Stock options by themselves are thought to encourage excessive risk taking, and there is some empirical evidence to support this premise. In practice, corporate officers tend to hold large upside and downside financial exposures to stock price movement and to near- and medium-term financial goals.

When Lehman collapsed, for example, management bore enormous losses. The general rule is that corporate management tends quickly to lose tens or hundreds of millions in incentive gains when things turn south. Risk concealment is a different matter, but it eventually sees the light of day as well, and long-term incentive gains fall steeply when it does.

Despite the popular perception, the executive suite is hardly a consequence-free environment, particularly for gamblers. Whether executives are seen as victims of risk or as its perpetrators, the effects are clear. For example, one study found that the total value of chief executive officer (CEO) incentive and stock holdings fell enormously in 2008. Stock ownership, outstanding equity awards, and bonus payouts decreased by 42 percent. The CEOs analyzed in the study lost a combined $53.7 billion—roughly $55 million for the average CEO. In face of this sort of illiquid, undiversfied downside, risk aversion should be the prevalent bias rather than risk taking.[2]

Clearly, incentives should expose executives to the risks and rewards of their decisions over time, and do so in clear and compelling terms. At the corporate level, though, one wonders whether incentive interventions are really the lead solution to risk problems. The typical incentive structure already displays a rather pitched down-slope. More focus on non-pay aspects of the problem— on basic risk detection and risk management—are the more pressing matters to pursue.

Consider that some banks did a better job than others of anticipating the mortgage meltdown and taking action. Incentive policy did not seem to make the difference here. Top officer incentives, in their broad strokes, were not that different from one financial company to another. They all had lots of money riding on near- and medium-term goals and lots more on stock price exposure.

Personal stakes ranged in size—from huge to really huge—but they had a big incentive all along to put the brakes on maniacal risk taking.

But many did not. Alan Greenspan noted that many financial CEOs were aware of big risks but thought they could get out quickly when their positions started to sour.[3] Apparently, they did not learn the lesson from the Long-Term Capital Management crisis of the 1990s, the "portfolio insurance" debacle of the 1980s, and many other such episodes. That is, your investment strategy cannot rely on getting out right at the moment when everyone else is trying to get out. The market crash in 2008 was due in part to new awareness of the size of financial market risks and their systemic-level linkages to the real economy. At that point, there really was no market for the most toxic assets and therefore no way to get out. Incentive tweaking is not Risk Priority One at the top officer level. Risk management is. And that includes managing any risk stemming from delusional thinking about incentive policy. Incentives won't cure a gambler.

Business-unit or profit-center incentives often appear more vulnerable to risk concerns. A rogue securities trader brought down Barings in 1995, in a loss of a few hundred million that seemed colossal at the time. "French bank" was a punch line for a few weeks in early 2008 after one lost several billion through unauthorized trades. Later in that inauspicious year, inhabitants of an unpatrolled quarter of AIG brought the company down and made the French and English rogues look like pikers.

If you do not keep your eye on people like these, they will take your credit cards and head to Vegas. In reference to subordinates and their clandestine risk taking, we read that former Salomon chair John Gutfreund said, "They're buttering you up and then doing whatever the f--- they want to do."[4] High business stakes and decision rights often are found at the business unit level, in both financial and nonfinancial companies. But, often, not much long-term incentive stake is based on unit results. At this level, instead, many people in big-ticket jobs get paid mainly for this year's results.

Where risk is concerned, incentive effects have much to do with who holds what information and which decision rights. We noted the senior management group holds more information than the CEO about the truest sources of business advantage within the company and also about where the risks lurk. The CEO's position vis-à-vis these executives is replicated in their own relation to successive tiers of subordinates, in a process cascading throughout the enterprise. Incentives are present at every level in that cascading process, and so is authority to make decisions balancing risk and return. Some solutions:

- Business-unit incentives can create accountability for long-term performance standards, in a framework in which participants are exposed clearly to the longer-term risks of their actions (but one offering a compelling degree of liquidity). This can be achieved well enough with a structure of bonuses and long-term incentive pay in which each element takes notable account of business-unit or profit center results.

- "Bonus bank" arrangements are being reconsidered, particularly in the financial sector. Under these programs, bonuses are held back for a year or more and left at risk based on ongoing financial performance. Some rule makers prefer bonus banks to stock-based deferrals, focusing on the idea of a direct *economic clawback* of bonuses paid based on the ongoing profitability of the profit center that funded them. The more common approach of deferring bonuses in stock is less effective in this regard. Bonus banks are not prevalent in general industry, disfavored for a range of good reasons we will examine shortly.

At the corporate or business-unit level, risk can be addressed through plan design—through metrics, standard setting, range setting, incentive testing, and calibration. Plans can use value-based metrics or risk-adjusted metrics, for example (see Chapter 8):

- Value-based metrics such as *economic value added* or *total business return* apply an explicit risk-based charge to the use of capital in a business.
- Risk-adjusted return metrics measure the return earned on the level of risk-adjusted or economic capital used (i.e., the level of corporate capital that is preempted by risk taking in a particular unit).

Risk assessment can be tricky, though. It is a risky world. Downturns and crises happen frequently. Early in my career I worked down the street from the staid Continental Bank of Chicago while it imploded, taking a chunk of my boss's money with it. A few years later in October 1987, I went to a noon meeting with a client in the trading room of their grain terminal in New Orleans. He announced that the Dow had lost nearly one-fourth of its value so far that day. The historical record shows that stock prices are partly erased on a rather frequent basis.

For many years, big mortgage companies were reporting that they had studied risks and that they did not need much capital. This was meant to hold them, they said, in all but one in a thousand annual scenarios. One big bank CEO, in contrast, candidly remarked in his annual report that a financial crisis is something that happens every five to seven years. If your ankles are getting wet every few years, you are not living in a thousand-year floodplain. Observers are reasonably skeptical about risk-adjusted capital metrics and the guesswork they entrain. Complexity must be cited as a challenge as well. Still, incentive policy in business units likely would improve if it took some sensible account of risk-based capital allocation. That process is designed to find where the risks are and measure them.

One way to apply these methods is in a comparative format only, one that ranks businesses in terms of risk rather than trying to set the absolute risk scale itself. Matters like market equity value and bond ratings (default probabilities) can be observed and used to set levels of overall risk and risk-based capital. The purpose of risk-based capital estimation is then to allocate capital among business activities, in a zero-sum exercise. Performance goals can be developed for the overall company as well (see Chapter 8), making goal allocation into another reconcilable, zero-sum exercise. Performance demands can then be scaled to risk taking. For example, a business unit with a ratio of economic capital to book capital that is 2.0 might have a marginal return on invested capital (ROIC) target that, all else equal, is twice the level applied to a unit with a 1.0 ratio.

There are many other incentive matters having risk linkages, whether any explicitly risk-cognizant metric is used or not:

- *Standard-setting* is improved when it takes account of risk and of the effect it has on the level of return, and of financial performance, needed from a given business.

- *Performance ranges* should reflect the potential variability in business results, and assessing this may involve looking at a number of indicators of prospective risk. A medical products maker widened its performance ranges for 2009, for example, to acknowledge higher uncertainty.

- *Incentive calibration and testing* can help identify situations creating moral hazard. Examples throughout this book include improperly high or low leverage, effects of being close to or out of the performance range, effects of kinks in the payout curve, and risks of unbalanced metrics and of poor accountability for longer-term decision consequences.

Risk management initiatives can be featured as elements of incentive plan goals or as inputs into performance management. This is like basing some pay on goals like customer service scores, employee engagement, or brand strength. Risk management may be a more urgent matter at some companies than these other examples, and a more broadly held concern. Such metrics can be a bit fuzzy when compared to well-specified financial goals (see Chapter 6), but they can work well if set well.

When considering risk effects on rewards, it is worthwhile to keep in mind that incentive plan participants are not always rational about risk. People systematically overassess small risks, for example. They may judge risks differently in regard to owned wealth rather than incentive gains (*house money*). Incentives that expose them to too much risk for too long may be counterproductive.

Controllable risks may be more palatable to them than uncontrollable ones. During the 2008 financial crisis, it appeared that capital markets were assessing risks very highly, charging a lot for them, or both. Executives may do the same thing when faced with oddly illiquid or risky incentive structures or with prospective gains they feel they can little predict or affect.

SHEEP IN WOLVES' CLOTHING

Observers have been busy looking for incentive risk as a kind of big, bad wolf. But risk is tricky to measure. Sheep may wear wolves' clothing:

- Lower-risk companies with more predictable results tend to use narrower performance ranges in bonus plans and performance plans. This means higher payout leverage, since payouts move up or down fast, based on small variances from target. But this does not mean the plans are driving risk taking. Payout leverage of 6:1 means payouts as a percentage of target move six times as fast as performance as a percentage of target, so ten points of performance above target could drive a payout at 160 percent of target. This could be inappropriately low leverage for a low-risk company (or metric), for example. And leverage of 3:1 could be too high for a risky business. Leverage, as an incentive risk measure, does not really tell you who is encouraging risk and who is not.

- Lower-risk companies tend to post lower stock price volatility, affecting their option valuations. Lower option valuation means, all else equal, a larger number of options must be granted to achieve a given guideline for grant value. A low-risk company granting a given amount of long-term incentive (LTI) value in the form of stock options will tend to make option grants with larger face value than those at a higher risk-company. If risk is measured by grant size, this mild-mannered business suddenly looks like Evel Knievel.

We should not rush to indict the high leverage company as the one with inappropriately high risk, since the opposite may well be true. The real wolf actually can be hidden in sheep's clothing. The trader bonus pools investment banks tend not to have high leverage, for example. Many such pools are set at a fixed percentage of income over some threshold so their payout leverage actually is quite low at 1:1. The volatility is in their business results, not their bonus plans.

INVESTORS VERSUS MANAGEMENT

Executive pay watchdogs have for years recommended that senior management hold a lot of company stock to align risk and upside between investors and executives. These demands reached a particularly high pitch after the financial crisis of late 2008. Each stock sale was seen as a betrayal, and expected holding periods were, it seemed, unlimited.

The all-purpose prescription of equity grants and holdings is flawed for many reasons. Remember that stock does not come with instructions on how to create value, and most of senior management cannot affect the stock price much anyway. This limits the efficacy of stock as a medium not only for generating performance-based gains but for clawing them back.

In the current context, another flaw is the proposition that equity-based incentive grants can, by themselves, unify perspectives of management with those of investors. We should not expect management and investors to see things in the same way. Investors hold generally liquid and diversified interests, so they are concerned about the risks that a particular company's stock adds to a diversified portfolio. Investors as a group—current and future—hold a perpetual stake in future results. Senior managers and executives have an interest in the company that is neither liquid nor diversified, and every bit of the overall variation in business results may affect them. Management runs the place. They are not anonymous, fractional claimants. They should be made to hold concentrated equity stakes. But their stakes should not be perpetual. They are people, not statues. It makes sense to permit executives to limit risks over a certain threshold and to take money off the table.

Career risks are a big issue from a management viewpoint, too, and a non-issue to investors. Here, management's inclinations may depart greatly from those of investors. They may depart farther due to individuals' risk aversion, illusions of control, and impatience. In a pay-related example of the "house money" problem, people often attach a lot of value to money they can withdraw from the company, becoming especially risk averse with any prospect that threatens that balance. These attributes have implications for the many detailed choices involved when setting up incentive plans, so it is worth taking a look at how they play out. If you are not looking for issues like these, many of which underlie the *behavioral school* of investing, you may end up being schooled by them.

Stock option granting policy seems particularly vulnerable to risk biases:

- *Asymmetric views on risk cause companies to waste a lot of money on stock options.* The economic cost of an option might be four or five dollars based on the gains it might generate and the chances of achieving those. An executive, however, might think it is only worth a dollar or two. Options involve long timeframes, and much complexity and risk—this is the kind of financial claim an individual will discount heavily. Cash and whole shares do not pose difficult valuation problems or excessive risk discounting.

- *Unless someone believes in the highest-gain scenarios, they are not likely to value options as highly as the market does.* The economic cost to shareholders of an executive's option grant has to do with future gains it might generate. A lot of the value of an option derives from relatively unlikely scenarios that generate huge gains.

- *Option risks and gains normally play out too late to create timely incentive effects.* As noted in Chapter 3, many grants stay underwater or close to it for the several key years following a grant, right at the time when the company was hoping for some engagement, retention, or risk-balancing incentive effects. Grants made more than a couple of years ago are mostly or wholly vested; they are not retaining anyone. Incentive effects at that point should be attributed to shareholding requirements or to individual risk appetites, rather than to incentive granting policy. And tying up grants with longer vesting will not be effective, either—it will just cause options to be seen as worth even less.

- *And, of course, their upside-only structure may encourage executives to roll the dice.* Options generate explicit, unlimited gain potential. Gains can be lost, but those losses stop at the exercise price. Performance shares and restricted stock, on the other hand, pose explicit downside ranges along with their upside (Within a balanced long-term incentive mix, options can simply add some upside leverage without creating dangerous payout asymmetries).

Companies should probably stand ready to up-weight option grants if people start to overvalue them again, as they did in the 1990s. Quotes on multiyear options remained high after the 2008 crisis, however, and so did the volatility levels they implied. In the meantime, the perceived value of options seemed to be falling, as participants often remained skeptical about prospective gains and their time-frames. Option perceived values would have had to rise greatly for options to appear favorable. There remains a pretty large gap to close before a typical option grant starts to look like a "good trade" from a shareholder perspective.

The typical incentive structure provides some outlets for risk reduction—earlier option exercises, fewer stock-based deferrals, lower elective participation in the rare "buy-in" incentive plan, and holding fewer shares above any stock holding requirements. If some executives have a high risk appetite or perceive options to be highly valuable, the same plans permit them to self-select into higher risk/higher upside positions as well.

THE RISK TRADE

Structuring incentive pay often means buying or selling risk, sometimes in surprising ways. In the overall pay structure, for example, the main kind of option

EXHIBIT 5.1   PUT AND CALL SCENARIOS

	Stock Plus Put Portfolio			Call Plus Debt Portfolio		
	Stock	Put	Total	Call	Debt	Total
Zero-Change Scenario:						
Start Price	100				100	
Ending Price	100				100	
Gain or Loss	0	0	0	0	0	0
50% Gain Scenario:						
Start Price	100				100	
Ending Price	150				100	
Gain or Loss	50	0	50	50	0	50
50% Loss Scenario:						
Start Price	100				100	
Ending Price	50				100	
Gain or Loss	−50	50	0	0	0	0

being granted may actually be a put option rather than a call option. Exhibit 5.1 leads us into this discussion by setting out a put-call parity table, showing how the terminal payoffs on puts and calls are related. If the stock price rises 50 percent, the stock-plus-put scenario generates a 50 percent gain on stock with no gain or loss on the put. The debt-plus-call scenario ends in the same place, as debt value is unchanged but the call options generate a $50 gain. The downside scenario generates zero net loss since stock losses are offset by put gain. The call and debt values do not change, either, so again the portfolios are equivalent. Either way, the investor has constructed an upside-only position.

Total direct pay can be read a bit like this exhibit. Salaries are cash annuities, like bonds. Stock options, it has been argued, bring the overall pay package in line with those of investors. The typical pay structure is a debt-plus-option deal, with a relatively assured debtlike claim in the form of salary combined with incentive plans whose variability creates optionlike upside (or that simply consist of actual call options).

But as the equation suggests, that does not add up to a stock–equivalent claim on the overall enterprise. If the company's value falls, executives typically keep their salary and may even get some bonus pay. So, their payoffs in either gain or loss scenarios are not like those of stockholders but rather like stockholders who own some puts.

This raises a question about the nature of the incentive claims we ordinarily convey—are they put options or call options? It also points up the standing argument for making executives bear both upside and downside, as investors do. This can be done by using whole shares and performance plans more heavily, rather than just stock options, in the long-term incentive structure.

Much of this has been accomplished already, though, as the LTI mix now creates much more whole-share exposure and so do executive stock holdings. As noted earlier, the sample average CEO lost $55 million when the market tanked in 2008. The put option effect is not very large when most of pay has a downside element.

Some observers believe companies should create even more complex forms of options than the vanilla grants used commonly now, perhaps ones with exercise prices that compound or move with an index. These have technical problems so they are rare, but they may function well under certain circumstances (see Chapter 10). Since they are even more complex and uncertain than regular options, though, they may invite even more discounting and create even worse pay trades. That should limit their use only to those cases in which their features are especially compelling.

Bonus banks have been prescribed in the past for use with plans based on the metric economic value added (or economic profit [EP]). In this arrangement, the executive's entire bonus is not necessarily paid out currently. Instead, all or part of it is placed in a notional bank. The entire bonus might be banked or just the amount over some cap. Typically, one-third of the bank is paid out each year. The bank normally is reduced by losses, so past bonuses banked are at risk of future elimination. The balance may also vary based on the ongoing range of performance.

So, the bonus payment each year is a function of cumulative performance for at least three years. It includes whatever part of this year's bonus is paid currently plus a third of the bank balance. Like payouts in a goal-based long-term incentive plan, payouts are made to reflect performance over a period of years. Given the wide use of stock-based bonus deferrals on Wall Street and the search for risk mitigation tools, the topic of bonus banking has taken on greater interest since the market meltdown.

It has also been promoted as a feature of incentive plans using the metric economic value added. In such cases, it can function as a *quid pro quo* for the unlimited upside often recommended. It may help overcome design problems with such plans, including harvest bias, volatile results, and uncertainties in targeting, ranges, leverage, and economic dilution.

Money in a bonus bank is pretty safe; normally, it is quite likely to be paid rather than wiped out by big losses in later years. As a liability to the corporation, it might be worth 90 cents on the dollar. But it often is worth less to participants since they see it as riskier. This devaluation scenario affects the bonus element of pay, which attracts high focus and normally is paid in cash at year end. So the devaluation can be expected to be large. Prevalence of these arrangements is very low in general industry.

Lots of design choices affect the maturity, risk, and perceived value of incentive programs. Long vesting terms sometimes are proffered as solution to risk issues, for example. But long vesting and golden handcuffs can move quickly past the point of diminishing returns. Goal-based long-term incentive pay, on the other hand, may allow investors to shift risk to management on terms that both parties favor (discussed in Chapter 10).

It is a question of balance. A good place to look is market norms. The company does act as a risk intermediary in labor markets, even at the executive level. In a process resembling asset securitization, it takes a portion of its general, uncertain income stream and turns it into the various tranches composing the executive pay structure. Management needs to be able to take some money off the table once in a while, and companies typically let them do this in the form of salary, bonus, and long-term incentive grants that are cumulatively liquid over time. Salaries, benefits, and perquisites are relatively sure; bonuses are iced at the end of each year, and long-term incentives are about as uncertain as shareholder wealth.

So where should you be in terms of mix? Well, the market mix has been set through informed market activity over a period of years, particularly now that the pro-option accounting bias has been neutralized. It apparently represents an overall approach that executives and companies find workable and to mutual advantage. At equilibrium, it probably is a fairly efficient outcome in terms of balancing the appeal to executives while getting reasonable performance for the company. It probably is a good cost solution, as well. If the company wanted to make pay substantially riskier or more illiquid overall, it would have to increase pay greatly in order to be competitive. In the market solution, investors basically are selling insurance and liquidity to the executive on voluntary terms that both parties regard as favorable. That would be a good risk trade.

Some companies hold salaries well below market and make up for it with a higher bonus. In some such situations, a portion of the bonus is pretty much like a salary from the company's viewpoint and not genuinely at risk. Putting these sure costs into the putatively "at risk" pay bucket simply invites participants to discount them. This brings the pay structure into conflict with a common judgment flaw. People systematically overassess small risks. That is why you can sell them flight insurance, and that is why nuclear power causes outsized concern. This also explains why it is not a good idea to subject an unusual amount of cash pay to risks, even ones seen as small. You would have to increase pay a lot to make up for that. Bonus banking poses similar risks of discounting, and perhaps the larger risk of simply not being able to hire the talent needed.

Companies do not have to muddle through every issue to have effective pay programs. They can move rapidly toward good decisions about how to structure pay plans, basing them on solid principles that apply in the bulk of cases. They can do this by narrowing choices and dismissing some of them early in the process.

In the instant case, that means they do not have to depart materially from the time frame, risk, and liquidity of the market's overall pay mix. They just need to redesign their elements using sound techniques. Companies should take care if straying far from the market's proportions. That might just invite discounting or worse.

Risk and Incentive Calibration

A short-term bias in the incentive structure will encourage executives to chase only those business initiatives paying off within the crimped time frame and performance interval of the current bonus plan. This almost certainly discourages good longer-run initiatives at many companies, simply because so many profitable business initiatives carry near-term losses and a multiyear time frame for generating high returns

Risk adds more problems when trying to figure out whether a given incentive structure will encourage high returns or not. Many business ventures become safer when their returns are allowed to run for a few years. Three years of performance causes a risk reduction similar to the diversification effects of holding three securities in a portfolio rather than one. But results look risky nonetheless to anyone who has a short view.

A mirror issue concerns "trailing risks," like securitized loan residuals or long-term warranty liabilities. In these cases, it is near-term profits that may be hyped.

Long-term performance plans can help with each issue, and so can the use of persistent and adaptive standards within annual incentive plans. These approaches subject executives to the several-year consequences of their own risk taking. In effect, they govern risk by piggybacking on the executives' personal risk tolerances.

Many incentive plans underweight the effect of capital usage. This can encourage many value-destroying decisions since people can be paid for putting capital into low-rent uses. Capital measurement also carries some risk-related consequences. Undercounted capital can encourage managers to gamble more than they otherwise would. They get all of the income-based upside of a gamble but suffer a disproportionately small loss if the capital is put to waste.

Getting capital into the right role normally means using capital-conscious metrics like ROIC or total business return (TBR), or setting targets that clearly ratchet up income goals over time when the company uses more capital. In all cases, there should be a clear emphasis on capital usage in plan-related communication.

Solutions based on "total return" metrics like TBR are worth note as well. These metrics judge financial performance based on the two main ways in which it serves the financial interests of investors:

1. By increasing the value of the business they own
2. By generating cash flows from operations that can be distributed to them (free cash flows)

If the incentive plan pays for growth only—ignoring the cash yield from a business irrespective of its growth rate—then it will favor the pursuit of high growth rates all of the time, in all business units and all business conditions, without full regard for the capital costs and risks involved. Total return plans create an explicit reward for business growth on the one hand and cash yield on the other. They clearly express the notion of balance rather than the more typical message that growth, no matter the risks and costs, is the only thing that pays. The total return incentive approach does not require the use of a value-based metric like TBR, it is worth noting. Rather, TBR-type approaches can be used to set pay-out schedules in plans that use traditional metrics like operating income, EPS, and ROIC (Chapter 7).

Incentive policy interacts with formal risk management practices as well. No matter what public companies do with incentive structure for the broad senior management group, they surely will end up with the few top officers having a lot of exposure to stock price movement. If the company wishes to use particularly distinctive risk management or hedging policies, the incentive system will encourage it to do so to the extent it increases share price. More intensive management of risk may appeal to investors. They may see the costs of the various hedging tactics as cheap in relation to risk reduction. By contrast, they may see many of a company's unique risks as largely diversifiable ones, or unlikely ones not worth going to unusual lengths to mitigate. In commodity, materials, and precious metals, some investors insist that hedging by the company works against their reason for investing in the first place, which was to create asset price exposure.

Overall, stock market judgments and pricing effects should motivate executives to do a proper job of risk management. Stock prices incorporate information so well that markets often are found to be highly efficient, with residual price movements resembling a statistical random walk. That is fine, one might say, until stock prices take a random walk off a short pier, as they did in late 2008. But, much of that movement was the risk evaluation process in action, apparently including a reassessment of firms' risk management policies.

Management, for their part, can go well beyond hedging or insurance tactics. They can decide what businesses the company is in. If risks are untenable and management cannot tame them on reasonable terms, they can sell them off.

THE WAGES OF RISK: ESTIMATING THE COST OF CAPITAL

Whether the cost of capital is at one level or another has strong effects on business value. Going back to the discounted cash flow (DCF) example at the beginning of this chapter, a decrease in the cost of capital to 8 percent has the effect of increasing the value of the enterprise by 25 percent.[5] An increase in the cost of capital to 12 percent reduces value by 17 percent. In many other, more typical DCF model scenarios—ones with moderate income growth, capital increases, and longer forecast terms—the effects of changes in the cost of capital are even greater.

The cost of capital for a business is the rate of return required by investors to compensate them for the risks they bear. The cost of debt to the company is equal to the overall interest rate paid on borrowings. Since debt is deductible from income taxes for a taxpaying corporation, debt financing has certain tax benefits commonly assumed to contribute to the value of the business. By convention, these tax benefits are taken into account by stating the cost of debt on an after-tax basis. A company with an overall borrowing cost of 6 percent and a tax rate of 33 percent would have an after-tax cost of debt capital of 4 percent (6% × [1 − 33%]).

Let us assume for the moment that the cost of equity capital is 10 percent. To figure out the company's overall cost of capital, the costs of debt and equity are averaged together based on the levels of debt and equity used. If the company's value consists one-third of debt and two-thirds of equity, its weighted-average cost of capital (WACC) is 8 percent (see Exhibit 5.2).

BETA COEFFICIENTS AND THE CAPITAL ASSET PRICING MODEL

The actual cost of equity for a company is trickier to determine than the cost of debt. Debt interest rates can be observed in the market, but expected returns on stock investments cannot. Companies have to use estimation methods to attach a reasonable cost to equity. There is no flawless or definitive way to do this. The capital asset pricing model (CAPM) is a technique used often by companies to

EXHIBIT 5.2	WEIGHTED-AVERAGE COST OF CAPITAL EXAMPLE		
Capital Source	**Weighting**	**After-Tax Cost**	**Weighted Cost**
Equity	67%	10%	6.67%
Debt	33%	4%	1.33%
Total			8%

judge the overall risk of a business and to attach a cost to the capital it uses.[6] CAPM is derived first by making certain assumptions about investor attitudes and the structure of capital markets. Then, investor behavior is predicted, as well as the mechanism investors will use to price risk:

- CAPM assumes that investors are risk-averse. For a given level of expected return, they prefer investments offering lower risk. Diversification reduces risk. A combination of risky securities—a portfolio—will have lower overall variability than the average of the individual securities in the portfolio. This is because the gains on some securities will offset losses on others as long as their returns are not perfectly positively correlated.

- Capital markets offer a wide range of investment choices. Investors, in their search to reduce risk, can be expected to hold broadly diversified portfolios. Investors can improve their investment risk/reward profiles even further by combining their risky asset portfolios in various ways with "risk-free" investments such as U.S. Treasury securities. Following CAPM's strict assumptions, investors actually all hold interests in the same market portfolio of risky securities. They combine such holdings with risk-free investments in various ways to suit their individual risk tolerances. This strategy allows investors to get the highest returns at every risk level and to create a portfolio whose risk/return trade-off suits them best.

- The relevant measure of risk for a particular security is how much risk it adds to the market portfolio that everyone holds. That risk contribution is measured by seeing how much the security's returns covary with returns on the market portfolio. The rest of the security's variability is unrelated to the market portfolio's movements, so it disappears in the diversification process. In a CAPM world, investors demand a return only on the covariant part, since that is the only part that increases their portfolio's risk and therefore subjects them to any incremental risk.

This covariant risk metric is called the beta coefficient. A company with average risk will post a beta of 1.0. Betas run mostly in the range of 0.6 to 1.4, with 0.6 being low risk and 1.4 being high risk. If a company's own beta cannot be observed (e.g., because it is a private company or a business unit), then betas of peer companies may be consulted as an indication of risk level.[7]

CAPM uses beta to figure out the cost of equity. A typical formulation expresses the expected rate of return on an equity security (K_e) as a function of the company's beta coefficient (b), the risk-free rate of return (R_f) and the market equity risk premium ($R_m - R_f$):

$$K_e = R_f + b\,(R_m - R_f)$$

The market equity risk premium is the higher return that market investors demand on an average stock investment, over a risk-free investment like a Treasury security, to compensate for the additional risks involved.

The risk-free rate in the United States typically is taken to be the yield to maturity on long-term U.S. Treasury bonds. Long Treasury bonds are hardly risk-free. They are subject to principal value risk if they are not held to maturity, reinvestment rate risk if they are, purchasing power risks depending on inflation rates, and even default risk. Nonetheless, they provide a baseline estimate of the real rate of return for investments with little risk plus the yield premiums associated with a long-term maturity and inflationary expectations.

Normalizing the risk-free rate at 5 percent and adding the risk premium for equity investments, for many years estimated in the 3 to 7 percent range, provides an overall equity rate of return centered on 10 percent for an average company.[8]

These numbers can move around. The financial crisis of late 2008 sharply increased the costs of risky corporate investments, for example. The premium over treasury yields for investing on highly rated junk bonds rose by an enormous 3.27 percentage points between early 2008 and early 2009, as shown in Exhibit 5.3.

John Maynard Keynes attributed market volatility in part to "animal spirits," which seem evident in the early 2009 premiums. They have been on a moderating path since then, however.

Returning to the more general guidelines of 5 percent risk-free rates and 5 percent equity risk premiums, a low-risk company with a beta of 0.6 would have an equity cost of 8.0 percent, while a high-risk company beta of 1.4 would warrant a rate of return of 12.0 percent. This range has covered the landscape for most medium to large companies under typical market conditions. Rates may remain elevated going forward.

FINANCIAL LEVERAGE AND THE COST OF CAPITAL

Start-ups, particularly those with venture financing, sometimes cite higher equity rates of return. Depending on the nature of the investment, venture capital and private equity firms cite expected portfolio rates of return from the mid-teens up to the 40 to 50 percent range per year.

Financial leverage explains some of these higher yields because it affects the risks built into the costs of debt and equity. Whether it affects the cost of capital overall or should affect incentive pay is another matter. For example, expected returns on equity in the 15 to 20 percent range would be reasonable in a leveraged buyout of a mature, moderate-risk company. See Exhibit 5.4.

EXHIBIT 5.3   MARKET RISK PREMIUMS

Maturity	AAA Minus Treasury			BBB Minus AAA			BB Minus BBB			BB Minus Treasury		
	2009	2008	Change	2009	2008	Change	2009	2008	Change	2009	2008	Change
3M	1.12	1.51	−0.39	3.04	1.05	2.00	4.229	2.5106	1.72	8.3907	5.0664	3.32
6M	1.09	1.32	−0.23	3.03	1.18	1.86	4.1395	2.2671	1.87	8.2619	4.763	3.50
5Y	1.04	1.59	−0.55	3.07	0.72	2.36	4.4174	2.7148	1.70	8.5273	5.0196	3.51
10Y	1.43	1.22	0.21	2.56	1.00	1.56	4.4295	3.252	1.18	8.4269	5.4773	2.95
15Y	1.20	1.02	0.18	2.70	1.38	1.32	4.2878	3.0362	1.25	8.1909	5.4351	2.76
20Y	1.52	1.06	0.46	2.39	1.39	1.00	4.3292	3.1457	1.18	8.2362	5.5922	2.64
25Y	1.69	1.13	0.56	2.14	1.28	0.86	4.4123	3.2865	1.13	8.2361	5.6948	2.54
30Y	1.98	1.18	0.80	1.97	1.32	0.65	4.4354	3.2457	1.19	8.3832	5.7515	2.63
Average			−0.06			1.77			1.56			3.27

Source: Bloomberg

EXHIBIT 5.4   **DEBT AND COST OF CAPITAL SCENARIOS**

Source	Market Value Weight	After-Tax Cost	Cost of Capital
Equity	75%	12.0%	9.0%
Debt	25%	5.0%	1.3%
Overall Cost of Capital, Typical Middle-Market Company			10.3%
Equity	25%	20.0%	5.0%
Debt	75%	7.0%	5.3%
Overall Cost of Capital, Releveraged			10.3%

Exhibit 5.4 shows how a big change in capital structure may simply re-distribute risk between equity and debt investors. The weighted-average cost of capital remains at 10.3 percent so enterprise risk, value and expected returns do not change. But holders of the small amount of equity have much higher and riskier expected returns. The average debt cost rises as well due to the higher-risk capital structure.

Whether leverage affects value, and to what extent, are subjects of ongoing investigation by academics, experimentation by companies, and marketing by fin-anciers. Historically, companies assumed that an optimal capital structure should be pursued, one balancing the risks and interest rate costs of higher financial lever-age with its tax benefits. Nobel Prize winners Modigliani and Miller identified conditions in which firms might be indifferent to capital structure, how tax policy might encourage firms to maximize debt financing, and how costs of financial distress would act to moderate levels of financial leverage actually used.

Further work has looked into matters like how investor arbitrage might elim-inate any discounts in the stock prices of the underleveraged. If there are signifi-cant valuation gains to be had by changing capital structure, after all, many actors in capital markets will try very hard to make such changes happen. Investors do not leave that kind of money lying in the street. They might substitute personal leverage for corporate leverage, for example, continuing to the point where they have bid up the company's share price and eliminated any discount. Or they might simply take over underleveraged firms, recapitalizing them and pocketing any gains. The mere threat of this would narrow any discounts in advance. Overall, one must conclude that effects of financial leverage on the overall value of an enterprise are modest and uncertain.

OTHER METHODS AND EVIDENCE FOR ATTACHING A COST TO CAPITAL

Besides CAPM, a range of other methods can be used to measure and price business risk for purposes like cost of capital estimation:

- For those uncomfortable with CAPM's dismissive treatment of diversifiable risks, there is the method of looking at overall risk rather than just its market-covariant "beta" element. Historical stock volatility can be measured, as an indication of overall risk. It can also be measured on a going-forward, *ex ante* basis by looking at long stock option quotes and solving for the level of prospective volatility that drives them. These estimates are called *implied volatilities*.

- Overall variance in financial results (against targets, trend lines, or peer norms) also is a valid risk indicator.

- Another method involves focusing on that part of risk that really frightens the risk-averse—the downside—by looking at the *semi-variance*.

- It is possible to disaggregate risks in various ways—splitting overall risk into business and financial leverage components (e.g., or foreign investment risks into business, currency, and expropriation elements). This allows some market pricing of risk by element, either through present value discounting or through risk charges like synthetic insurance or hedging costs.

- One method is known as *arbitrage pricing theory* (APT). It specifies numerous drivers of the cost of capital, attaching coefficients to them through data-dredging and aggregating them into a predictive model.

- A less sophisticated method, but one that effectively remains in wide use, simply takes a risk-free rate or cost of debt rate and adds a rough risk premium to it based on the judged risk of the deal or the investment.

- Bond yields and default spreads provide good information about the prevailing prices for various elements of risk, as we saw in Exhibit 5.4. The risk premiums among high-quality corporate bonds, T-bonds, and junk bonds (net of expected defaults) say a lot about how much risk investors are willing to bear for another point or two of yield. T-bonds convey information about the base level of returns needed on any long-term investment, and inflation-adjusted bonds expose inflation's contribution to them.

New methods surface periodically in the financial press. For a wide range of companies over more than 25 years, I have used weighted-average costs of capital mainly in the 7 to 15 percent range. Readily observable risk levels typically have placed companies clearly into one segment or another of the range.

In business valuation, costs of capital matter greatly. Small differences in expected returns can have big impacts on security prices. In the incentive design arena, in contrast, simplicity is more powerful than precision. Here, it is counterproductive to argue about a few basis points. Using a rounded figure for the plan's cost of capital—like 10 percent, for example—has the material advantage of allowing break-even returns on investment to be cal-culated easily. Within incentive plans, simply giving rough justice to the cost of capital is a huge improvement over the current state of economic lawlessness. Overdetailing the cost of capital complicates the plan and makes it less effective. It is one of the areas in which value-based incentive plans sometimes fail.[9]

As in business valuation, measurement of shareholder expectations requires more precision about costs of capital. Over the past 15 years or so, precrisis, I have used cost of equity assumptions centering roughly in the 9 to 11 percent range for larger companies. This consists of normalized long treasury yields in the 4 to 6 percent range and a market equity risk premium of 3 to 7 percent. Actual market levels of total shareholder return (TSR) for companies in the S&P 500 index centered in the 10 to 11 percent range over the past 20 years, including the crisis year 2008 (see Chapter 3). This lends general credence to this range of costs of equity. The last two decades have seen a net disinflationary trend, however, so securities yields may have been a bit elevated during this period.

Cost of equity in that range lead to weighted-average costs of capital in the 8.0 to 9.5 percent range most of the time. If companies have no debt or very high debt, I have not hesitated to confirm their costs of capital with a separate computation using a "normalized" capital structure, often using a ratio of debt to total capital (market value) between 20 and 40 percent.

Regarding post-crisis costs, one has to consider risks of high and unstable tax, borrowing, spending, and regulatory effects in the United States. My assumption is that the new equilibrium range will be at least somewhat higher for years. Call it a Colbert effect, after the seventeenth-century finance minister who origi-nated the French habit of government control of the economy, known as *dirigisme*.

I often have seen analysts' forecasts using weighted-average costs of 9.5 to 11.0 percent. To get there, I think you have to assume that medium- to large-cap equities as a category were priced to yield 12 percent or more, compounded, over the long-term. Investors, when polled in the past, did not estimate expected returns to be that high.[10] Actuaries did not either, and they have to make such assumptions in a big-ticket context of pension accounting. When I see high rates used by analysts, I assume the financial forecasts being used in their DCF models have some high side bias that would have to be offset by an above-market discount rate in order to square with the stock value.

Back to the big picture, note that the economic guidance provided by incentive plans will not replace the company's other tools of financial govern-ance. Almost all corporations evaluate large investments and other initiatives with a fairly close eye on the risks involved and returns needed. That is where the company has the opportunity to apply precise, up-to-date, project-specific costs of capital, fine-tuning business decisions to create the most value. Incentive plans, in contrast, are blunt instruments. Their overall effects on the company's investment evaluation process can be very positive, to be sure. They can create new accountability for capital outlays and their general opportunity costs. To achieve these effects, though, incentive plans need not use exactly the same costs of capital used for project evaluation, treat them with nearly as much precision, or apply them in a variable, piecemeal way to each of a company's business initiatives.

Incentive plans can provide consistent thematic and directional guidance to business decision making, and they can do so in a way that is comprehensive and compelling. Just do not ask them to take you to the third decimal point on each initiative.

My general prescription for the cost of capital's effect on incentives is to use a reasonable, rounded figure for the entire company, allowing it to vary among business units or over time only when material differences emerge:

- Keep the cost of capital fixed for the duration of individual grants like bonuses, phantom stock grants, or performance share or unit grants.

- If the cost of capital changes materially, take this into account when setting up future long-term incentive grants and bonuses.

And, to be clear, incentive plans do not have to feature an explicit cost of capital. They can take account of capital and risk simply by imposing appropriate income hurdles. They can accomplish that in several ways, which we will see in later chapters. (Techniques presented in later chapters include applying a capital charge within a residual income metric or using a capitalization rate within metrics like shareholder value added [SVA] or total business return [TBR], discussed in Chapter 7.) Companies also can set up award schedules that trade off income and capital effects in accordance with the cost of capital by, for example, using combinations of metrics such as operating income and ROIC (Chapter 6). They also can use a range of target-setting methods that take account of shareholder criteria for returns on new capital (Chapter 8). Granting levels under incentive plans of all kinds can be benchmarked for their overall dilution effects, taking into account the effects of cost of capital on shareholder resources (one TBR-based example appears in Chapter 9).

In their agency role, executives decide many things on behalf of a company's owners. Risk taking, risk management, and risk-adjusted investment hurdle rates are among those things. The incentive structure can improve business governance by encouraging executives to balance risk and returns over time as an owner would wish.

■ NOTES

1. Richard N. Ericson, *Pay to Prosper* (Scottsdale, AZ: WorldatWork, 2004).
2. Watson Wyatt's "2009/2010 Report on Executive Pay: Moving Beyond the Financial Crisis" is based on public data from 982 companies in the S&P Super 1500 that filed proxies before July 2009.
3. Remarks from Alan Greenspan during a televised appearance on March 15, 2009.
4. Michael Lewis, "The End," Portfolio.com, November 11, 2008.
5. The initial example is a zero-growth perpetuity, so it can be valued by taking the annual free cash flow (FCF) and dividing it by the cost of capital. At a 10 percent cost of capital, the enterprise is worth $1,000. At an 8 percent cost of capital, it is worth $1,250 ($100/8%).
6. See for example Robert F. Bruner, Kenneth M. Eades, Robert C. Higgins. Robert S. Harris, "Best Practices in Estimating the Cost of Capital: Survey and Synthesis," *Financial Practice and Education* (Spring/Summer 1998), excerpted in *Harvard Business Review* (September 1996). The authors found the capital asset pricing model is by far the method used most commonly by companies to set costs of equity capital.
7. Financial leverage affects betas. More highly indebted companies have more variable equity returns, so they have higher measured betas. Peer betas may need some adjustment if the peers have capital structures differing greatly from those of the subject company. In those cases, the observed betas on peers can be "unlevered" to a zero debt equivalent beta (an asset beta), then levered back up to the level of the subject company.
8. Roger Grabowski and Shannon Pratt set forth a thorough review of market evidence of the equity risk premium in their book *Cost of Capital: Applications and Examples* (Hoboken, NJ: John Wiley & Sons, 2008).
9. A similar, common issue is the procedures used to adjust targets and results for various business events. That is another area in which a preference for financial precision simply overcomplicates the plan and reduces its efficacy. This issue is detailed in the discussion of metrics in Chapter 8.
10. Roger Grabowski and Shannon Pratt, *Cost of Capital: Applications and Examples* (Hoboken, NJ: John Wiley & Sons, 2008).

CHAPTER 6

Motive, Means, and Method: Evaluating Incentive Performance Metrics

Since the onset of option expensing, companies have been remixing and redesigning their long-term incentive grants. In particular, they have been placing much more weight on goal-based vehicles like performance units and shares and delivering more pay based on business-unit results. In the United States, restricted share grants to top officers now are much more likely to be triggered by explicit performance goals, in compliance with I.R.C. section 162(m). Again, partly in response to section 162(m), annual incentive pay targets have risen rapidly as well.

These trends all take formal goals and metrics, place a lot more weight on them, and bring them much closer to home. The value of executive pay packages has risen greatly over time, with most of that growth coming from incentive pay. Goal-based pay is not only a much bigger slice of the incentive pie, but of a greatly expanded pie. Company processes for incentive performance measurement and goal-setting were always a big deal. These incentive changes have made them a far bigger deal.

With purely stock-based pay, it is the stock market that sets expectations for performance and decides what gains have been earned. The market is remarkably astute and efficient, to be sure, when it values company shares. But, to most, its mechanism is mysterious, distant, and unsteady. It does not work as an incentive for many people. We need better solutions, and those hinge on well-designed goal-based pay.

In our search for designs, we should keep in mind the principle that "form follows function." Senior management's work product is sustained financial success for owners. Incentives for people in senior management should be based preponderantly on financial performance—particularly on the controllable elements and those linked most closely with value creation. That is the approach best fitting their roles. It is also where there are big design problems that, if remedied, hold the promise of improving business results.

This chapter reviews a range of traditional measurement approaches used in goal-based incentive plans. It starts with a general discussion of the types of measures that can be applied, discussing individual measurements, financial metrics, and nonfinancial metrics generally. It then reviews the range of specific financial metrics used most often in executive incentive plans. Lastly, it examines the use of indexed or immunized performance measurement approaches.

ROLE OF INDIVIDUAL PERFORMANCE IN INCENTIVE PAY

Few long-term incentive plans use individual goals to deliver payouts. Where annual incentives are concerned, individual performance is assigned a low weighting, if included at all. More than half the companies in our design surveys have assigned a specific weight to individual team or departmental performance.[1] Among these, a typical weight for top officers is 25 percent. So, individual performance carries something like 12.5 percent of the explicit weight of bonus goals in a market sample. From there, it falls, for several reasons:

- Individual or departmental performance sometimes is used as an award modifier. Therefore, it is valued or devalued explicitly, based on financial results rather than being rewarded as an independent matter.

- The overall bonus is often subject to financial performance thresholds, clipping 10 percent or more of financial performance scenarios and making it more unlikely that individual goals will be funded.

- The individual part of awards may be administered less generously when financial results are poor (and much less often is it increased as an offset), again putting financial results more firmly in the driver's seat.

When bonus time arrives for someone in top management, there simply is not much money payable based on individual performance as a truly separate matter from financial results. That means zero is a rounded approximation of the typical weighting of bonus pay on individual performance—of the sway that it actually holds when plans pay out at one level versus another. Stock grant sizes may be affected by individual performance, but normally the goals amount to modest contingencies. To have impact, a goal needs to be applied across a scale and accompanied by appropriate leverage. What incentives say, in effect, is that when top executives are spending a lot of time on things that do not help financial performance over time, something is wrong in their priorities.

There is plenty of reward for individual performance though. That is how executives got themselves into the high-paying jobs and, normally, they cannot stay for long without it. The excellent performer will move along faster to higher salary levels, which in turn scale up incentive targets. So, individual performance is hardly underrepresented in the typical system of executive rewards, even if it has no role in incentive payout determination.

It can be risky to put cash bounties on too many items in a bonus plan. Many priorities are matters that people in management should just be doing as part of their job. Paying money for a task may have the effect of taking an assumed duty and making it contingent on pay. The book *Freakonomics* tells a good story about such effects.[2] Patrons of a day-care center were admonished to pick their kids up on time at day's end. Common courtesy kept the patrons on their toes. They would try hard to get there on time to avoid being inconsiderate to the staff. Then the center put in a policy of modest fines. The incidence of lateness rose sharply. At that point, lateness did not mean inconsiderateness. The staff seemed prepared to be importuned, for a price.

Courtesy-based compliance had always been the higher road. In the workplace, having generally high expectations and standards is the higher road. Aligning overall success with pay can reinforce those standards for everyone. Putting cash targets next to each item in the job description may not.

NONFINANCIAL GOALS

Respondents to our design surveys cited customer satisfaction, safety, and strategic objectives most often as nonfinancial goals, with prevalence of 16 percent, 17 percent, and 27 percent, respectively. Other nonfinancial yardsticks include metrics such as employee satisfaction, brand recognition, and market share.

These metrics may be very rich in concurrent business insight and very worthwhile to measure and pursue. They may be critical elements of business literacy efforts and may even be effective in delivering variable pay in the broader workforce. But they do not broaden the basic system of goals and accountabilities at the senior management level. Senior management priorities are, for the most part, things that show up in financial performance within a reasonable amount of time. Brand recognition is not inherently valuable unless it shows up in the form of better economic results. Economic impact is a proper test. The performance being captured by valid nonfinancial goals normally is subsumed over time by actual financial performance.

Nonfinancial metrics are often leading indicators of future business health and financial success. Surveyed companies have cited a desire to support future value creation, when using such goals, more than one-third of the time. But their "leading" aspect is not necessarily needed at the senior management level.

Incentive structure should be long, and forward-looking in its focus. Senior executives are meant to see matters through before cashing in. So, at this organizational level, nonfinancial goals normally do not stem any important time gap.

Wharton School professors surveyed 157 companies about their use of nonfinancial metrics, finding their systems poorly specified and inadequate to the task of delivering management pay.[3] Here are some of their anecdotes:

- Patent-based incentives encouraged managers to increase new filings irrespective of whether it made more sense to license someone else's technology or whether the patents ever earned back their cost or were even put to work.

- A bank based customer service scores on polling of actual visitors to bank branches. A manager coaxed in visitors and plied them with food and drinks.

- Quality targets of an automaker were reached when management reclassified certain flaws as acceptable.

Goals of all kinds can be hard to set. But nonfinancial goals are trickier. They can lead much more easily to distortions. Some companies believe that all their stock-based grants form an effective bulwark against the various risks of nonfinancial goals. Why would management do that kind of thing, they argue? The stock price would fall and they would lose some of their stock gains. But stock and options by themselves do not man this barricade very well. What keeps management, especially those in business units, from chasing easy money tied to bad goals—some vague threat of marginally reduced option gains? I don't think so.

Balanced scorecards began to attract some chatter once again after the 2008 crisis, due to skepticism about metrics and goals of all types. Such approaches can be very helpful when used in communication efforts and as part of broad-based variable pay. The process of coming up with them may be marvelously revealing and insightful. But, in the end, balanced scorecards convey many potentially problematic nonfinancial metrics, with lots of ways to go wrong. If the company wishes to use nonfinancial goals in this effort, it should draw them from a rigorously set system of value drivers.

Strategic initiatives are often seen as a reason to use nonfinancial metrics in a big way. However, incentive plans that emphasize financial success over time will be very supportive of a good strategic plan, just as they are for any other value-creating initiative. And what if the strategic plan is economic nonsense? It could happen. A scan of any month's *Wall Street Journal* headlines makes it clear that big, bad business strategies are commonplace. Well-designed incentive plans will discourage those just as they do other actions likely to destroy value. If the strategy really is a loser, then management and investors should be happy that incentives are helping to put on the brakes. Observers sometimes argue that the bigger problem at many companies is not strategy formulation but implementation. Companies can win with less-than-perfect strategies, but they probably cannot win with mediocre execution. Decisive incentive plans draw a straight, bold line from strategy formulation right through any successful execution.

Lots of financially driven incentive designs connect rather thoroughly, even subtly, with tenets of the strategic plan. Here are examples comparing terms of a client's strategic plan to key messages of its performance share plan design:

- The strategic plan has a strong operational/strategic focus. Incentive plan goals are based on results of operations—earnings before interest and tax (EBIT) and overall capital usage—rather than on metrics like earnings per share (EPS) that are more susceptible to nonoperating effects. This choice is meant to pursue higher "line of sight" and engagement effects.

- The strategy's overarching goal is to drive *sustainable* competitive advantage and profitable growth from sustainable revenue sources. Incentives use explicit long-term goals within an overlapping structure, ones set to pay out most when results flow from sustainable sources over time. Stock price increases—through multiple expansion—hinge on this as well.

- Strategic initiatives at the company are set to improve the clarity of focus with shareholders. The incentive plan pays for actual financial results, in amounts easily funded by financial results—not for nonfinancial goals. It is denominated in shares, creating important linkages with shareholder wealth.

- Strategic success hinges on driving behavior change and alignment deep in the organization. The performance share plan deliberately creates high line of sight in pursuit of behavior change. Payouts hinge heavily on operational results, those offering greatest line of sight for the overall participant group.

- The strategic plan pursues cross-functional alignment and better decision making, with authority better enabled below the senior officer group, and with clear expectations from the top to the bottom across the company. It encourages high-quality decisions in precise terms. Incentives are designed to create a strong shared interest, one meant to encourage teamwork and alignment toward overall success—across functions and levels.

- The strategic plan will involve a mix of strategic acquisitions and selective investments. The incentive structure folds in mergers and acquisitions, divestitures and investments flexibly, paying for investments offering good returns over time. This creates an undisrupted financial interest in underlying financial results and value creation.

- Plans indicate the financing picture may be fluid (debt, repurchases). Performance share plan goals are based on operational decisions that participants can affect. The strategy also pursues sustainable cash flow, which is emphasized explicitly in the incentive payout schedule.

- The plan hinges on some portfolio effects, with some units meant to provide a stable source of funds. The long-term incentive (LTI) structure reflects the important contribution of free cash flow (FCF) to investor returns, balancing it against the value gains that stem from income growth.

Leadership of corporate functions like human resources and information systems do not always feel very strong line of sight to corporate incentive pay. For them, individual, department, or other nonfinancial goals are often said to be more compelling. Their incentive plans usually do not work that way, though. They are driven mainly by corporate financial results and stock performance, as for other senior managers.

A general move toward more goal-based pay is a big step in the direction of improving line of sight for all of senior management including functional leaders. It strips out the more vague aspects of stock performance, centering pay closer to matters executives can influence. And functions do have a great deal of influence. Information systems performance is almost always seen as essential. Systems success was the gate to growth in a start-up home improvement chain, for example. Growth company chief financial officers (CFOs) and heads of planning are charged with mergers and acquisitions and other big-ticket investing— matters whose results often decide whether the company creates any value. The impact of human resource (HR) is very strong as well. Companies often have per-share compensation and benefits costs that are greater than EPS, as one indication of the scale of impact. If they are worried about finding the next 5 or 10 percent gain in EPS, they can look to more efficacious rewards design. Return on investment is a pressing, high-stakes matter across all functions.

Functions are sometimes seen unfairly as cost centers rather than sources of value creation. Their nature, though, may indeed require closer performance monitoring; a more intensively managed meritocracy. At the senior management level, though, that is already happening much of the time. These roles interact closely with the corporate chief executive officer (CEO) and, at times, the board. As service providers, they feel performance pressure within the senior management ranks. And, with executive pay pending more heavily on shared financial goals, they are not getting out of the crucible any time soon.

Moving pay to the business-unit level can be helpful for staff function incentives, as well. Companies placing the most pay on unit results, particularly long-term incentives, often are the ones in which units are more autonomous. In these more devolved organizations, function heads at the unit level have more independent impact on unit results. Delivering pay based on unit results in this situation is one of the most properly engaging approaches available.

When the reporting lines to corporate functions are bold rather than dotted, the corporate-level function is one with more control and impact. Heavier corporate authority means the corporate-level functional cadre is a comparatively influential one. This is matched properly with a higher stake in consolidated performance.

Just as companies should not leave incentives largely in the hands of the stock market, they should not atomize them into a lot of compartmentalized and subjective goals. Nor, most of the time, should they revert to a system of moving targets like the indexation and immunization tactics discussed at the end of this chapter. They should take on the task of choosing proper financial metrics and goals, and run their incentive system mainly on that basis. The balance of this chapter reviews the main metrics on the typical menu. Chapter 7 then reviews value-based financial metrics.

Evaluating Financial Metrics

A colleague likes to remark that the difference between a good golfer and a bad golfer is that the good golfer knows where his bad shots are going to go. We next examine the pros and cons of various financial metrics, clarifying the cases where their results can depart from value creation. This should help companies improve the state of their game, when it comes to incentives, by seeing where they run afoul of shareholder interests and how they can get back in bounds.

Companies rely mainly on familiar, traditional measures to judge results and deliver rewards within their annual incentive plans. Income-based metrics, taken together, dominate bonus pay delivery, with sales and return-type metrics having large overall impacts as well. Here are example results from a recent poll of annual incentive plan metrics:

Performance Measure	Prevalence
Sales/revenues	34%
Cash flow	26%
Earnings per share (EPS)	26%
Net income/earnings/profit	24%
Pretax income	5%
Gross margin	4%

(Continued)

Performance Measure	Prevalence
Earnings before interest and taxes (EBIT, or EBITDA)	25%
Net operating profit after tax (NOPAT)	2%
Operating income/operating profit	25%
Operating measures, e.g., operating margin	7%
Economic profit/Economic Value Added (EP/EVA)	4%
Return on assets/return on net assets (ROA/RONA)	3%
Return on equity (ROE)	7%
Return on invested capital (ROIC)	8%
Cost/expense control/reduction	17%
Volume/production	7%
Customer satisfaction	16%
Employee satisfaction	4%
Safety/environmental	17%
Strategic objectives	27%
Team/department objectives	16%
Individual objectives	44%

Note the percentages total more than 100 percent due to multiple responses. We will recategorize these shortly for purposes of our discussion, treating operating income and EBIT together, for example, and ROIC and RONA as the same thing.

Revenue, Volume, and Gross Margin

Revenue is used often at both the corporate and business-unit levels in many kinds of incentive plans, including those focused on senior management. Performance against revenue goals captures a lot about business health and success, since it reflects growth in the volume of business as well as selling prices in the marketplace. In a growing company, it is often a leading indicator of profitability.

Companies that see organizational scale or market presence as a strategic variable sometimes use revenue and volume as pay metrics. Consumer products companies are a good example. Incentive plans used by Coca-Cola have been based partly on case volume, for example. Market share is always used as a performance indicator in such settings and sometimes enters into pay programs. Revenue growth versus peers gets at many of the same matters covered by market share, measuring the company's ability to expand along with the size of the market and to get a bigger piece of it.

Gross margin is an indicator of some aspects of business health, as well. It has particular interest for companies with up-market brands, for example, since it testifies to the strength of consumers' preference and their willingness to pay more in response. Companies whose products offer performance advantages expect higher gross margins as well when the market pays them for their innovation and technical prowess. BMW provides a good example of both the cachet and performance effects.

Using a metric to judge business success is one thing. Linking executive pay to that yardstick is another. When we start attaching pay to these metrics we see some potential problems. Too much focus on revenue can lead the organization to chase unprofitable growth. Revenue by itself misses most of the basic drivers of value creation. Volume has the same shortcoming. Too much emphasis on growth in and of itself surely is a driving force behind many failed acquisitions.

Revenue is used often in incentive plans. On the whole, though, most established companies do not place much emphasis on revenue as an independent matter from more complete measures of financial results. Rather, they tend to attach a weight of less than 50 percent to any revenue goal for a senior management team, less at the corporate level.

That is good, but it is not enough to keep companies entirely out of the trouble that can attend the practice of basing incentive pay on revenue. In a typical incentive plan attaching some separate weight to sales goals, management can make more money by increasing sales without increasing profit, through sales that bring zero incremental profit. Exhibit 6.1 is an example of a plan that includes a revenue goal and some scenarios of performance and reward it implies.

Let us say that it is a bad year and performance appears to be on track toward threshold levels: $90 in revenue and $8 in operating income. The scenarios show three ways to get performance up to targeted levels:

1. *The hard way.* This involves winning profitable new sales. Sales end up at $100 and profits at $10, so this performance scenario involves getting $10 in new revenue with incremental profit margin of 20 percent.

2. *The easy way.* This one cuts prices to the point where marginal profit is zero. In this case, revenue increases to $110 but profits stay at $8.

3. *The middle way.* This involves $105 in revenue and profit rising by $1.

| EXHIBIT 6.1 | INCENTIVE PLAN WITH REVENUE AND OPERATING INCOME GOALS |

	Bonus Award Percent of Target			Weighting	Scenarios		
	0% Threshold	100% Target	200% Maximum	Percent of Target	Hard Way to Target	Middle Way	Easy Way to Target
Revenue Range	90	100	110	50%	100.0	105.0	110.0
Operating Income Range	8	10	12	50%	10.0	9.0	8.0
Payout					100%	100%	100%
Management's Order of Preference					3	2	1
Investors' Order of Preference					1	2	3

Consistently profitable new revenue is best for investors. It results in higher income and value. The scenarios bring equal pay for management, so they encourage the easiest one first: unprofitable new revenue. This plan puts investors' interests at odds with those of management. The same is true to a lesser extent in plans placing lower weightings like 40 percent or 25 percent on revenue.

This basic example of plan testing exposes the kind of issue we encounter in many incentive plans. Before rolling out plans, companies should test them to see how they reward good and bad business decisions. In Exhibit 6.2, revenue is

| EXHIBIT 6.2 | INCENTIVE PLAN WITH REVENUE GOAL AS AWARD MODIFIER |

	Bonus Award Percent of Target			Scenarios		
	0% Threshold	100% Target	160% Maximum	Hard Way	Middle Way	Easy Way
Operating Income Range	8	10	12	10.0	9.0	8.0
Award on Operating Income				100%	50%	0%
Revenue Range	90	100	110	100.0	105.0	110.0
Revenue Award Modifier	0.8	1.0	1.25	1.0	1.125	0.8
Payout				100%	56%	0%
Management's Order of Preference				1	2	3
Investors' Order of Preference				1	2	3

featured in an incentive plan without putting management at odds with investors.

Revenue is a big factor in this plan, but operating income is in the driver's seat. Operating income places a value on management's performance, which is then modified by revenue performance. The effect of revenue is important, but it plays out more consistently with owner preferences.

When revenue is indeed a leading indicator, it can be used to set future performance targets. This year's revenue growth can increase next year's operating income goals based on a standard margin. We used this method as part of the procedure used to set targets for a diversified manufacturing company. This created a pro-growth incentive plan, but one in which it would not make sense for the business to expand with unprofitable volume. Mechanical algorithms like these sometimes function better than negotiated goals. They can create financial stakes and accountabilities that have both a memory and a shelf life.

A new venture will often base bonuses on early milestones and revenue. Short-term profit can be an especially counterproductive metric in such cases. The relevant issue is mainly one of timing. Success of the venture can be judged perfectly well based on financial performance over time. In such cases, a potential solution is to put in place a long-term incentive plan based on the venture's cumulative financial results. Such a plan encourages taking all actions with an eye toward longer-run, sustained profitability. In this case, the pitfalls of revenue and other financially incomplete goals are not corrected within the bonus plan. Instead, they are counterbalanced by LTI.

Gross profit is equal to revenue minus the cost of sales, so it does reflect at least one cost category. But it attaches no importance to other costs. It might discourage a company to outsource manufacturing, for example, even when such a move would be greatly beneficial. The gains to the company could be felt heavily in opportunity costs of capital and in unabsorbed selling, general, and administrative expense (SG&A). These do not count in the gross profit computation. It might also encourage overspending on costs such as advertising that do not enter into cost of sales.

Gross profit is a widely quoted indicator, but it is not used much in incentive plans. Too much emphasis on margins can encourage price gouging that reduces revenue, profit, and value creation over time.

USING VALUATION CRITERIA TO CHOOSE METRICS

We have seen problems with revenue, volume, and gross margin as incentive metrics and what can be done about them. These are just a few of the dozens, even hundreds, of measures that a company might consider. Companies bat around new measurement ideas all the time. What is needed is a general method for reviewing measures and their suitability for use in incentive plans, and in particular for plans directed at senior-level management.

Valuation criteria are well suited to this task. We applied them when defining *earnings quality* in Chapter 2. Let us use them as our method to assess metrics for use in a management incentive plan:

Step 1. Compare the metric to the primary value drivers in the discounted cash flow (DCF) valuation model: income, capital usage, and the cost of capital.

Revenue reflects only part of the first driver and neither of the next two. So it is a very incomplete metric and, in many cases, it will conflict with value creation. We can test this by moving other variables around. What if revenue rose while profits were flat (the unprofitable sales growth example)? What if revenue and profits rose, but capital outlays wiped out any economic gain?

Step 2. Ask this question: As a practical matter, are plan participants in a position to take material advantage of the gaps in the metric? If the revenue-heavy incentive plan is a sales commission arrangement, one dealing with equally profitable products over which participants have no pricing control, then it may not conflict at all with value creation. If the whole top management team is in it, it may pose real risks of distortion.

Step 3. Look for solutions based on valuation precepts. In the case of revenue-based plans, that means looking for an offsetting emphasis on expenses, capital usage, and the cost of capital—upon the elements of DCF value not covered by revenue. These already may exist within the incentive structure. If the plan features revenue as a modifier rather than as a separate goal, then it may not need adjustment.

CONTEXT FOR EVALUATING FINANCIAL METRICS

A value-based review of performance metrics takes some work. High standards of rigorousness fit the context, however. Financial metrics have a range of important roles in incentive pay. They may act:

- As the basis for all or part of award potential, independently of other metrics, within a goal-based annual or long-term incentive plan
- Within a performance/award schedule that determines awards jointly as a function of several measures (e.g., EPS and ROE)

- As a basis for the valuation formula used in a phantom stock plan
- As a basis for setting targets denominated in other measures (e.g., setting payout schedules for operating income and return on investment [ROIC] based on their valuation implications, as estimated by the metric total business return [TBR])
- As a multiplier or modifier of performance or awards
- As a threshold condition on overall award payment within plans—that is, an overall bonus funding "circuit breaker" set at the corporate level, or as the trigger for issuance of performance-contingent stock grants (e.g., to comply with U.S. I.R.C. section 162(m))
- As the basis for setting the number of shares or options granted in a stock-based incentive plan, for accelerating grants already made, or for determining the cash or shares earned in a long-term performance plan
- As part of a method of judging dilution related to incentive plans

Let us continue to assume the metrics we are reviewing are used in the first context—as a basis for earning material amounts of reward within an incentive plan for senior management. That is the role in which metrics must meet the highest standard.

Operating Income, EBIT, and Return on Invested Capital

Operating income is revenue minus cost of goods sold and operating expenses. It may be stated in pre- or post-tax terms—we will assume pre-tax, here. In an uncomplicated company—one without much in the way of nonoperating sources of income and expense aside from interest expense—operating income is the same thing as EBIT. Operating income is a commonly quoted measure of business performance and size that is used more often than any other when devising incentives for business units. It is the "sweet spot" of the income statement for our purposes, being stated after subtracting the operating costs that most management team members can influence, but before the financing costs and other odd income sources and costs they cannot influence much.

ROIC is equal to operating income divided by capital. It is stated in percentage terms and, like operating income, it comes in pre- and after-tax versions. ROIC is the same general metric as return on capital employed (ROCE) and return on net assets (RONA). Return on investments (ROI) is defined the same way, and it also serves as the more general term for getting an economic yield from a business outlay. Return on assets (ROA) is net income divided by total assets. It is used mainly in financial intermediaries like banks.

Do operating income and its peer metrics work well as incentive plan metrics? Let us roll out our three-step procedure:

Step 1: Operating income after tax is one of the three main drivers of valuation, along with capital usage and the cost of capital. Operating income differs from operating income after taxes only to the extent of taxes. So, taxes, capital usage, and the cost of capital are the value drivers missed by pretax operating income. The tax issue normally is addressed by:

- Stating performance in after-tax terms
- Capturing taxes through its effects on FCF or net capital usage (e.g., lower taxes mean higher FCF and perhaps higher cash and lower net debt)
- Using a pretax metric in cases where tax policy and effects are seen as being outside of the participant group's main focus

An incentive plan based on operating income ought to do a good job of encouraging the income growth that drives value creation. So far, so good. Now, how about those matters of capital and its cost? These drivers take us to the heart of problems with operating income and other income metrics as incentive plan yardsticks:

- Operating income does not by itself take capital usage into account. If operating income after tax rises from $100 to $110 with no change in capital, then the value of the company's operating performance goes up. If it used $2,000 in new capital to increase income by $100, however, the low return of 5 percent surely destroyed value. Operating income alone does not tell you whether actions taken in its pursuit created value or not.

- The other blind side of operating income is the cost of capital. If the investment in the earlier example had been $1,000 rather than $2,000, the return on the investment would have been 10 percent. Is this enough of a return to create value? Probably, but it depends on the cost of capital. Investors need to get a return on the investment in the business to compensate them for the risks they bear in funding it. That "hurdle" rate of return is the cost of capital as we saw in Chapter 5.

If the cost of capital is 8 percent, a $1,000 investment needs to generate an annual after-tax return of at least $80 to create value. This investment generated a return of $100, so it did create value. Operating income by itself does not tell us anything about the cost of capital, so it again is an insufficient basis by itself to judge success in the value creation realm. Other income-based metrics we'll see shortly—pretax income, net income, EPS, and cash flow—have various degrees of blindness to capital usage and its cost.

Return on invested capital, however, does take into account the capital involved in business initiatives. ROIC on new investments can be benchmarked directly against the cost of capital. However:

- The ROIC measurement alone does not include the cost of capital, so it does not by itself signal whether value creation occurred.

- ROIC is based on historical capital. Company histories and accounting practices can affect the amount of capital reported. These differences could cause Company A to have ROIC of 5 percent of historical capital, while Company B might report 20 percent, even if it has exactly the same income prospects and valuation. So ROIC, like operating income, does not by itself identify value creation in a consistent way.

Each factor can be a problem depending on the role of ROIC within an incentive plan. If the plan bases awards on ROIC improvement, for example, then a company with initial ROIC at 5 percent would take on an investment that offers ROIC of 5 percent or better, including many value-destroying investments with ROIC under the cost of capital of 10 percent. Another company might turn down any investment offering ROIC below its starting point of 20 percent, including many with value-creating yields above 10 percent.

We have run into this problem with some frequency. One example was a manufacturing company whose goal-setting procedures for ROIC required business units to improve ROIC from existing levels, whether they started at 35 percent or 3.5 percent. The proper standard, in contrast, is that new investments must earn yields in excess of the cost of capital. The beginning level of capital, and therefore the existing level of ROIC, is irrelevant.

Differences in capital measurement are often serious enough that ROIC cannot even be used to benchmark results among peers or business units, much less against absolute standards of value creation. And speaking of absolutes, note that ROIC is not one. It is stated in percentage terms. Value creation is stated in terms of absolute value. Two business performance scenarios may involve the same ROIC, but one may be far larger than the other and may have created much more value. This indifference to quantity leads to problems like those ascribed earlier to margin measures. In pursuit of ROIC by itself, companies may wish to sell off assets and shrink the business to where it consists mainly of assets with high yields in relation to historical capital, even if this course of action creates no value. We will look at some other return-based metrics later—return on equity (ROE), cash flow return on gross investment (CFROGI)—that have the same set of problems.

Step 2: Are these problems with operating income and ROIC a concern, considering who is in the participant group? If senior management is in the plan, then you bet it is. They make the decisions about capital, and these two measures pose a range of problems in that area.

Step 3: So, how do we address these problems? We get income, capital, and its costs represented in proper proportion. That means amending the plan's metrics, target-setting methods, award schedules, or all of these.

Some solutions to the issues associated with operating income and ROIC are as follows:

- As is the case with revenue metrics, target-setting methods can be helpful. Let us take a company that uses operating income as its sole measure of business performance. If the company increases capital by $1,000 and it has a 10 percent cost of capital, it does need to get after-tax operating income on the new investment of at least $100 to create value. Jacking up the operating profit target for the next year by an additional $100 creates accountability for this goal and encourages the company to make only value-creating investments. As we will see in Chapter 7, this is the equivalent of an incentive plan based on a form of the metric economic profit.[4]

- Where ROIC is concerned, we simply recommend not using it as the sole measure within an incentive plan, but instead combining it with absolute measures of business scale or income. It is combined most readily with operating income. In these cases, the emphasis on growth in operating income provides a scale to the ROIC criterion. The presence of ROIC in the plan addresses the fact that operating income does not reflect capital usage.

TWO WRONGS CAN MAKE A RIGHT

Balancing ROIC and operating income (OI) is a somewhat common general approach, but it often is flawed at the detail level. It needs to be constructed carefully. Exhibit 6.3 is an example of an incentive plan format based on operating income (after-tax in this case) and ROIC.

The plan is typical, using performance ranges of +/− 20 percent on each metric, a 0 percent to 200 percent award payout and a symmetrical award schedule. This plan has metrics constructed from an "operating" or "total capital" perspective, as recommended in Chapter 2. It has wide, straight-line performance and payout ranges, ones meant to avoid payout distortions that could occur at borders or bends in the payout line. The ROIC performance range uses the cost of capital, 10 percent, as its minimum level, so it appears to discourage lower, value-destroying ROIC levels. The matrix format hints at certain valuation dynamics, too, according less payout to income growth when associated

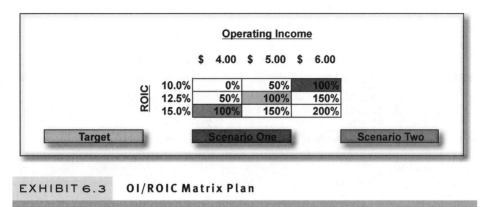

EXHIBIT 6.3   OI/ROIC Matrix Plan

ROIC is lower. Overall, it appears to reflect many value drivers. Let's put it to the test.

The center cell of this award matrix pays awards at 100 percent of target if levels of income and capital are at $5 and $40, respectively, so that ROIC is 12.5 percent. Last year's income was $4 and capital was $40. This target scenario and each to follow involve a $1 increase in income from the "base" business. Let us examine some other outcomes that reward management equally:

- **Scenario One.** What if performance ends up in the upper right hand corner of the matrix, with operating income at $6? Last year's income was $4 and there was a $1 increase in base business, so there is an additional $1 income gain here that came from some initiative that we can set apart and evaluate. Let us say it is a wholesaler stocking up to carry a new line of products.[5] ROIC landed at 10 percent, so ending capital must have been $60 because $6 is 10 percent of that. Capital last year was $40 and the base business had no additional capital demands, so this separate investment apparently amounted to $20. A $1 income gain on a $20 investment is a poor return at 5 percent, yet the incentive plan pays out at target.

    How bad was the investment decision? The $1 permanent income gain is worth $10, or $1 divided by the 10 percent cost of capital, as learned in Chapter 2. The investment outlay was $20, however, so the company is worse off by $10, net. The plan nonetheless pays out 100 percent at target because it does not recognize this destruction in value. Investors would have been better off if management had not made the investment, but the incentive plan treats the two outcomes equally.

- **Scenario Two.** Target awards also can be earned with ROIC of 15 percent and $4 in income. Income at $4 is a dollar off the base case of $5, while ROIC at 15 percent suggests that capital fell to $26.67 ($4/15%).

		Operating Income				
		$ 4.00	$ 4.50	$ 5.00	$ 5.50	$ 6.00
	10.00%	0%	0%	0%	0%	0%
	11.25%	44%	50%	56%	61%	67%
ROIC	12.50%	80%	90%	100%	110%	120%
	13.75%	109%	123%	136%	150%	164%
	15.00%	133%	150%	167%	183%	200%

Target	Scenario One	Scenario Two

EXHIBIT 6.4   OI/ROIC Matrix Based on Value Creation

These could be effects of selling or liquidating a line of business. That performance level pays out at 100 percent as well. But it actually involves value creation of $3.33. Sale proceeds apparently were $13.33 because net assets fell from $40 to $26.67, but the reduction value from the $1 income loss was only $10 ($1/10%).

This award schedule appeared reasonable at first glance. When we got into the details—the level at which the incentive plan actually operates—we saw some serious flaws. Many plans apply separate payout schedules for ROIC and operating income, often resulting in the same problems. Payout misspecification is common in incentive formats of all types. One should look for holes in the measurement scheme, fix them if needed, and test the overall plan before rolling it out. In this case, a solution could be to change the existing award matrix so awards are aligned with value creation. Exhibit 6.4 is such a matrix.

Value creation or destruction at each cell in the matrix is compared to the company's $50 base case value, with the difference used to set up the award schedule. These percentage deviations from target are leveraged up by a factor of five in order to create 200 percent upside. The value-destroying scenarios in the matrix are zeroed out and made ineligible for reward. In this matrix, scenarios 1, 2, and all others are made to pay out based on their estimated degree of value creation.

This is a good general solution for incentive plan award schedules. We build on it several times in later chapters. The matrix format for the payout table is one that allows the dynamics of value creation—the trade-off between capital usage and income gains—to be specified at many different performance levels.[6] It is a generally underused format, however, noted by only 10 percent of respondents to our annual incentive design study.

On the Importance of Being Earnest

The value-based payout example was more complicated than typical design, but this level of complexity will not make the plan ineffective. The end result of this financial calibration exercise was simply a table linking payouts with some ordinary metrics. It took some work to think through the schedule, but that is work worth doing in view of the consistently proper incentive effects it creates. The executive teams that get paid by plans like these look closely at the details. If their plans had a bunch of economic loopholes in them, they often figure, it makes sense to find out what those loopholes are, so, at least in a pinch, they might be pursued.

We do more of this kind of detailed payout "calibration" analysis in later chapters dedicated to incentive design, as opposed to this chapter dealing with measurement. However, this initial example warrants a look here because the OI/ROIC matrix is an example of a *system* of financial measurements, one that makes up for the deficiencies of single metrics by combining them in productive ways.

Traditional metrics hold the serious advantage of being simpler and more familiar than value-based ones. If you're going to use them in a prominent, high-stakes way, though, you have to pay close attention to how you tie them to pay. That can take some time. Traditional approaches can take up a lot of time as well. Their adverse side effects can create many one-off problems over the full course of the measurement term. These require time to correct, often requiring staff, consultants, management, and board members to remediate. Worse, the innate biases in the metrics can cause problems with decision making and performance that may or may not be correctible. The better path is the more earnest one—making incentive promises that are thought through thoroughly at the outset.

Pretax Income, Net Income, EPS, and ROE

This is the mainstream of corporate performance measurement. These metrics are used often to deliver bonus pay to top officers of public companies:

- Pretax income is EBIT minus net interest expense and other sources of nonoperating income and expense.
- Net income is pretax income minus income taxes.
- Return on equity is equal to net income after tax divided by stockholder's equity. Return on common equity is equal to net income after taxes and preferred dividends (that is, net income available to common shareholders) divided by common equity.

- EPS is equal to net income available to common shareholders divided by common shares outstanding. Basic EPS is based on the number of shares actually outstanding, while diluted EPS reflects effects of in-the-money stock options and other contingent, equity-equivalent claims.[7]

EPS is the main yardstick of financial performance cited by analysts and the business press. Companies often act as if shareholder expectations are denominated in near-term EPS. This seems to force them into a constant game of next-quarter capitalism. Often, it leads them to tie pay to EPS. In reality, EPS has no monopoly on investor attention. The stock market consistently looks past EPS toward longer-run expectations for free cash flow. Much of the market mystique and incentive prevalence of EPS is undeserved.

A review from the standpoint of valuation principles provides these major findings:

- The pretax income measure that initiates the computation of these metrics is stated net of interest costs. This departs from the total capital perspective that describes value creation in the DCF model, as mentioned in Chapter 2. It can leave financing and investment policy open to distortion, and can make it hard to benchmark performance.

- These metrics carry some problems cited in the cases of operating income and ROIC. Income-based metrics are not sensitive to capital usage. Return-based metrics do not explicitly comprehend the cost of capital, can be affected by inconsistencies in historical costs of assets, and can distort some target-setting methods.

- EPS does reflect effects of both debt and equity capital usage and in this regard is more complete than other income-based metrics. It is stated net of interest paid on net debt investment as well as the per-share effects of equity investment. As we will see next, though, these factors can be sources of EPS distortion.

Debt, Share Repurchases, EPS, and Stock Price Gains

We have seen some but not all of the ways financing decisions can distort metrics and pay. There still is big money to be made on share repurchases. In the first scenario (Exhibit 6.5), a company with zero debt and zero growth in operating income can produce EPS growth of 10 percent per year by repurchasing shares with all of its available cash flow (ending shares were used in these example EPS computations). Exhibit 6.6 involves 5 percent income growth with increases in

Year	0	1	2	3	Residual Value
Operating Income, After Tax	$100	$100	$100	$100	$100
Total Capital	1,000	1,000	1,000	1,000	1,000
Increase in Capital		0	0	0	0
Free Cash Flow		$100	$100	$100	$1,000
(Income Minus Capital Change)					
Cost of Capital 10.0%					
Present Value as of End of Year:					
FCF for Remaining Forecast Term	$249	174	91		
Residual Value	751	826	909	$1,000	
Enterprise Value	1,000	1,000	1,000	1,000	
Valuation at Beginning of Year		1,000	1,000	1,000	
Value Gain		0	0	0	
Free Cash Flow		100	100	100	
Total Investor Return		$100	$100	$100	
Return as a Percent		10.0%	10.0%	10.0%	
of Beginning Value					
Book Value of Equity		$1,000	$1,000	$1,000	
(Capital Minus Debt)					
Share Price:					
Debt % of Ending Value	0.0%	0.0%	0.0%	0.0%	
Ending Debt	$0	$0	$0	$0	
Equity Value	$1,000	$1,000	$1,000	$1,000	
Number of Shares Outstanding	1,000	909	826	751	
Stock Value per Share	$ 1.00	$ 1.10	$ 1.21	$ 1.33	
Earnings per Share:					
Interest Expense (4% cost after tax)	$0	$0	$0	$0	
Net Income	100	100	100	100	
EPS	$0.10	$0.11	$0.12	$0.13	
Outstanding Shares:					
Equity Cash Flow					
(Free Cash Flow − Interest + Debt Change)		$100	$100	$100	
Equity Value Before Repurchase					
(Including Equity Cash Flow[ECF])		$1,100	$1,100	$1,100	
Stock Value per Share Before Repurchase		$1.10	$1.21	$1.33	
Number of Shares Repurchased with ECF		91	83	75	
Number of New Shares Outstanding		909	826	751	

Effect of Debt and Repurchases:					3-Year Avg. or Growth Rate
Operating Income Growth		0.0%	0.0%	0.0%	0.0%
EPS Growth		10.0%	10.0%	10.0%	10.0%
Growth in Enterprise Value		0.0%	0.0%	0.0%	0.0%
Total Investor Return		10.0%	10.0%	10.0%	10.0%
Growth in Stock Value		10.0%	10.0%	10.0%	10.0%
Total Return to Equityholders		$100.0	$100.0	$100.0	$100.0
Return on Invested Capital		10.0%	10.0%	10.0%	0.0%
Return on Equity		10.0%	10.0%	10.0%	10.0%
Shares Controlled by Management	10.0%	11.0%	12.1%	13.3%	1.1%

EXHIBIT 6.5   Repurchase Effects with Zero Growth and Debt

capital based on 20 percent incremental ROIC. In this case, debt is held at 33 percent of enterprise value. This scenario turns 5 percent income growth into EPS growth averaging 16.4 percent. This is not a bad game, and it is one that can be played year after year.

Management's control of the enterprise grows each year in the first two scenarios. Exhibit 6.7 shows an example like the one in Exhibit 6.6 except with

Year	0	1	2	3	Residual Value
Operating Income, After Tax	$100	$105	$110	$116	$116
Total Capital	1,000	1,025	1,051	1,079	1,079
Increase in Capital		25	26	28	0
Free Cash Flow					
(Income Minus Capital Change)		$80	$84	$88	$1,158
Cost of Capital 10.0%					
Present Value as of End of Year:					
FCF for Remaining Forecast Term	$208	$149	$80		
Residual Value	870	957	1,052	1,158	
Enterprise Value	1,078	1,106	1,132	1,158	
Valuation at Beginning of Year		1,078	1,106	1,132	
Value Gain		28	27	25	
Free Cash Flow		80	84	88	
Total Investor Return		$108	$111	$113	
Return as a Percent of Beginning Value		10.0%	10.0%	10.0%	
Book Value of Equity (Capital Minus Debt)		$656	$673	$693	
Share Price:					
Debt % of Ending Value	33.3%	33.3%	33.3%	33.3%	
Ending Debt	$359	$369	$378	$386	
Equity Value	$719	$737	$755	$772	
Number of Shares Outstanding	737	669	607	549	
Stock Value per Share	$0.97	$1.10	$1.24	$1.41	
Earnings per Share:					
Interest Expense (4% cost after tax)	$14	$14	$15	$15	
Net Income	86	91	96	101	
EPS	$0.12	$0.14	$0.16	$0.18	
Outstanding Shares:					
Equity Cash Flow (Free Cash Flow − Interest + Debt Change)		$75	$78	$81	
Equity Value Before Repurchase (including Equity Cash Flow [ECF])		812	833	853	
Stock Value per Share Before Repurchase		$1.10	$1.24	$1.41	
Number Shares Repurchased with ECF		68	63	58	
Number of New Shares Outstanding		$668.93	$607.00	$549.23	

Effect of Debt and Repurchases:					3-Year Avg. or Growth Rate
Operating Income Growth		5.0%	5.0%	5.0%	5.0%
EPS Growth		16.6%	16.3%	16.5%	16.4%
Growth in Enterprise Value		2.6%	2.4%	2.2%	2.4%
Total Investor Return		10.0%	10.0%	10.0%	10.0%
Growth in Stock Value		13.0%	13.0%	13.0%	13.0%
Total Return to Equityholders		$93.40	$95.90	$98.20	$95.83
Return on Invested Capital		10.2%	10.5%	10.7%	10.5%
Return on Equity		13.8%	14.2%	14.5%	14.2%
Shares Controlled by Management	10.0%	11.0%	12.2%	13.4%	1.1%

EXHIBIT 6.6   Repurchase Effects with Moderate Growth and Debt

rising debt levels. High share repurchase levels sometimes are described as a "slo-mo LBO." That title seems fitting for this scenario since management doubles its share of the company's equity. It takes the same 5 percent annual growth of operating income and turns it into 31.6 percent average EPS growth. If not adjusted out of incentive plans, these effects can drive payouts. Repurchases can distort gains on stock-based pay, too, by converting money that might have gone to dividends into higher stock distort gain on stock-based pay, prices instead. The former does not pay out, explicitly, in most stock option plans, but the latter does.

Year	0	1	2	3	Residual Value
Operating Income, After Tax	$100	$105	$110	$116	$116
Total Capital	1,000	1,025	1,051	1,079	1,079
Increase in Capital		25	26	28	
Free Cash Flow (Income Minus Capital Change)		$80	$84	$88	$1,158
Cost of Capital 10.0%					
Present Value as of End of Year:					
FCF for Remaining Forecast Term	$208	$149	$80		
Residual Value	$870	$957	$1,062	$1,158	
Enterprise Value	1,078	1,106	1,133	1,158	
Valuation at Beginning of Year		1,078	1,106	1,133	
Value Gain		28	27	25	
Free Cash Flow		80	84	88	
Total Investor Return		108	111	113	
Return as a Percent of Beginning Value		10.0%	10.0%	10.0%	
Book Value of Equity (Capital Minus Debt)		$693	$598	$500	
Share Price:					
Debt % of Ending Value	20.0%	30.0%	40.0%	50.0%	
Ending Debt	$216	$332	$453	$579	
Equity Value	$863	$774	$680	$579	
Number of Shares Outstanding	774	623	486	363	
Stock Value per Share	$1.11	$1.24	$1.40	$1.60	
Earnings per Share:					
Interest Expense (4% cost after tax)	$9	$9	$13	$18	
Net Income	91	96	97	98	
EPS	$0.12	$0.15	$0.20	$0.27	
Outstanding Shares:					
Equity Cash Flow (Free Cash Flow – Interest + Debt Change)		$188	$192	$196	
Equity Value Before Repurchase (including Equity Cash Flow [ECF])		962	872	775	
Stock Value per Share Before Repurchase		$1.24	$1.40	$1.59	
Number of Shares Repurchased with ECF		151	137	123	
Number of New Shares Outstanding		623	486	363	

Effect of Debt and Repurchases:					3-Year Avg. or Growth Rate
Operating Income Growth		5.0%	5.0%	5.0%	5.0%
EPS Growth		31.0%	29.1%	34.8%	31.6%
Growth in Enterprise Value		2.6%	2.4%	2.2%	2.4%
Total Investor Return		10.0%	10.0%	10.0%	10.0%
Growth in Stock Value		11.5%	12.6%	14.0%	12.7%
Total Return to Equityholders		$99.20	$97.30	$95.10	$97.20
Return on Invested Capital		10.2%	10.5%	10.7%	10.5%
Return on Equity		13.9%	16.2%	19.5%	16.2%
Shares Controlled by Management	10.0%	12.4%	15.9%	21.3%	3.8%

EXHIBIT 6.7   Repurchase Effects with Rising Debt: "Slo-mo LBO"

Capital structure effects can trouble the effective use of net income, EPS, and ROE in incentive plans, though these are the yardsticks used most commonly. When companies make choices regarding how to finance investments, whether to restructure their capital sources, whether to pay, stabilize, or increase dividends, or whether to repurchase shares, they are doing two things. They are doing something that almost no one in an incentive plan can influence, and they are affecting incentive pay for most members of company management, perhaps materially.

This is not good, if the objective is to create line of sight. It may not be affecting the valuation of the overall enterprise very much, either. Capital structure probably works mainly like the bookkeeping choices set forth in Chapter 2, producing potentially huge effects on financial reporting in the near term and modest or zero effect on FCF and investor returns over time. Many company financing moves may simply trade risks and cash flows among investor classes at market transaction prices.

Changes in capital structure may bring benefits. Perhaps more debt can better exploit the corporate tax benefits of debt finance, without being wholly offset by risk effects. Perhaps repurchases will deliver free cash flows to investors in a more tax-efficient and flexible way. Share repurchase actions may contain a positive new signal; that management is paying closer attention to capital usage. If any of these are true, they will improve stock performance. The few decision makers involved, all with heavy equity exposure, will gain. If anyone else in incentive plans has their pay driven much by capital structure, they're just free riders or victims of policies they cannot control.

Remedying Issues with Pretax Income, Net Income, EPS, and ROE

We have identified the issues with these metrics. Let us move on and look at some solutions:

- *Focus on overall results of operations, through metrics like operating income and return on capital—rather than their equity-based counterparts, EPS, net income, and return on equity.* Do you feel it is hard to disconnect folks from EPS, given what a big deal it seems to be for shareholders and the board? Put in plans that encourage the best possible operating results for the enterprise over the long haul—that encourage the greatest return to all holders of enterprise capital—and these plans will encourage the highest quantity and quality of EPS performance over time.

- *Shift the incentive structure from an exclusively annual one to one with a longer horizon.* This increases line of sight for most people. It also increases the role of core performance from operations vis-à-vis shorter-term distortions including changes in capital structure

- *When necessary, immunize plans formally from capital structure changes.* A financial services company did this in a phantom stock plan, restating net income each year based on a normalized equity capital-to-assets ratio. Some corporate bonus plans compute EPS before effects of repurchases.

There are other approaches. ROE and EPS can be combined in a matrix format like the one presented earlier in terms of operating income and ROIC.

Metrics in this category can also be combined into systems of drivers, down-weighting the effect of capital structure on the metric's outcome.

CASH FLOW METRICS

Next, we address a range of cash flow metrics: Earnings before interest, taxes, depreciation, and amortization (EBITDA), operating cash flow, cash flow per share, CFROGI, and free cash flow. These metrics are often used in industries in which heavy depreciation charges and debt costs make reported earnings low, negative, or in any event difficult to benchmark. They are common in the broadcasting and real estate industries, for example.

High-debt companies, including leveraged buyout (LBO) companies, often use cash flow metrics since they focus closely on the critical matter of cash flow coverage of debt service. Part of the performance play in an LBO is to take a stable business with low reinvestment requirements and commit much of its cash flow to external debt service. Proponents assert that this forces new discipline on management of company costs and capital outlays, improving efficiency and value and funding high returns for holders of the company's sliver of equity. The deals are meant to maximize tax benefits of borrowing. They also may take advantage of imprudent lenders. Cash flow measures sometimes are used to try to synthesize these LBO-like incentives within other types of companies. Companies also implement measurement systems based upon cash flow because they consider them to be better indicators of the ongoing earning power of an enterprise.

Here are definitions of the major cash-flow-based metrics (excluding the value-based ones like CFROI and CVA that are covered in the next chapter):

- *EBITDA* is earnings before interest, taxes, depreciation, and amortization. The "A" is vestigial: U.S. accounting rules no longer require companies to take regular periodic amortization charges for the goodwill they acquire, so this measure might more properly be called EBITD. It is EBIT plus depreciation, or pretax operating cash flow. This metric is used very often as a valuation yardstick, since it focuses more clearly on persistent earning capacity, in comparison to the more heavily accrual-based metrics found farther down in the income statement. Some phantom stock plans use EBITDA for valuation purposes, a practice we evaluate with some skepticism shortly.

- *Operating cash flow* is equal to operating income (usually after tax) plus depreciation. It is the starting point of the *free cash flow* (FCF) computation defined in Chapter 2. FCF is the amount of cash flow that can be distributed from operations after satisfying the company's capital reinvestment requirements. It is computed as operating cash flow minus net capital expenditures and additions to net working capital and to other assets. (More briefly, it is operating income after taxes minus the overall change in capital.)

- *Cash flow per share* is EPS plus depreciation per share. There is another metric called "cash EPS," but that is a bit different. It is EPS plus per-share effects of amortization charges like goodwill amortization (now discontinued) or option expense, depending on the presenting analytical issue.

- *Cash flow return on gross investment* (CFROGI, pronounced *see froggy*) is a cash version of ROIC, computed as operating cash flow divided by gross capital (the customary definition of capital or net assets, plus accumulated depreciation). Since the income metric used in the plan—operating cash flow—is gross of depreciation, the capital construct should be as well.

To apply a valuation perspective to cash flow metrics, we need to learn about something called *recapture*. Mark Twain once said, "I'm not so much concerned about the return on my money as the return of my money." To create value for owners, a company must generate enough cash flow not only to provide a return *on* capital, but also to provide a return *of* capital that is used up as assets wear out and need replacement over time.

A company might hold land parcels for investment, for example, leasing them out for use as parking lots while waiting to sell them for development. This company does not need cash flows to fund the replacement of these assets. Land does not wear out and require replacement in the way that buildings and equipment do. Investors in this company have certain expectations for return, but they expect to receive these returns mainly in the form of gains in value on company investments.

The developer who buys the land and puts a hotel on it, however, needs cash flow from operations sufficient to replace depreciating assets as they wear out—things like furniture and fixtures and HVAC systems. If instead of hotels the company has shorter-lived assets—if it operates a fleet of taxicabs or runs a chain of photocopy shops, then it needs to devote even greater cash flows to asset replacement before it can be said to earn any return on investment for owners.

The fact is that all cash flow is not created equal. The measures considered until this section deal with the issue in a simple way; they are all stated net of depreciation charges. The common cash flow measures, in contrast, are all stated after the "add back" of these charges.

In the context of an incentive plan, the recapture issue may cause companies to waste capital or overpay incentives. EBITDA, for example, can be a very useful yardstick for expressing value. However, it can have adverse consequences when used within an incentive plan. In an example of a phantom stock plan of a general type described in Chapter 9, a company is valued at seven times EBITDA. The plan subtracts new investments from the FCF element of a "total return" computation (value gains plus FCF). Or it may characterize the inflows as debt and subtract "net debt" at each valuation date (or present them as purchases of new shares). An example is shown in Exhibit 6.8.

Such a plan imposes a break-even EBITDA-yield requirement of 14.3 percent on new investments. That is 1/7, or one divided by the valuation multiple. The $25 investment reduces FCF by $25. The EBITDA gain from the investment is $3.57, or a 14.3 percent yield. When capitalized at a 7.0 multiple, the EBITDA gain creates a $25 gain in enterprise value, so the net effect on TBR is zero.

The problem with the 14.3 percent yield requirement is that it is economically inadequate for many investments, particularly those involving depreciating assets that need to be replaced over time. In the example, the asset has a ten-year life and depreciation (or recapture) charges are 10 percent per year. This reduces pretax return on invested capital to 4.3 percent, falling farther to 2.7 percent after taxes. If WACC were 8.5 percent, then economic profit would be 5.8 percent to the negative. The rightmost columns in the exhibit show the extent to which the valuation multiple would need to be reduced—to 4.25 for the investment and 6.8 for the company—in order to restore a proper break-even outcome.

EXHIBIT 6.8   EBITDA-BASED VALUATION EXAMPLE

	Base	Before	Investment	After	Investment	After
EBITDA	90.0	100.0	3.57	103.6	5.88	105.9
Multiple	7.0	7.0	7.0	7.0	**4.25**	**6.8**
Enterprise Value	630.0	700.0	25.0	725.0	25.0	725.0
Value Gain		70.0	25.0	95.0	25.0	0.0
FCF		30.0	−25.0	5.0	−25.0	5.0
TBR-Based on EBITDA Multiple		100.0	0.0	100.0	0.0	100.0
Gain in TBR				0%		0%
EBITDA/Outlay				14.3%		23.5%
Depreciation @ 10-Year Life (Inv. Recapture)				10.0%		10.0%
EBIT				4.3%		13.5%
Taxes @ 36%				1.6%		5.0%
ROIC				2.7%		8.5%
WACC				8.5%		8.5%
Economic Profit Indication				−5.8%		0.0%

Simplified example ignoring tax benefit of depreciation, FCF-based gains in TBR, other factors

In this example of an EBITDA-driven approach, many value-destroying scenarios would pay out for a time. The other shoe would drop eventually, at asset
replacement time. The company will have to pay another $25 to replace the asset
once it is fully depreciated, or give up the earnings stream—either way substantially revising the performance picture. But by then, incentive payouts may have
been distorted materially for years. The EBITDA model would bias outlays
toward short-life assets, encourage sale of long-life assets and discourage leasing
generally.

This suite of cash-based measures poses some other issues as well, but they are
not new ones. Cash-based income metrics do not provide for a complete overall
return on the capital used in the business, just as operating income and net income do not. The return-based metric, CFROGI, poses the same set of issues
cited for ROIC.

There are solutions to issues associated with the metrics based on cash flow:

- *Apply them only in cases where asset composition and life are largely fixed, as in
  real estate or cable television.* In this case, criteria for return simply need to be
  set at levels high enough to reward only those investments that create
  value.

- *Accompany the measures with some accountability for gross capital usage.* Over
  time, gross capital requirements will reflect the recapture criterion. The
  award schedule used in an independent power producer's phantom stock
  plan, for example, balanced operating cash flow against gross capital invested in the enterprise. As an alternative, cash flow and CFROGI can be
  combined in a matrix format in much the same way as ROIC and operating income were earlier in this chapter.

- *Use an EBIT-based multiple rather than an EBITDA-based one when estimating
  valuation effects of performance.* This is a simpler approach because, as noted,
  the EBITDA multiple would have to vary based on asset life and mix in
  order to indicate proper linkages from value to rewards.

In other examples in Chapter 7, the CVA and RVA metrics each involve capital charges that include both return and recapture elements. The CFROI metric
addresses the problem through an "internal rate of return" computation.

INDEXATION AND IMMUNITY

In many situations, it makes sense to try to insulate incentive pay from big "uncontrollable" or "unearned" influences like input prices, interest rates, and so
on. Otherwise, incentive payouts will have a lot more to do with exogenous
factors than with management performance.

Before considering complex remedies to this situation, though, companies should consider an ordinary one. Basing pay more heavily on actual financial results partially immunizes senior management from the largest source of pay variation they face now, which is the large movements in stock price—unrelated to actual business results—that drive much of the gain on stock-based incentives from one year to the next. Goal-based pay is a pretty strong form of immunity, but it is proper for senior management whose strongest impacts are on business results.

Many companies want to take their plan designs farther down this road, however, putting in place an extensive apparatus of immunization or indexing. They might use performance plans based on the indexed metric "relative total shareholder return," for example, or immunize results from uncontrollable matters (e. g., fuel costs, interest rates, exchange rates, housing starts, commodity prices). This can be done by:

- *Upweighting the more controllable aspects of business performance.* Consider a simple profit equation:

$$\text{Profit} = \text{Price} \times \text{Volume} - \text{Cost}$$

  If cost were, in this case, the big uncontrollable driver, then it would make sense to try to construct metrics placing a higher weight on the more controllable ones—price and volume—to use alongside profit as incentive goals. Revenue, volume, and price-driven metrics would be examples. If price were the swing factor, metrics might include cost/unit of volume or again, volume.

- *Formally immunizing results from exogenous effects.* Selling price variances could have wild effects on profit, as they did for a client in the oriented-strand-board (OSB) business. They ran profit and loss calculations based on actual selling prices and again based the selling prices that had been projected at the outset of the year. The average of these results provided a partially immunized basis for measuring performance. A simplified example appears in Exhibit 6.9.

Many businesses have a lot of exposure to outside factors, to be sure. However, the basic structure of goal-based incentives can be made to deal with them. Paying based on medium- to long-term financial results—through more enduring and adaptable target-setting approaches in annual incentive plans, for example, and through greater emphasis on the goal-based part of long-term incentive pay—increases the signal-to-noise ratio within the incentive structure.

The general target- and range-setting and measurement dynamics of a longer-term incentive structure provide plenty of opportunity to deal with garden-variety uncertainty and volatility. Companies can use wider ranges when they

| EXHIBIT 6.9 | SIMPLIFIED IMMUNIZATION EXAMPLE | | |

	Plan	Scenario Actual	Scenario Adjusted	Avg. of Actual, Adj.
Price	$ 200	$ 400	$ 200	
Times Volume	1,000	1,100	1,100	
Equals: Revenue	200,000	440,000	220,000	
Minus Cost (@50%)	100,000	220,000	110,000	
Equals: Profit	100,000	220,000	110,000	165,000

face high volatility, for example. New-cycle goals can ratchet up or down in response to business conditions. This reorients opportunity each year to an updated set of specific challenges, ensuring more strongly that payouts are earned. Some very strong exogenous factors (e.g., the home construction outlook) are predictable enough that they can be handled through annual target setting.

Value-based target setting and measurement techniques can help companies to see around corners in the outlook, to some extent, and also to be more adaptable (see Chapters 7 and 8). Another client in the OSB sector took this road, studying measurement and targeting techniques and how they can tame the variances and focus in on persistent, core management performance.

Most companies are in charge of their own destinies. They can set some standards for themselves and be accountable to them. There is a lot of ambient correlation among stock prices, suggesting that a rising tide does raise all boats. But, over time, winners and losers emerge. So everyone is not in exactly the same boat.

Even among the few legitimate cases for indexation or immunization, such methods are a mixed bag. For one thing, investors may expect management to take actions to reduce some exogenous risks, through formal hedging, for example, or through tactics like diversification, integration, shifting risks to customers or suppliers, or insuring certain risks more fully.

OVERALL PERSPECTIVES

The metrics debate has a lot of moving parts. Many of the commonly cited *metric* problems in the incentive structure actually stem from its short-term nature. When you shift the term structure of incentive goals from the short term to the medium term, you're addressing a lot of what is wrong with senior management's pay.

Operating income measured over three to five years, for example, is not the same metric for incentive purposes as operating income measured over one year. The longer-term version allows many events to be folded into results, over time, and to be averaged out over the course of several years and performance cycles. Targets for long-run operating income can be set more confidently than with its annual version. External capital market information can be applied more readily, for example, and so can internal hurdle rates for returns on new capital usage.

We have also seen in this chapter that many of the problems with traditional metrics can be addressed without abandoning them as a group. We will see more solutions later. Companies, no doubt, will continue to evaluate dozens of variations on financial metrics as they set up incentive pay plans.

It is possible to address the flurry of issues involved in this area without memorizing all of its moving parts. Value creation is our guide in every case, and it has only three simple parts. None of the incentive metrics discussed in this chapter make full use of those moving parts. They need to be approached with awareness and care.

Most of the metrics discussed here are familiar and commonly quoted ones. That is a strong advantage, so it often is worthwhile to examine their deficiencies and patch them up in various ways for more productive use. Another choice would be to ditch traditional metrics and use value-based ones, and that is what the next chapter is about.

NOTES

1. This figure also includes the prevalence of team/department results since it is construed here as another form of individual performance when applied to a senior management role.
2. Steven D. Levitt and Stephen J. Dubner, *Freakonomics: A Rogue Economist Explores the Hidden Side of Everything* (New York: William Morrow, 2005).
3. "Coming Up Short on Nonfinancial Measurement," *Harvard Business Review* (November 2003).
4. It is equivalent to a plan using the "beginning capital" version of economic profit in particular.
5. Large business investments such as new plant construction, development, and rollout of new products or acquisitions also would work as examples, but these normally don't generate performance at intended levels within a year.
6. I have used the matrix format and seen it used in a wide range of business contexts for 30 years. It is a perfectly acceptable method for expressing payout opportunity in an incentive context, one particularly suited to setting out pay/performance scenarios.
7. The gross number of new shares issued is netted by items like the exercise price to be paid or the value of bonds to be tendered, transaction tax effects, and the unamortized balance of stock-based incentive grants.

CHAPTER 7

Value-Based Performance Measures

What if you held a war and nobody came? In the 1990s, business journal headlines trumpeted new metrics like economic value added and cash flow return on investment. *CFO* magazine covered the "metric wars" among promoters of these two metrics and a few others, and *Fortune* began to force-rank corporate America based on economic value added. It looked then as if big changes were afoot in the performance measurement arena. Most companies seemed on course to dump the primary methods they used to judge and reward business success and to adopt wholly new ones.

It didn't happen. Companies continue to use traditional metrics such as earnings per share (EPS), return on equity (ROE), and operating income (OI) to deliver cash incentive pay. The best-known value-based metric, *economic value added,* was cited as a bonus plan metric by fewer than 5 percent of the companies polled in our design survey. If a company is not using a value-based metric as a performance measure in its executive pay programs, it is not really using it at all. The metric wars are over, and traditional metrics won.

It did not look back then as if value-based metrics by themselves were going to take over the world. Rather, the interest in these metrics derived from a bigger trend that has been in place for decades. That story concerns the ascendancy of basic, powerful principles of corporate finance. It is about their advantageous use in more and more areas within businesses and in their markets for commerce and capital. I learned about this kind of thing while a graduate student in the business school at University of Chicago and over nearly 30 years as a financial advisor to industry. I have been thrilled to see the string of Nobel prizes awarded to the leading lights in financial economics. That story is still going strong. The value-based management (VBM) movement of the 1990s was a chapter in this bigger, ongoing story.

Facing option expensing and environment of new, higher standards, companies have been taking the huge pile of resources they use for senior management incentive pay and putting it into some very different buckets, ones with more explicit goals, more focus on long-term results, and more business-unit stakes. This has intensified the focus on metrics and goal setting. It has also compounded the ills caused by inadequate metrics and payout calibration and greatly raised the stakes on getting them right. Here are the key objectives for metrics and payout calibration, ones fitting the the new standards for incentive pay:

- Focus on long-run performance of operations rather than short-run performance results distorted by traditional metrics.

- Apply market-vetted goals rather than setting performance standards based purely on internally negotiated budgets and plans.

- Eliminate the more common sources of bias without adjusting incentive plans to the point of incomprehensibility.

- Pay close attention to the overall use of capital by the enterprise. It is a decisive matter in determining whether business decisions create value and is one addressed poorly in many plans.

- Balance risk effects, and take them consistently into account. Risk and cost of capital effects are often present in incentive plans, but usually they are unclear, off mark, and very inconsistent.

- Emphasize that management has a tangible ownership stake in every dollar of enterprise income and investor capital—rather than the distant and weak accountabilities often present in a company's incentive structure.

- Provide a proper, fiscally prudent basis for delivering rewards—whether it is at the corporate, group, division, profit center, or venture level.

To do it right, companies have to take another look at how they approach measurement. Metric efficacy and connections with value creation have always been near the center of the debate. This chapter reviews that subset of metrics that link explicitly with value creation—value-based financial metrics.

The standards set out in this book do not require the use of any specific metric, traditional or value-based. Nor do they endorse any one-size-fits-all target-setting algorithms or incentive plan formats. Proper standards do require reasonably complete fiscal control over the use of incentives in the business. They do require that incentive plans adhere to consistent financial criteria and be administered with integrity. Where the choice of metrics in senior management's pay is concerned, that means taking account of the basic financial drivers of value: income, capital usage, and the cost of capital. Standards like these can be satisfied in a wide range of ways.

VALUE-BASED MEASUREMENT

We know from Chapter 6 that traditional metrics like EPS, operating income, and ROE do not by themselves consistently encourage value creation. Rather, incentive plans based on those metrics often allow many scenarios in which value-destroying decisions are rewarded and vice versa. A value-based measurement approach, in contrast, is defined strictly by the following:

- It can be reconciled with business value. Normally, this means that the present value of a given scenario for company performance, when measured by a value-based metric, can be reconciled directly to results of a discounted cash flow (DCF) valuation of the same scenario. We will do those computations for each of the value-based metrics presented in this chapter.

- When used in an incentive plan, it encourages management to make business decisions that create shareholder value. This can be set out as three conditions:

  1. It encourages management to maximize long-run operating income.

  2. It encourages business investments offering returns in excess of the cost of capital. At the same time, it encourages management to sell off assets if net proceeds are higher than the value the assets would contribute to the enterprise over time.

  3. It encourages management to balance risk and return so as to favor value creation.

We will be reviewing six value-based metrics:

1. Economic profit (EP, a.k.a. economic value added)
2. Total business return (TBR)
3. Shareholder value added (SVA)
4. Cash value added (CVA)
5. Cash flow return on investment (CFROI)
6. Real value added (RVA).

A seventh metric was introduced in Chapter 6 as the basis for an award matrix driven by operating income and return on invested capital (ROIC). This metric, "net value added," is a derivative of EP, so it is not presented among the separate metrics we evaluate over the course of this chapter. However, the matrix technique that was used does add a seventh genuine alternative. Rather than using an explicitly value-based metric, a company can combine traditional measures into systems that consistently align results with value creation. This general technique assembles traditional measures into combinations that sync up with value drivers, and it can be accomplished based on other metrics, such as TBR or SVA. Several incentive plans in Chapters 9 and 10 base award schedules on TBR, for example. In this chapter we will also describe a metric called *return on economic capital,* one based on the risk-based capital concept used in the financial services industry.

Each of the value-based metrics reflects income, capital usage, and the cost of capital in proportion to their effects on valuation. These connections are depicted in Exhibit 7.1.

The exhibit might look a bit like the Rosetta Stone at first glance, but we can decipher it more readily. A few things are apparent on its face. The first four metrics are computed using just the three drivers of the DCF model: income, capital usage (i.e., ΔC, or the change in capital), and the cost of capital. The measures below are based on operating cash flow, so they require that depreciation (d) be added back to income. Consistently, cash flow metrics include capital on a basis gross of depreciation, so we add back accumulated depreciation (AD) in those computations. The only other general factor considered is inflation, and that affects the inflation-adjusted metrics, RVA and CFROI (i denotes the inflation rate, while AI refers to accumulated inflation).

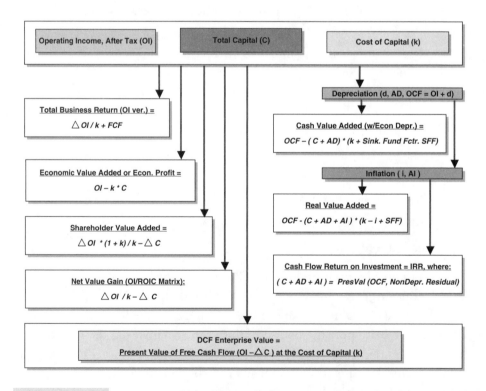

EXHIBIT 7.1   **DCF Valuation Drivers and Value-Based Metrics**

These value-based metrics are all drawn from the same well. The exhibit, dense as it is, does make it clear that if we simply consider the three drivers of DCF, and sometimes set apart the effects of depreciation and inflation, we can construct the full range of value-based metrics. This should help in demystifying this subject matter. We will now examine the definitions and initial computations and see the best uses of each approach.

ECONOMIC PROFIT OR ECONOMIC VALUE ADDED

EP is defined as operating profit after tax, minus a charge for the use of capital. It measures the extent to which operating results exceed basic investor demands for return on their capital. It is a form of the *residual income* or *economic rent* concepts in longstanding use in business and economics.[1]

The basic idea of EP is that a business creates value for owners if it is able to generate returns on invested capital that exceed the opportunity cost of capital. DCF makes the same implication, as do other value-based metrics. EP takes this maxim of value creation and converts it into an operationally focused, periodic measure of performance.

The economic profit example in Exhibit 7.2 shows Year 1 operating income after tax of $150. The capital charge is $120, based on a 10 percent cost of capital and $1,200 in capital. EP is equal to $30, or $150 in income minus the $120 capital charge.

EP in its basic form is a simple, complete metric that can be used productively in annual and long-term incentive plans. It is the simplest way in which income, capital, and its cost can be combined into a single metric. EP should be used when companies want to take a decisive step toward value creation and break away entirely from traditional measures. Economic profit and other residual measures also make sense in other cases. For example, we implemented EP at a gas turbine manufacturer. The company already had ROIC as a measurement and had allocated capital costs as part of predecessor plans, so moving to EP represented little change and added complexity.

Even in their most basic form, residual income metrics do have some communication problems. Measured residual income is low or negative at many companies, rendering "percent change" comparisons meaningless. Residual income metrics also have a format that just does not resemble the most familiar modes of business judgment, troubling not only growth assessments, but other familiar frames of judgment like margin, yield, or turnover. Though simple and accurate, residual income simply does not reconcile easily to the typical suite of quantitative metrics executives are used to applying. For these reasons, award schedules using metrics like income and

Year	0	1	2	3

Forecast of Results of Investment Outlay:

	0	1	2	3
Capital	1,200	800	400	-
Operating Cash Flow		600	630	662
Depreciation		400	400	400
Operating Inc. After Tax 25% Tax Rate		150	173	196
Free Cash Flow		550	573	596

Discounted Cash Flow Valuation:

		1	2	3
Present Value of FCF	10% Cost of Capital	500	473	448
Net Present Value	221			

Economic Profit (Economic Value Added):

		1	2	3
Operating Inc. After Tax		150	173	196
Capital Charge		120	80	40
Economic Profit (EP)		30	93	156
Present Value of EP	10% / 221	27	76	117

Cash Value Added:

		1	2	3
Operating Inc. After Tax		150	173	196
Depreciation		400	400	400
Operating Cash Flow After Tax		550	573	596
Capital Charge (2.49 Capital Charge Factor)		483	483	483
Cash Value Added		67	90	114
Present Value of CVA	10% / 221	61	74	85

Real Value Added:

			1	2	3
Operating Inc. After Tax			150	173	196
Depreciation			400	400	400
Operating Cash Flow After Tax			550	573	596
Inflation Adjusted Cost of Capital	7.84%	2% Expected Inflation			
Capital Charge (2.58 Capital Charge Factor)			474	483	493
Real Value Added			76	89	103
Present Value of RVA	10% / 221		69	74	78

Cash Flow Return on Investment:

		0	1	2	3
Capital		1,200	800	400	-
Accumulated Depreciation			400	800	1,200
Inflation Adjustment			24	48	73
Current Dollar Gross Investment		1,200	1,224	1,248	1,273
Asset Life			3	3	3
Operating Cash Flow	10% / 221		550	573	596
CFROI			18%	19%	20%

EXHIBIT 7.2   **Present Value Equivalency or Discounted Cash Flow (DCF), Economic Profit (EP), Cash Value Added (CVA), and Real Value Added (RVA)**

return, but calibrated in value-based terms, typically provide a better solution than EP.

Capital charges in EP plans are often subject to distortion based on issues affecting the measurement of beginning capital. Another general alternative to the basic formula of EP is to base the capital charge on the change in capital. After all, valuation methods reviewed in Chapter 2 are not affected by beginning capital levels. The only thing affecting forecast free cash flows is the *change* in capital. This overcomes two issues with residual income metrics: capital measurement inconsistencies and low or negative levels of residual income that throw off percentage change comparisons. A large energy company chose to implement a residual income metric but based its capital charge only on the change in capital as a way of avoiding this problem.

Like the other metrics, EP accretes performance at a distinct periodic rate. Basically, dollar one of any income increase is a dollar's gain in EP terms, and dollar one of capital increase reduces EP by a dime, at a 10 percent cost of capital. Whether any particular interval of EP gain pays anything to senior management, and how much, depends on the separate matter of plan design and standard setting. A plan that shares a percentage of any EP with the management group will pay out based on that same dollar year after year. A plan based on EP improvement, or one using some other ratcheting device as part of standard setting, will tend to reward it only once. This is a design choice, not an outcome dictated by the metric itself. A percent-of-EP plan will make a company that has low or negative EP—that is close to 50 percent of the population in any given year—ineligible for much if any reward. A plan based on EP gains often will systematically underreward cash flow generation. These issues should obviously be addressed in some way. It can be done using the standard-setting methods covered in Chapter 8.

USE THE METRIC, LOSE THE REST

Usually, companies using the EP metric should adopt it in its basic form with only a few, obvious contingent adjustments for things like acquisitions and divestitures. Such adjustments apply to just about any value-based metric. They often apply to traditional metrics as well, if not already taken into account when setting targets. This means that the basic metric is not subject to any standing adjustments as part of its routine computation. Rather, it consists entirely of income, capital, and the cost of capital.

There are complex methods for metric adjustment stereotypically linked with EP or economic value added. Promoters of residual income metrics have cited over 100 possible metric adjustments, often advising companies to adopt a great number of these. For example, a large German manufacturer adopted about a dozen such adjustments in connection with its global, EP-based annual incentive plan. That company's culture is very centered on its high-quality engineering. Accustomed to working with very low tolerances, it has a high tolerance for complexity and a high interest in precision. When it comes to pay plans, most companies do not. Such adjustments usually render EP plans incomprehensible to most participants. For most people, the incentive plan simply cannot work in any clear or direct way.

Many of the EP adjustments are unnecessary when the incentive structure rests on valuation precepts. Metric adjustments sometimes involve reversals of basic accruals like the company's bad debt reserve. Most such reversals simply move a bit of income from one year into another. This approach simply takes too much trouble to isolate performance in any one year, perpetuating the troublesome preoccupation with near-term results. A better approach is to lengthen the effective time frame of the company's incentive structure.[2] That creates an incentive stake in longer-run results, rendering small issues such as reserve manipulation pointless. Ironically, EP's typical accrual adjustments do not include the reversal of depreciation expense, though depreciation is the mother of all accruals.

Some companies spread out expenses incurred in areas like research and development and marketing, running them through the profit and loss statement over a period of several years. From a motivational perspective, this is meant to stem any temptation to cut back on discretionary items like advertising or research and development outlays in an attempt to make the numbers at the end of a particular bonus year. As seen in Chapter 2, spreading such costs has no impact on free cash flow or on longer-run earning power. Nonetheless, this is a reasonable adjustment to consider in a bonus plan in cases where R&D commitments are very large. But again, the more complete response is to create a serious stake in longer-run results (we review some normal adjustments toward the end of this chapter). Also, many matters can be reflected in the target-setting process rather than as metric adjustments. For example, expected results of acquisitions can be built into incentive targets in ways that can formalize accountability and, potentially, improve decision making. The metric, unadjusted, is then left in a clearer state.

EP plans often involve their own methods for plan structure and target setting. Examples include bonus banks, multiyear targets set by standard formulas, and award ranges centered on EP improvement. They are meant to overcome many of the EP issues cited so far. However, these features often simply add up to an unworkably complex apparatus. The human resources head of one of the world's largest retailers properly asserted this about the EP plan he inherited, "Hey, I'm a smart guy and I don't understand this thing."

TOTAL BUSINESS RETURN

TBR is the term for any of a range of metrics that track the increase in the value of a business plus the income or free cash flow it generates.[3] This two-part measurement approach is like computing total shareholder return (TSR)—dividends plus capital gains—on a stock investment.

Working with a client team, I developed an income-based version of TBR for use in the company's phantom stock plans. In constructing it, we drew on the format of other TBR metrics, my experience with measurement and valuation principles like those in the DCF model, underpinnings of the EP metric, and the "capitalized" format of the SVA metric.

Value, in this version of TBR, is based on the perpetuity valuation methods and assumptions mentioned in Chapter 2. In the example in Exhibit 7.3, this company's income is $600 at the outset so its value is $6,000, or $600 divided by the 10 percent cost of capital. In Year 1, income rises by $150, so the value gain is $1,500. Free cash flow (FCF) is negative at –$450, resulting in total business return of $1,050.

This version of TBR, when used to measure multiperiod results, simply adds up FCFs for a period of time like three years, irrespective of their timing. The DCF model, in contrast, is highly concerned with the timing of FCFs, with positive ones that occur earlier being worth more, and so on. A version of TBR that is more precise in this regard is shown on the next line of Exhibit 7.3 and that is the one that is reconciled to the DCF model. The imprecision of the simpler TBR formula tends to be offset within the usual workings of the incentive plan. For example, the payout structure piggybacks on executives' personal costs of capital. Also, high nominal costs of capital like 10 percent often are offset by phase-ins of large capital outlays into TBR results. Most often, the simpler version of TBR works better. Simplicity is a powerful advantage, when communicating incentive terms.

A dollar of forecast-term income or capital reduction has a similar effect on FCF and so on TBR. Increases in income over the forecast term have a multiple impact based on the cost of capital. The multiple is 10 when the cost is 10 percent, for example. A basic TBR phantom stock grant on 1 percent of a company entitles holders to 1 percent of income over the forecast term, charges them 1 percent of any capital increases, and gives them 10 percent of any increases in income. So income increases are worth 10 times as much to the holder.

The TBR phantom stock plan isolates value creation by trading off investments, which reduce FCF, against income gains, which have a multiple impact on value. The trade-off between these two factors means that new investments generally need to generate returns in excess of the cost of capital in order to increase incentive pay. That is where TBR takes the interplay among income, capital usage, and the cost of capital and brings it home within an incentive plan.

A TBR computation is more complex than most metrics. It requires thinking about capitalized earnings. But it does not necessarily drag you through the precise, perpetuity-valuation calculation of capitalized earnings. Rather, TBR's

Year		0	1	2	3	Residual
Forecast of Business Results:						
Operating Inc. After Tax (OI)		$600	$750	$900	$1,050	$1,050
Capital		5,000	6,200	6,500	6,800	
Free Cash Flow			($450)	$600	$750	$10,500
Discounted Cash Flow Valuation:						
Present Value (PV) of FCFs	10% Cost of Capital		($409)	$496	$563	$7,889
Enterprise Value	$8,539					
Shareholder Value Added (SVA):						
Operating Inc. After Tax (OI)		$600	$750	$900	$1,050	
Capitalized Change In Income			1,650	1,650	1,650	
Change in Capital			1,200	300	300	
Shareholder Value Added			450	1,350	1,350	$3,150
Present Value of SVA	10%		$409	$1,116	$1,014	
Value of Initial OI Level		$6,000				
Enterprise Value	$8,539					
Total Business Return:						Total
Operating Inc. After Tax		$600	$750	$900	$1,050	
Value Gain			1,500	1,500	1,500	4,500
Free Cash Flow			(450)	600	750	900
TBR, Annual			1,050	2,100	2,250	5,400
Three-Year TBR with FCFs Compounded			($545)	$660	$750	$5,366
Present Value of TBR, Residual		$4,508				$4,031
Enterprise Value	10%	$8,539				
Net Value Added (Capitalized Change in Economic Profit):						
Operating Inc. After Tax		$600	$750	$900	$1,050	
Capitalized Change In Income			1,500	1,500	1,500	
Change in Capital			1,200	300	300	
Net Value Added, Prospective, on New Outlays			300	1,200	1,200	2,700
Present Value	10%		273	992	902	
Present Value of Annual Base OI Level		$6,000	$136	$124	$113	
Enterprise Value	$8,539					
Reconciliation of Metrics:						Total
Change in Economic Profit			$30	$120	$120	$270
Capitalized			10%	10%	10%	
Equals: Net Value Added			300	1,200	1,200	2,700
Plus: Annual Increase in Base Income Level			150	150	150	450
Equals: Shareholder Value Added			450	1,350	1,350	3,150
Plus: Initial Income Level			600	750	900	2,250
Equals Total Business Return, Annual			$1,050	$2,100	$2,250	$5,400

EXHIBIT 7.3   Present Value Equivalency of Discounted Cash Flow (DCF), Shareholder Value Added (SVA), and Total Business Return (TBR)

valuation conventions can be described in the usual price-earnings ratio format. Value is 10 times earnings, in our earlier example, so a dollar of increased earnings means a $10 rise in value.

To understand TBR, you also have to get your head around FCF. Getting management to think about this subject matter in the context of value creation is a good idea. The situation should be seen as an opportunity to use incentive pay to support an important process: financial training for a broad range of decision makers.

FCF is part of TBR, so TBR-based plans normally include FCF within the stream of financial results eligible for reward. This tends to lead to fairer and more competitive outcomes than with other value-based approaches.

The TBR metric itself is used most often within phantom stock plans. In a phantom stock context, business units and private companies are trying to create well-functioning incentives and compete with stock-and-option-dominated executive pay in the marketplace. TBR is helpful here. Its value-gain plus cash-flow format stands up well next to the analogous mechanism of stock-based pay.

Like the other value-based metrics, TBR can be used to set up payout schedules that are stated in terms of traditional metrics like OI and ROIC. The technique applies to bonus plans, performance unit plans, and performance share plans. In performance share plans, it is a very good way to blend the line of sight of a value-based metric, especially at the business unit level, with the benefits of denominating senior management pay in corporate shares. A complete example of that method appears in Chapter 9.

We will see in Chapter 8 that TBR can also be used to set targets for business performance within incentive plans using other measures. Companies can use customized sets of goals for various business units, for example, while conforming them to a uniform TBR scale. TBR is also useful in the performance comparisons that sometimes enter into target setting as well as measurement within indexed plans. The total return format of TBR works some financial magic in these settings and some others because it allows the performance of very different businesses to be benchmarked in a consistent way. Low-growth companies with high FCF, for example, can be measured on a reconcilable scale with units having high income growth and capital needs. This approach remedies quite a number of the issues that throw off comparisons made in terms of other measures. This OI-based variant of TBR has been implemented in various ways in scores of companies.

Another version that is at least as common is one based on earnings before interest, taxes, depreciation, and amortization (EBITDA). EBITDA-based versions, as commonly applied, have deficiencies that mean they do not comport with value-based measurement principles (this was noted initially in Chapter 6 and will be examined further in Chapter 9).

SHAREHOLDER VALUE ADDED

SVA is equal to the valuation effects of improvements in income minus concurrent increases in capital. It is basically the same thing as net value added, or capitalized change in EP, except for its "annuity due" convention, which assumes that increases in income occur at the beginning of each year and are receivable then.[4]

In the SVA format, the $150 increase in income is worth $1,650, equal to the $1,500 present value of the income stream used in the TBR computation ($150 in Year 1 and every year thereafter) plus the current-year income of $150, receivable now and therefore not discounted. The change in capital is $1,200. SVA is equal to the value of the income, $1,650, minus the concurrent $1,200 increase in capital, or $450.

SVA seems a perfectly valid construct for use mainly in long-term incentive plans. EP is better for annual plans. SVA would function well as a valuation formula in phantom stock plan as well (I prefer TBR in most phantom stock design situations because of the host of favorable dynamics described here and in Chapters 8 and 9). Like other value-based metrics, SVA can be used as a calibration device for incentive plans stated in terms of other measures like OI and ROIC. My experience has been that SVA is not seen often in incentive applications.

CASH VALUE ADDED

CVA, in general form, is a cash version of EP. In CVA, the income construct is operating cash flow rather than income. Capital should be stated gross of accumulated depreciation, for consistency.

In most CVA applications, the capital charge simply equals the company's cost of capital multiplied by gross capital. This causes the recapture problem noted in Chapter 6 in the discussion of EBITDA: in particular, the risk of encouraging investments with high cash flows even when they are not sufficient to a reasonable return on investment as well as recapture of its depreciating component. This flaw can bias corporate investment and divestment policies in a range of harmful ways. My solution is to build a *sinking fund factor* into the CVA capital charge so it demands both a return on capital invested in depreciating assets and a return of that capital.

This version of CVA is presented in Exhibit 7.2. In it, the entire $1,200 investment consists of depreciating assets so the return-and-recapture charge applies to its full amount. The capital charge is equal to $483 per year, an amount sufficient to provide a 10 percent per year return on the $1,200 investment and also fund its replacement (assuming zero inflation) at the end of Year 3. Year 1 operating income plus depreciation is $550, so CVA is $67 after subtracting the capital charge.

CVA accretes value differently than EP. Its economic depreciation format has the effect of leveling the capital charge and leveling CVA when income is fixed. The EP capital charge, in contrast, falls each year as the asset depreciates, making EP drift upward until the asset is replaced. CVA is more accurate in this regard, since the performance of the asset does not actually rise in real terms each year (and RVA is more accurate still, when inflation is a material concern). The upward drift of EP is said to cause something of a "harvest" bias, and EP does tend to rise during any of the short intervals when management can patch up fixed assets, keep them running, and put off replacement outlays. That is more perception than reality because EP generally encourages economically optimal replacement policies when management has a long-term interest in it. Actually, all these value-based metrics are said, unfairly, to cause a harvest bias simply because they create new, proper accountability for capital usage. But that is not a bias. It is the removal of one.

CVA is a good metric for annual or long-term incentive plans when the company has a strong focus on cash flow. Two of the power generation companies cited in Chapter 9 adopted cash versions of value-based plans, for example, one using CVA in a bonus plan and the other using a cash version of TBR in its phantom stock plan. A high priority on cash flow in some companies often is related to the fact that net income is very low once high financing and depreciation costs are subtracted.[5]

CVA actually does not encourage cash flow generation any more strongly than other metrics like EP or TBR; if it did, it would cause an anti-investment bias. Rather, CVA's format simply signals the cash flow part of the message, just as TBR signals an economic balance between growth and yield. Again, choices among the major value-based metrics mainly are format and communication choices, rather than choices based on one metric having true analytical superiority over another.

CASH FLOW RETURN ON INVESTMENT

CFROI is unlike the other metrics in that it adjusts for inflation in an explicit way, generating economically more meaningful results in cases where inflation would otherwise distort them.[6] General computational procedures are complex. Their general steps proceed like this:

1. Restate gross capital to a current-dollar, inflation-adjusted basis. CFROI advocates assert that operating cash flow is stated in current dollars, so capital must be in current dollars if the metric is to be used reliably for

many comparisons. The restatement involves digging into the gross fixed asset account, dividing it into "vintages," or the past years in which the constituent assets were placed in service, and restating these outlays in current-dollar terms.

Alternatively, it is possible to estimate the past pattern of asset placement based on asset life and the accumulated depreciation ratio. Past outlays then are adjusted to current value using an inflation factor like the gross domestic product inflator, resulting in current dollar gross investment, or CDGI (CDGI is the current replacement cost of the dollars invested in the past in fixed assets and not the replacement cost of the assets themselves). To this, add the current balance sheet figures for other assets (assumed here to be close enough to a current-dollar basis of presentation). In the Year 1 example, the only asset is the $1,200 outlay, and an inflation adjustment would be a mere $24 at a 2 percent inflation rate, so CDGI is $1,224. Many companies have older assets or ones in highly inflationary markets. In such cases, these adjustments are material and can help to judge results on a more consistent basis.

2. Determine the average life of depreciating assets. This typically is approximated by dividing the gross asset balance by the annual depreciation charge. In this case, the asset life is three years.

3. Assemble an "internal rate of return" calculation, using CDGI as a current investment amount, current after-tax operating cash flow as the level annual income amount, asset life as the number of years, and the nondepreciating portion of the balance sheet as the residual value. The resulting internal rate of return (IRR)—that is, the discount rate that equates present value with CDGI—is CFROI. In this case, it works out to be 18 percent.

This is a cash flow-based measure, so we need to ensure that we are handling recapture of investments in wasting assets. CFROI handles this implicitly within the IRR computation, assuring that asset depreciation is funded out of cash flow before any genuine return accrues.

CFROI is not a simple metric at a conceptual or computational level. Also, it does not stand alone as a value-based measure and needs a sibling metric, just as ROIC does, to get outcomes that comport with valuation principles. CFROI-based goals can be combined with cash flow within incentive plans in the same way that ROIC and OI were in Chapter 6. It was counterbalanced with CDGI growth, in one wood products company. Overall, though, CFROI is too complex as a practical matter for use in most incentive plans.

If inflation and cash flow issues are serious ones, I would suggest remedying them through the target-setting process or within plans driven by other metrics (e.g., through differing inflationary expectations impounded in nominal costs of capital in one country versus another). If an inflation-adjusted VBM standard truly is useful, I recommend RVA over CFROI.

REAL VALUE ADDED

I developed RVA based on inflation-adjusted valuation work I had done with multinationals in the 1980s. In the context of incentive metrics, I wanted to get at the inflation adjustment and cash flow basis of the metric CFROI without having to deal with its complexity in quite so overt a way. Real value added is equal to operating cash flow minus an inflation-adjusted charge for the use of capital. All of the complicated bits of CFROI are handled within the RVA capital charge, simply called *rent*. Like the capital charge factor used in the CVA computation, it accounts both for return on capital and recapture of depreciating assets. It also addresses inflation. The rent computation of RVA works just like the CVA capital charge, except that the rate of return used to determine it is adjusted for inflation, as in this example:

$$\text{Real cost of capital} = (1 + 10 \text{ percent cost of capital})/$$
$$(1 + 2 \text{ percent inflation rate}) - 1 = 7.84 \text{ percent}$$

The RVA capital charge is like a rent expense, and rent is a rhetorically efficient term for the computation. Everyone knows what rent is and what causes it to rise or fall, and this helps explain the complexities in computing this inflation-adjusted charge. It actually is useful as well as a more general description of the concept of an opportunity cost for business capital. All of our metrics include a cost of capital concept just as the DCF model does, so it is worth sketching out the ideas behind the RVA rent charge. All else equal:

- Rent is higher (in relation to gross cost) if the property or asset has appreciated in value since acquisition. Rents and property values tend to rise together, irrespective of the historical cost of the property on the books.

- Rent is lower to the extent prospective inflation and related capital gains (rather than rent cash flow) are expected to provide a portion of expected return to owners. An urban land investor might be content with rental income of only 2 percent of value (to a parking lot operator, for example) if the expected net rate of gain on land value is 10 percent. In that situation, expected total return on the asset could be 12 percent, and higher with financial leverage.

- Rent is higher to the extent wear and tear is expected to occur. A piece of equipment wears out but land does not. Investors need to get enough cash flow from that asset to replace it at the end of its life, not just to get a current cash return on the cost of its investment. Rents are higher not only for depreciable assets over nondepreciable ones, but also for depreciable assets with shorter lives.

What we should expect is that rent, at equilibrium, equals the level required to provide a total return to investors (cash flow plus capital gain) equal to the cost of capital. If a business is earning more money than the economic rent on its assets, then it is economically profitable.

The trick of RVA is to address inflation, and the idea of an inflation-adjusted return on gross investment, entirely within the intuitive framework of a rent expense. Results are stated in the residual income format of EP rather than the percentage-return format of CFROI, so the metric has more valid stand-alone use as an analytical device. However, it makes sense only in cases in which inflation is a serious issue (e.g., a multinational wanting to state local currency performance on a consistent basis) and cases in which inflation is not seen as covered adequately by the nominal cost of capital or by target-setting procedures.

The rent analogies are useful in covering the general idea of a capital charge, but inflation has not been a prominent part of the discussion of value-based metrics in recent years. Many central banks around the world got the message from Milton Friedman that inflation is always and everywhere a monetary phenomenon. There has not been much inflation so it does not have the distorting effect it once did. That could change in coming years. U.S. monetary policy was hugely reflationary in response to the financial crisis in 2008. Central bankers are meant to stand by and "take away the punch bowl" at the proper time. If they do not, inflation may become a measurement issue once again.

Summarizing metrics and their main uses:

- EP is useful in performance-based plans for companies intending to make a substantial commitment to VBM precepts and break away from traditional measures. CVA is more complex, but useful in cases placing a premium on its cash flow format.
- TBR is effective for many phantom stock plans. It offers a stock option format with value-based functionality and can be used in important target-setting contexts.
- All the metrics can be used to calibrate award schedules for other types of plans. The most broadly applicable approaches are those based on income and ROIC, calibrated using TBR.
- The CFROI framework is useful in analytical and planning applications, but the metric's complexity and return-only format make it hard to use

in a pay context. CFROI's analytical benefits can be gained using other constructs in target setting, nominal cost of capital determination or, in the unusual case in which an inflation adjusted metric should be used in an incentive plan, through the metric RVA.

COMMON VALUES

We have talked about a range of value-based metrics. Now, to prove they warrant their *value-based title,* we will reconcile them to the DCF model:

- Exhibit 7.2 shows how EP, CVA, RVA, and CFROI indicate that the net present value of a given business decision is equal to that indicated by the DCF model. A business decision with a finite life is used for this purpose because these are measurements of periodic performance rather than valuation formulas. CFROI is a return-based metric, not one stated in dollars that can be discounted to present value. A present value is shown for CFROI simply to demonstrate that it is composed of the same original cost and operating cash flow elements as the other metrics.
- TBR and SVA are valuation formulas. They are meant to estimate how current financial performance translates into enterprise valuation and return. In Exhibit 7.3, we reconcile their valuation implications with those made by the DCF model. Results are presented in terms of the "net value added" computation as well, for reference.

The metric TBR captures all forecast-term FCFs as well as any value gain arising from increases in income. The present value of these two items, when combined with the beginning income level and the contribution it makes to the DCF residual value, add up to the same set of cash flows being valued in the DCF model.

SVA, in contrast, does not give credit for all of the forecast-term income and its effects on FCF. Rather, SVA focuses on valuation effects of *increases* in income only. To reconcile SVA value with DCF value, you must add the capitalized value that the beginning income level contributes to DCF value.

The DCF reconciliation is a bit more complex than a cursory scan of the metrics, but it is worth doing. Metric proponents have argued for over two decades that value-based measurement approaches differ greatly among themselves. But the more rigorous process brings us to a different conclusion: in terms of our basic mission—linking results and value—these metrics are all the same. If they really were capturing economically distinct messages, they would have different implications for value. They would have different views on important matters like whether a particular business decision creates value or what a particular company is worth. They do not.

They would also have different views on whether a particular level of performance warrants being paid. But the metrics, by themselves, do not say much about this. Many plans using economic profit pay out top-of-range awards when the metric is negative, for example, so the result of the metric computation itself apparently does not clinch the matter. Whether a particular performance level warrants being paid mainly is a matter of what target was established for company performance. SVA for Year 1 was $450 in our example, while economic profit came in at $30, but either could result in targeted levels of payout if it was used as the target performance level.

TBR would seem to come close to being a prescription for how to pay management. As noted in Chapter 2, it does advance the idea that a comprehensive measure of "return" including FCF is a good way to define the stream of financial results that are eligible for reward. Here again, though, the devil is in the details. Gains on a TBR phantom stock grant are not settled definitively by TBR performance, for example. Choices regarding grant size and structure link various performance levels with participant gains.

You would have similar choices to make when using TBR to calibrate incentive payouts using traditional metrics (as we did using the OI/ROIC matrix in Chapter 9). In Chapter 8, we will do it using target-setting methods, again within incentive plans featuring no VBM yardstick. For now, let us just note that metrics and target setting are separate matters. A financial metric by itself does not have anything conclusive to say about what level of performance merits reward.

METRIC ADJUSTMENTS AND BUSINESS GOVERNANCE

Companies using both traditional and value-based measurement approaches are obliged to adjust actual financial performance from time to time to deal with certain events like acquisitions, divestitures, or large, nonrecurring variations in income. Specifying these matters has always been important. Participants need to know that their incentive will accommodate business events in predictable ways. If executives can't rely on sensible accommodation for good business decisions, shareholders can expect fewer of them. And adjustment procedures need to be set out well enough to comply with applicable tax and accounting rules (e.g., I.R.C. section 162(m)).

Adjustments can be controversial, though, and not all observers take a balanced view of them. One commentator[7] excoriated a company, an apparently successful one, judging by its stock performance, for using an adjusted "cash EPS" metric when triggering annual stock granting. The metric had add-backs for stock-based pay costs, ones that accelerated based on performance. It also added back intangible amortization. Grant design and administration at that company may have been good or bad, to be sure, and payouts may have been inappropriately high or low. But the article did not enable the reader to judge those points decisively. It did proceed to indict the simple presence of an add-back as a corrupt matter by definition—"In any other universe, costs reduce earnings. But in (the company's) happy world, expenses actually increase the bottom line." I wonder if the writer should redirect the outrage toward the thousands of incentive plans that use revenue as a metric, since revenue is profit with *all the expenses added back.*

In pursuit of transparency, executives and board members do sometimes state a desire to base incentives purely on results as reported in the financial statements. Practically speaking, however, most companies must at least stand ready to adjust when needed. The pay watchdog groups reviewed in Chapter 4 had a lot to say about incentive design, but their principles did not require an adjustment-free regimen. One of them made the practical observation that companies are obliged to keep a separate set of books for payout calculation purposes.

The trick is to keep adjustments to a minimum while enabling them to do their job, which is to keep effects of the overall incentive system functioning properly across a wide range of business decisions and events. Companies using value-based metrics such as TBR or EP usually adopt some guidelines for plan adjustments when adopting incentives. For the majority of plans using traditional metrics, we find a rather mixed range of market practices:

- Some companies define the common measures net income, EPS, and ROE from a continuing operations perspective, thereby sidestepping much below-the-line effect.

- One-time or temporary effects on income commonly are spread out over time or simply removed from measured performance.

- Many such events are contemplated during the company's incentive target-setting process (normally based on budget), so actual performance does not necessarily require adjustment. Budgeted income for a particular year might be higher or lower than it otherwise would have been, due, say, to an acquisition made in an earlier year or planned in the current one.

- Events clearly outside of management's control are often removed at least partly from incentive plans, but companies do this most often through the budget process (basically by taking into account business conditions) and through the metrics (generally, by up-weighting more controllable measures of results).

- When adjustments occur, they are often made in reaction to events that not only are seen as out of management's control or otherwise outside the scope of the performance and reward criteria of the incentive plan, but also as surprises.

How to best to deal with special events depends on the metrics and the target-setting methods used. It is also affected considerably by pay strategy, including how the general notion of accountability is applied within such plans. That is probably why treatments vary so much from one plan to the next. The strict form of the adjustments often hinges on compliance with of I.R.C. section 162(m) and, potentially, other accounting and tax provisions. The subject matter here, however, is the economic character of the adjustments rather than trends in technical compliance.

We will sketch out a model treatment for making adjustments within incentives under these assumptions:

- The plan uses a value-based measurement approach and therefore places reasonable weight on income, capital usage, and the cost of capital.

- The matters requiring adjustment were not anticipated during the target-setting process.

- Incentive plans are meant to impose full accountability on management for any events affecting business results, whether the current participant group caused them or not.

When these things are true, it is pretty simple to devise a general set of rules for dealing with most contingencies and still be assured that they do not short circuit the intended incentive effects of the plan. The compulsory adjustment features needed in a value-based incentive plan are the same ones commonly addressed when administering more traditional plans:

- How to deal with large outlays like acquisitions, capital expenditures, and costly initiatives in areas like marketing and research and development

- How to deal with reorganization costs, divestitures, and other material effects seen as nonrecurring

In these cases, the goal is to maintain a continuous stake in business results and full accountability for them, often by spreading out their effects over two to three years. This takes some effort, but it is easier than some of the notable alternatives. One client in early 2009 spent $1 million on legal fees and other outside costs to make a tender for underwater options. Another, in contrast, had a performance share plan that held up through the financial crisis. Payouts came in low and so did share prices, but the plan was not invalidated by a downturn or complex business events. Instead, it folded them into metrics over time in a reasonable way. A consumer products company made a big acquisition that invalidated the parameters of its performance plan. It had not been prepared to accommodate a big deal, common as such things are. It elected to cash out the plan and start over.

Acquisitions are the best place to start when talking about incentive plan adjustments, because methods in these cases cover most of the issues involved. Often, acquisitions are expected to take several years before they pay off at normal levels—before their financial performance reaches a level high enough to warrant having made the acquisition in the first place. The general solution is to spread the deal outlays over time, commonly over a period of two to three years. If the company wishes to have strict adherence to DCF results, it may add an interest charge to these capital deferrals, one usually assessed at the cost of capital. A Spanish food company, for example, elected to treat capital expenditures in this way. It wanted greater precision and was prepared to bear somewhat greater complexity in plan communication and administration.

However, that choice was unusual. Instead, costs typically are phased in without interest, with the understanding that this method imparts a modest pro-investment bias. The pace of the phase-in may be as simple as a straight-line pattern. It may also be set in such a way as to allow gains for executives to accrue at an agreed pace when deal performance is on track with expectations. In those cases, the agreed phase-in could be as specific as this example:

- 10 percent of capital in Year 1
- 35 percent in Year 2
- The balance in Year 3

Some businesses expect to generate losses for a year or two after acquisition, often while pursuing synergies or investing in capabilities of the target. Since these forecast costs are one-time (or temporary) and investment-related, they may be eligible for capitalization and phase-in as well.

Metric adjustments, like metrics and other incentive design choices, are elements of business governance. These terms can be structured strategically, to encourage the best business planning, decision-making and results. Acquisition phase-in procedures provide a good example of how to exploit these potential benefits of incentive policy. Most corporate acquisitions fail, after all. At many companies, a serious look at incentive policy needs to consider terms that act positively on the underlying decision-making dynamics.

Here as in many matters, timing is everything. The best time to set the phase-in schedule for pay purposes is right at the time of the deal. This way, management is obliged to come up with a deal projection and use that same projection for incentive plan purposes. They should not use one optimistic set of projections for deal purposes and diminishing ones later when negotiating incentive goals. But that is a common approach. Deal-year effects often are stricken from the record. Disappointments simply reduce later budgets and business plans. Acquisition failure rates may well stem in part from the fact that goal-based pay accountability tends to dissolve. Indeed, the key matter in such determinations is accountability:

- All outlays should be subtracted from performance over time.
- Management should be held accountable for getting returns on the investment in the deal and for the timetable they set, since these were what the board relied on when approving the deal.

In certain "strategic" acquisitions, companies permanently relieve their incentive goals from all or a portion of the cost of such deals, viewing the possible returns as too distant and uncertain to be included within the normal term of incentives. In "bolt-on" acquisitions, corporate management buys a company and then assigns it to one of its business units, which is expected to run it successfully even though it may not have had much input into deal selection or pricing. This is another case in which goals at times are lightened.

The overall dynamics of decision making at many companies would be improved if they accounted for all capital used, including in these two instances of common exception. For example, if business units are held accountable for bolt-ons, they might resist more strongly when corporate is about to make a bad deal. They might participate more actively in developing an achievable integration plan.

Business unit management possesses much operating expertise. They can be asked to step up in this way. To do so is, here again, a basic tactic in the face of informational asymmetry.

If strategic acquisitions are made with an expectation of longer-run returns, they should be assigned longer phase-in schedules rather than having their costs stricken out of the system. The critical governance dynamic is this: The incentive plan treatment of big deals should be used to *encourage the truest projections to emerge at the time of the deal.* For this to happen, management must know they will be held to account both for the deals costs and for the timeframe promised for earning threshold returns. This encourages the best information to be made available, and the highest quality business decisions to be made, when stakes are highest.

Why would management subject itself to such rigors? They get the upside of any deals that go well. They do not necessarily have to achieve the deal pro forma to see their reward rise in scale. A better general rule is this—measured performance should rise based on any "excess" returns. Take a company whose performance expectations do not include any forecast gains from large acquisitions. If they do one, and they get returns in excess of the cost of capital, those returns should increase their performance and pay over time in scale with economic results.

That is a tougher goal than just getting paid for any old deal, to be sure. But it certainly does not fail to encourage good investing activity. It is easier than hitting an inflated pro forma, for example. Remember, this approach does not necessarily use the deal forecast to set payouts. Instead, it is driven by the amount of the outlay, the cost of capital, and timing. Let's take a $300 million acquisition that needs to generate ROIC of ten percent in order to cross a threshold for value creation. The incentive plan may phase in the outlay at $100 million per year, applying an effective income threshold of $10 million in year 1, $20 million in year 2, and $30 million in year 3. Income over that threshold will increase performance and pay. If the company's investors fairly expect 15 percent ROIC performance on large new deals, they would apply higher thresholds. The fact that the deal pro forma may involve returns of 20 percent is not at issue. Such above-standard performance would expand payouts in this case as well.

As additional encouragement, consider that phasing in the deal without interest has the effect of bringing the cost of capital down by a point or two (often from a simple, rounded level like 10 percent down to a more economically accurate 8 to 9 percent).

The traditional approach to incentives and acquisitions involves incomplete metrics on the one hand and dissolving accountability on the other. Acquisition time is when the stakes are highest and governance and incentives matters most. At this key time, the traditional approach is a failure. These matters need to be set out and calibrated properly, and not only for performance effects but also for the separate matter of compliance with relevant tax and accounting rules.

METRIC ADJUSTMENTS: COMPULSORIES ONLY

Major capital expenditures such as new plant construction often are phased in like acquisitions. However, their timetables for returns are often shorter since premium acquisition prices are not involved. Simply excluding construction in progress from the capital computation is one method—outlays do not enter into capital until the new asset is placed in service. We have applied a one-year "suspense" approach in a couple of retail chains, deferring recognition of new-store outlays until after an absorption period.

Many incentive plans discourage divestitures because their metrics are heavily weighted toward income. Others encourage divestitures of those units that can be sold at a book gain since the gains can be taken into income for incentive

purposes. Value-focused incentive plans work differently. Their general workings, as well as their divestiture adjustments, help explain how these transactions
should be treated for purposes of executive reward. These plans convey a claim
on longer-term value creation, so they create the same economic trade-offs facing owners, encouraging a business sale when its economic benefits exceed
those the asset would have generated over time if retained.

In such plans, divestitures get the opposite treatment of acquisitions. The
gain or loss on sale in these cases is removed from income and treated in the
capital or free cash flow computation. Take a company with beginning capital of $400. If a unit with a book value of $40 is sold for proceeds of $100,
assets rise by $60 ($100 in new cash net of a $40 reduction in business assets).
This difference is a book gain that shows up in equity as well (ignoring
taxes), so capital ends up at $460. Next, we assume the $100 in proceeds are
used to pay dividends, repurchase shares or to pay down debt, so capital falls
to $360. Or we assume the money is characterized as "nonoperating cash"
for purposes of the plan and therefore is not included in capital. (If proceeds
are redeployed into other operating assets, they will not reduce capital, but
that is a separate matter.) In this example, $40, net, goes out of the company
for capital measurement purposes, and capital falls to $360. The drop in capi-
tal adds $40 to free cash flow. The gain adds $60 to income, so the total free
cash flow impact simply equals the sale proceeds at $100. Deal proceeds
increase free cash flow within the incentive plan.

Income lost as a result of the sale reduces the plan's income construct. A drop
in prospective earning power has multiple effects on valuation. If proceeds of
$100 exceed the unit's valuation, it is a sale candidate, and vice versa. In a long-
term incentive plan, this dynamic usually works well enough by itself. Participants are encouraged to weigh the near-term effects of sale proceeds against the
value the business unit would have contributed over time, just as shareholders
would wish. In situations in which short-term sale bias is seen as a risk, divestiture proceeds may be phased in.

Since major initiatives in areas like marketing or product development are
often like capital expenditures, made in pursuit of long-run returns, these can
be spread out and charged against income over time rather than all at once.
They also may be removed from the income computation and charged against
capital or FCF, so long as they represent major, one-time, separable outlays and
not just a ramp-up in ongoing expense levels. Removal is rather lenient. Spreading out such costs and charging them into income normally is a sufficient solution. In one case, a supermarket company did not permit payouts from profit
gains if they came from cuts on advertising and promotional spending. That is a
sensible message, but a bit difficult to calibrate across the full range of results that
might occur.

Research and development expenses are the clearest candidates for regular adjustment, pivotal as they are to long-term business results in many industries. But they do not always have to be adjusted. The company's internal governance of such activities may mean they end up having perfectly appropriate incentive effects. When adjusting, though, taking these costs out of the income statement and phasing them in over two or three years is the simplest approach. This mutes any gains to be had by cutting back on research and development in an attempt to hype short-term earnings.

There is a potentially better approach, however, and it applies in many such cases. It is one addressing the incentive structure more generally. This approach involves lengthening the effective time frame of the incentive structure. It renders pointless many short-term tactics. *If executives hold a sustained interest in capitalized business results, the company need not regularly capitalize short-term influences on those results.*

Speaking of capitalization, noncapitalized leases are a common, material adjustment to business results in the EP framework. Companies can rent facilities or equipment. This reduces income statement impacts relative to longer-term leasing or cash purchase, in amounts that can be very large in companies with big facility investments like retailers.[8] In cases like these, the question is: Should the company police this particular category of decision making, made by a small part of the management cadre, using an adjustment that makes metrics cloudy for all participants? Rent expense is a pretty good indication of the cost of asset usage anyway, particularly over time.

In most cases, the possibility of distortion in this area is best handled episodically, if it becomes a problem, under the normal administration powers of an incentive plan. In this example and others, what is most important is that management understands the ground rules. Asset rental is not left open to manipulation in that case. Nor are other forms of off-balance-sheet financing and a myriad of other potential distortions. Adjusting for everything all the time is not effective as a deterrent.

Restructuring charges are major income hits incurred with the expectancy of benefits over several years. In these instances, the arguments for one-time treatment as FCF have validity. However, some companies do "restructurings" every year or two. In those cases, the charges may have at least a partly recurring nature. If so, they ought not to be seen as one-time events. Spreading them out over a couple of years makes sense in many cases.

Major, temporary volatility in income is another possible object of adjustment. Some long-term incentive plans use current income levels as a basis for attaching a rough valuation to the company, a valuation that can be described as the enterprise value evidenced by current operating results. That is explicitly the case when plans use capitalized metrics like TBR or SVA. It is implicitly true in some other plans like ones in which operating income and ROIC goals are set up based on how they affect enterprise value and returns. Finally, continuous earning capacity is an implicit assumption underlying most incentive pay for senior management. If a plan at a typical company pays out targeted awards at $10 in income, or its equivalent in EPS or ROE, this normally is premised on the idea that $10 is at least a sustainable earnings level and, more often, a level on which future years can improve. Without that promise, many goal-based incentive plans would pose intolerable costs in relation to economic earning power.

If the income level being used to value the company is not expected to persist, then it should be adjusted to a more representative level. Think of it this way: the stock market does not regard obviously one-time, temporary fluctuations in income as something causing multiple changes in valuation. Incentive plans should not, either. Companies need to review income levels each year to see whether they are obviously unrepresentative of the future, being affected by clear, material one-time effects. If so, they may warrant adjustment in the current cycle or future ones. The general treatment would be to include such events in the capital (or free cash flow) element of measured results and not in the periodic income part. This kind of adjustment usually is not needed in a TBR-based long-term incentive plan unless there is a purely nonrecurring fluctuation in income of at least 20 percent. Otherwise, the basic plan mechanism (overlapping grants, "ratcheting" targets, subtraction of incentive plan cost accruals to arrive at income) smoothes out such effects reasonably well over time.

RISK-BASED CAPITAL REQUIREMENTS AND RETURN ON ECONOMIC CAPITAL

We began to address these approaches back in Chapter 5 in our more general discussion of risk. Risk is a subject affecting the design of incentives and how they work in a wide range of ways. Methods for risk-based performance measurement merit a look from companies in many industries, since formal tools of risk analysis and management have become more prominent generally. Example process includes the following:

- *Risk-based or economic capital levels generally are equal to the capital needed to offset practically all losses (e.g., up to the 99.9th percentile) arising from all sources of risk.* These capital requirements sometimes exceed loss reserves and book equity, resulting in a larger level of notional risk-based capital, or "economic capital," by business.

- *Business performance is often measured by a metric like return on economic capital (ROEC).* That is equal to net income (typically restated as if the business actually did have a lot more equity capital) divided by economic capital.

- *Consolidated levels of economic capital are set by adding up the risk of various business units and taking into account portfolio diversification effects when they are combined to produce consolidated results.* ROEC benchmarks generally are equal to a low-risk cost of equity or to ROE norms for heavily capitalized peers.

I do not suggest working up a risk-based capital adjustment apparatus purely for purposes of an incentive plan. Instead, companies should piggyback the design on financial indicators that the company otherwise would be producing and communicating during the normal course of business. I also suggest harmonizing the relevant messages about risk assessment and business decision making so the incentive rollout and risk-based capital management initiative are consistent. At the same time, companies should be on guard not to instill pay-related biases in the important risk management process, just as they should work to ensure that incentive concerns do not bias business planning.

How Not to Choose Among Value-Based Metrics

Proponents of value-based metrics often argue that one metric is better than another if it achieves better correlation with value creation. I recommend that the choice of metrics be based on *ex ante* correlation with value creation at your specific company. That is, it should be based on the approaches that are most likely, in your specific setting, to encourage business decisions that create most value.

VBM proponents often support their metrics based on statistical data: *ex post* correlation of metrics with value creation across broad samples of companies. But that assertion suggests that one of the metrics somehow has achieved a much better tracking of market value than the others. However, we have seen that these metrics are mostly the same, each reflecting value through the same three basic drivers.

Most high-quality studies of these matters accord little statistical explanatory power to value-based metrics beyond the level held by income, capital, and the cost of capital. That means operating income and ROIC will predict value just as well as value-based metrics. The various metric adjustments may work to align measures better, empirically, with value creation. Spreading out research and development costs is a genuine example. But these adjustments could be applied within any metric, so they can hardly be used to attribute greater empirical power to one metric over another.

I have always been a bit skeptical of studies claiming high predictive power for particular metrics. In some such cases, statistics are used in the way that the proverbial drunkard uses a lamppost—for support and not for illumination. Consider the example shown in Exhibit 7.4. The first panel in the figure

The ROIC Fallacy

	Income	Value	Capital	ROIC	Value/ Capital
Company 1	2	20	100	2%	20%
Company 2	4	40	100	4%	40%
Company 3	6	60	100	6%	60%
Company 4	8	80	100	8%	80%
Company 5	10	100	100	10%	100%
Company 6	12	120	100	12%	120%
Company 7	14	140	100	14%	140%
Company 8	16	160	100	16%	160%
Company 9	18	180	100	18%	180%
Company 10	20	200	100	20%	200%

The Economic Profit Fallacy

	Economic Reality			Metric Correlation	
	Income	Value	Capital	EP @ 10%	EP/ Capital
Company 1	2	20	100.0	−8	−8%
Company 2	4	40	100.0	−6	−6%
Company 3	6	60	100.0	−4	−4%
Company 4	8	80	100.0	−2	−2%
Company 5	10	100	100.0	0	0%
Company 6	12	120	100.0	2	2%
Company 7	14	140	100.0	4	4%
Company 8	16	160	100.0	6	6%
Company 9	18	180	100.0	8	8%
Company 10	20	200	100.0	10	10%

EXHIBIT 7.4   **Metric Fallacies**

describes a ten-company universe in which value is based entirely on income. Converting operating income into ROIC or EP, in contrast, actually weakens the connection with market value by introducing a variable—capital, in this example—that has no connection with market value. Nonetheless, ROIC is made to look like an omniscient metric in the second panel; it correlates fully with value simply because capital appears in the denominator of both ROIC metric and the market value/capital ratio being used to validate it. The second example does the same favor for EP.

Each measure has a 100 percent correlation with value. But that does not mean these measures are good predictors. It just means they are piggybacking on the power of income to explain value. Metric correlations are often presented in this format, and distortions are common. This denominator issue gets even bigger when, as often is the case with value-based measures, capital is a heavily adjusted construct. Statistical results sometimes are inflated as well by the presence of statistical outliers within the sample. A grain of salt is prescribed.

SCOPE AND PURPOSE FOR VALUE-BASED METRICS

Proponents have claimed that value-based metrics need to be implemented into every business process within a company, in a metric-centered kind of reengineering. They claim that implementing a metric like EP upgrades a company's financial processes. They insist that financial analysis and reporting needs to be reformatted into a single metric. Some believe the metric needs to be featured in all of the company's incentive plans, irrespective of organizational level. And some regard the use of value-based methods as a business strategy in itself. I do not agree with any of that.

Proper incentive metrics and calibration are not a business strategy, but they should support high-quality strategy formulation and execution. That is an explicit underpinning of the kinds of new standards set out in Chapter 4. In Chapter 6 we saw a company example of how strategy tenets can intertwine with specific incentive terms. Jack Welch made his views known rather clearly on this point. In an online exchange, he called maximizing shareholder value a "dumb idea" when used as a business strategy. "You would never tell your employees, 'Shareholder value is our strategy.' That's not a strategy that helps you know what to do when you come to work every day." Instead he said that value creation flows from sound practices leading to long-term growth.[9]

Some insist that a metric like EP must be used as the single unit of denomination for all analytical and reporting contexts. They note that reporting centers on revenue and EPS, capital outlays are evaluated by metrics like net present value (NPV) and IRR, success for owners is often cited in terms of TSR, and that incentives commonly use a range of metrics for incentive purposes. This Babel of tongues, they sensibly assert, poses significant translation costs and risks on a company.

Similar, reasonable arguments were made by linguists, years ago, ones promoting an invented universal language called Esperanto. Esperanto got some attention for awhile. It had a nice little run. Someone even talked William Shatner into making one movie spoken entirely in Esperanto.

Notice that I said *one* movie. Esperanto never really caught on. And neither did the idea of using EP, or economic value added, for every analytic and communication purpose. We are two decades into this story and corporate practices have not changed.

Value-based methods and incentives can indeed provide instructions on how to create value. They can show how to evaluate long-run effects of strategic plans and projections. My experience is that companies are accomplishing these things while using the metrics in a much more focused role. "Using" value-based metrics boils down to including them in sensible ways within senior management's pay plans and in related training and communication.

They can be used in broader-based incentives and business literacy efforts, but those efforts should focus most often on drivers of operating income. Companies can apply them in other areas—in project evaluation, for example, valuation of an acquisition, assessment of a strategic plan, or performance benchmarking. When applied in these areas, value-based metrics tend to be used as one among many tools.

In most applications, value-based metrics do not really amount to an improvement to financial tools already in use. The metrics are DCF-based, after all, and most companies use DCF or equivalent tools already. For the same reason, value-based metrics do not add much to a securities analyst's toolbox, either. Analysts normally can address matters like long-run income from operations, capital deployment, risk taking, and inflation when important.

When a company implements value-based metrics for pay purposes, it does not have to run out and change all the company's other financial processes. What it is doing, instead, is to conform the pay plans to the DCF procedures already in use. In the end, it is the link to senior management pay plans that decides whether a company really uses a particular value-based metric.

Beyond the realm of senior management incentives, these metrics are used most effectively in broader-based pay plans and in business literacy initiatives. Companies have undertaken many insightful and effective approaches in these matters. Successes can be attributed to the compelling and detailed value drivers often identified in the process, as well as the creativity and impact of the rollout. These are the keys, not the choice of one overarching metric or another. In more broadly based initiatives, the focus of performance improvements often is on income anyway, not capital or its cost, since that is where most employees can contribute. That does not prevent companies from using value-based metrics effectively in broad-based pay and communication efforts. Rather, it simply encourages them to focus most strongly on the income element of whatever metric is used and on those value drivers that participants can influence most strongly.

The place where VBM metrics bring their strongest differential impact, where their rubber really hits the road, is within a senior management incentive plan. At that level in the company, people can influence longer-term income, capital usage and business risk. When incentive designs comport with value-based standards, they are meant to talk to these people as their primary audience. Chapters 8, 9, and 10 continue to expose how to do that, laying out methods for devising incentive targets and ranges and for designing and implementing cash and stock-based incentive plans.

█ NOTES

1. Stern Stewart & Company developed the "economic value added" version of this metric and trademarked it as EVA®.
2. This is done by improving the target-setting and range-setting procedures used in annual incentive plans (Chapter 8) and by creating more compelling long-term incentive plans (Chapters 9 and 10).
3. Eric Olsen of Boston Consulting Group coined the general term TBR.
4. SVA was developed by the consulting firm ALCAR.
5. Keep in mind that, in high-leverage companies, it is necessary to size the incentive plans properly in relation to the small amount of shareholder resources involved. In extreme cases, a poorly designed incentive plan may risk being regarded not as an "incentive" but as a "conveyance."
6. This metric was developed by a consulting firm called HOLT Value Associates and, we understand, by a predecessor firm called Callard Madden.
7. Gretchen Morgenson, "Benchmarks as Flexible as Gumby," *New York Times*, July 26, 2009.
8. The adjustment in such a case is to compute the present value of the lease expenses, include it in capital and amortize these costs into income. Rent policy can distort financial results. My general recommendation is to use unadjusted results unless the issue is material and cannot be addressed properly otherwise. As the discussion of rent in the RVA section of this chapter noted, I regard rental expense as a fairly complete representation of the cost of asset use over time.
9. David Bogoslaw, "Shareholder Value: Time for a Longer View?" *BusinessWeek* (March 17, 2009).

CHAPTER 8

Ownership, Not Gamesmanship: Setting Targets and Ranges for Performance-Based Plans

At this point, we have examined many serious issues in incentive structure and the rules for a new framework have been set. A big step has been taken by filling in that framework with metrics. Specific metrics have been identified, along with techniques to combine them. Lastly, we have used valuation-based rules to evaluate any new metrics that may arise. With the addition of targets and ranges for pay and performance, the key parts of goal-based incentive plans will be in place. This chapter reviews a range of ways to set financial targets and ranges in a senior management incentive context.

Companies typically use budgets or other internal, negotiated standards to set performance targets in their annual incentive plans. Most respondents to our design surveys cited budgets as one source of annual incentive goals. Nearly half noted that management and the board determine goals, with half also citing growth or year-over-year improvement standards as the basis for their targets (many companies cite several benchmarks). Companies have also reported a growing focus on externally based standards and criteria like shareholder expectations, peer group performance, and the cost of capital.

These findings indicate that the majority of plans are still subject to the standing criticism: that management can get paid for managing expectations and not just for managing the business. Performance targets normally reflect an internal negotiation. At some companies they are sandbagged routinely. At many companies, aggressiveness is penalized from an incentive standpoint because aggressive goals simply raise the bar for a given pay opportunity. The process is often seen as unfair. Important resources—capital and management time—may be misspent. These outcomes are the opposite of what the process is meant to accomplish: strong performance standards, high-quality resource allocation, and overall fairness.

One *Harvard Business Review* contributor put it in these provocative terms, "The corporate budgeting process is a joke, and everyone knows it." Another *Harvard Business Review* commentator advocated doing away with the budget process entirely.[1] And some companies have done just that. The Beyond Budgeting Roundtable, an organization of planning and finance executives of leading companies, includes many innovators who are upending the norms of budgeting and incentives.

As we saw in Chapter 4, the Conference Board in late 2009 set out a broad range of potential methods for potential use in incentive standard setting:

> [C]ommittee should consider appropriate information regarding the company's industry and company growth rates, historical targets and actual performance relative to those targets, investor expectations, and key competitors and their performance levels. External expectations regarding the company, such as analyst reports and models and expectations built into the current stock price can also be useful sources for assessing appropriate targets for incentive compensation."[2]

We have been doing analyses of these types for our clients for many years. This chapter reviews and illustrates the methods involved.

BEST OF BOTH WORLDS

We saw in Chapter 2 that investor expectations, not internal budgets, determine whether a particular performance level causes a company's share price to rise or fall. If a company wants to set targets that align senior management's rewards with their contribution to investor return—and it should—it will have to take account of these external standards and expectations.

Does this seem like a novel idea? It is not. The bulk of senior management's incentive pay is already delivered on this basis. Most incentive pay is stock-based, so it reflects the performance assessments that underlie the stock price. Companies have overrelied on stock-based incentives, particularly upon options during their expense-free heyday. But one of the things that stock-based incentives do well is to reflect shareholder expectations.

As we have seen, the market value of a company's shares corresponds to the discounted value of expected future performance. Option and stock grants start out at the current stock price. Getting a gain from that starting point usually means performing well enough against the expectations contained in the strike price. Of course, the specific performance scenario held by the market may change after the grant, and so may other valuation criteria like views on longer-run business prospects and the price of risk. Nonetheless, a policy of equity-based grants is, in gross terms, an incentive framework that is recalibrated periodically based on prevailing shareholder expectations.

The problem, of course, is that these expectations may be a mystery to grant holders, the subsequent movement in share prices may be as well, and most participants do not have much influence over most of the matters involved anyway.

Goal-based pay is a solution when it reflects strong line of sight as well as proper calibration. It does require proper targeting as well, though, and that can carry some risks and concerns. Sandbagging (arguing incentive performance targets down to easily achieved levels) is a problem acknowledged by many. It is surely a serious problem at some companies, but probably not endemic at most. If it were, pay surveys would show bonus payouts consistently above target. The numbers do sometimes exceed target notably, but that tends to occur in years that were really great for corporate profit, when performance did exceed expectations broadly.

When sandbagging is a big part of the system and a big concern for executives, the company has a bigger problem than unfairness. The company's planning processes (including the annual budget) serve as an important governance tool. Companies that plan badly put themselves on track to make decisions badly and to commit their resources badly. The target-setting process probably is made unnecessarily time-consuming and adversarial, too, because of its connections to incentive pay.

Those problems are now playing out on a much larger stage. Setting incentive goals was always a high-stakes matter. The stakes are now enormous since there is so much more goal-based pay. Compensation committees are expressing a strong interest in seeing more data, particularly more outside benchmarks, when they approve goals. And shareholders and their advocates now expect board members to review more closely the economic effects of incentive pay (e.g., goals, risk effects, costs). Proper performance benchmarks can do the following:

- Enable boards to make decisions about incentive target setting that do not rely exclusively on management's representations.

- Introduce outside evidence and directional guidance, supplementing decision-maker insight.

- Help companies avoid misunderstandings and missteps in the high-stakes area of incentive target setting.

TRIFOLD GUIDE TO BENCHMARKS

In practice, companies can apply a range of procedures to help determine the performance levels at which a market-based target award opportunity is earned.

Often, this consists of setting a level having a typical average-to-stretch degree of difficulty. An initial review process can be assembled from three main sources:

1. Comparisons of historical performance against specified peers, in terms of common financial metrics like revenue growth, earnings per share (EPS), and return on invested capital (ROIC), supplemented by concurrent stock market performance metrics like total shareholder return (TSR).

2. Analyst forecasts of future revenue, EPS, and other metrics, often in a multi-year format and accompanied by commentary regarding concerns and prospects for the company and its sector.

3. Market capitalization multiples (e.g., price/earnings ratios, enterprise value/earnings before interest, taxes, depreciation, and amortization [EBITDA] multiples) and risk indicators, each of which provide evidence of the shape of future performance expectations.

This approach is designed to expose some of the more evident directional indicators regarding company performance and prospects. A multifactor process encourages decision makers to consider and reconcile information from several different meaningful sources—a basic procedural tactic when pursuing judgment accuracy.

Results may assist management by providing information useful to the business planning process more generally. These steps can add information sources to the benchmarks used at present, enabling more balance and reconciliation. It can also be an informative first step that may improve resource usage (e.g., helping to solidify matters to investigate during the planning process, streamlining commitments of staff time).

Using the results of a review like this is an exercise in judgment. There is no magic bullet in the area of incentive target setting. Some formulaic algorithms can be useful in standard setting when applied flexibly over time, but none can provide reliably unbiased point estimates. There are, however, techniques and principles that can be applied broadly. Here, we discuss a range of them. Many of the principles at issue concern the connection between financial results, risk, and long-term value creation for investors.

The Past Is Prologue

Past results almost always warrant a close look when setting targets for company financial results. Exhibit 8.1 is an example of a comparison format for a Fortune 50 company and similarly sized peers.

The figures make clear the central ranges of selected metrics over the past five years. The subject company's growth against peers can also be assessed by

EXHIBIT 8.1 EXAMPLE SUMMARY OF HISTORICAL FINANCIAL PERFORMANCE INDICATORS

Historical Financial Performance	2002	2003	2004	2005	2006	2007	Growth Rate (CAGR)			Avg. Growth	
							One Year	3-Year	5-Year	3-Year	5-Year
Revenue	**$487**	**$535**	**$605**	**$732**	**$816**	**$841**	**3%**	**12%**	**12%**	**12%**	**12%**
Peer 25th Percentile	$453	$532	$663	$701	$743	$688	7%	6%	6%	6%	7%
Peer 50th Percentile	$616	$662	$809	$1,129	$1,425	$1,421	11%	12%	10%	13%	10%
Peer 75th Percentile	$1,359	$1,508	$1,654	$1,713	$1,787	$1,965	13%	19%	16%	20%	16%
Percent Rank	28%	25%	22%	26%	28%	29%	17%	46%	64%	46%	64%
EBITDA	**$131**	**$148**	**$179**	**$215**	**$252**	**$261**	**4%**	**13%**	**15%**	**14%**	**15%**
Peer 25th Percentile	$60	$61	$71	$63	$63	$75	4%	8%	9%	8%	10%
Peer 50th Percentile	$84	$95	$115	$150	$194	$199	10%	17%	12%	17%	14%
Peer 75th Percentile	$146	$170	$189	$215	$248	$275	22%	28%	17%	29%	18%
Percent Rank	63%	69%	69%	75%	79%	69%	25%	40%	67%	40%	57%
Net Income	**$76**	**$87**	**$109**	**$126**	**$150**	**$153**	**2%**	**12%**	**15%**	**12%**	**15%**
Peer 25th Percentile	$19	$21	$27	$24	$37	$39	6%	12%	12%	11%	11%
Peer 50th Percentile	$33	$34	$36	$61	$92	$89	13%	29%	28%	21%	31%
Peer 75th Percentile	$52	$55	$88	$110	$130	$152	29%	47%	37%	49%	52%
Percent Rank	93%	91%	90%	87%	90%	76%	15%	21%	28%	30%	31%
Pre-Tax Income	**$112**	**$128**	**$161**	**$189**	**$224**	**$229**	**2%**	**12%**	**15%**	**13%**	**16%**
Peer 25th Percentile	$32	$32	$41	$48	$55	$57	-1%	13%	17%	6%	9%
Peer 50th Percentile	$50	$52	$56	$91	$131	$123	14%	28%	23%	15%	19%
Peer 75th Percentile	$85	$83	$134	$158	$190	$219	30%	56%	31%	43%	37%
Percent Rank	93%	93%	90%	91%	92%	77%	29%	16%	23%	35%	40%

Source: Standard & Poor's Research Insight.

examining whether its percentile ranking rises or falls. Setting out the raw data, rather than just percentages or percentiles, enables subperiod comparisons at a glance. Such analyses can be compiled for a wide range of metrics.

TSR can be examined alongside these data, adding a range of helpful insights:

- If years of high financial performance are accompanied by years of high TSR, those results probably should be interpreted as ones that exceeded relevant performance standards: 15 percent income growth may be the history, but 10 percent income growth may have been the appropriate target rate during that period of time. Saddling the company with a 15 percent growth rate based on past performance may be unfair. To do so could be like issuing stock options with exercise prices well above the current stock price when the agreed policy was to issue them at the money.

- What if company TSR was well above the overall market but only in line with industry peers? In that case, high performance may have been earned in part due to a sector tailwind.

- What if performance was equal to peers but TSR lagged far behind? The market may have been looking for higher performance from the company than from its peers and may have been disappointed when it came in at the middle of the pack.

Another possible interpretation is that the company's own outlook may simply have dropped, for its own reasons, with no part being linked to its past results against peers. Stock prices are forward looking at every measurement date, while historical performance is seen in the rear-view mirror. Long-term comparisons are helpful in this case; if the stock price drop occurred earlier in the period being examined, it's reasonable to infer that the decline stemmed from disappointments that played out in historical results for that time period.

The analytical tactic is to use stock-market-based comparisons as an overlay of economic context when interpreting historical comparisons of financial results. Capitalization multiples can be consulted as well, as assistance to a reading of past standards and performance. If multiples were average but TSR was high, company performance may have been outperforming modest expectations each year. Again in this instance, a risk is that too-high standards would be applied going forward. Low multiples at the end of the period could imply that high performance levels still are not expected to persist. If multiples rose over time, apparently in response to high performance, then those raised expectations may well be the relevant ones going forward.

Note that we are not saying that history will repeat itself—that the average earnings growth rates reported by peers or the company in the past, for example, actually constitute the right standards going forward. But we are saying the past is useful as prologue. The past can often be read for signals about the future. TSR was shown to be of use, just now, in interpreting what norms and expectancies actually were in the past. And what if a set of norms—seen raw or through the lens of TSR—had lasted for 10 or 15 years rather than just a year or two? All else equal, this strengthens the chances of history repeating itself. Organic growth rates in the food sector are a good example of this. They have for decades been comparatively stable and tightly clustered. That is a sector in which a review of past growth rates lends comparative confidence about persistent trends in the future.

ROIC comparisons require some interpretation and context as well. Higher-ROIC companies tend to have been better cumulative performers than others, in terms of taking investor capital and using it well. But rankings can be affected strongly by matters like how much of past growth was fueled by acquisitions, and how many of those deals happened before the game of merger "pooling" expired a few years back. It might also be affected by matters like advertising and promotional spending and research and development—currently expensed outlays that have a kind of product capital investment character.

Norms for pretax versions of ROIC and incremental ROIC are shown in Exhibit 8.2. Incremental ROIC is equal to the change in earnings before interest and tax (EBIT) divided by the change in capital, in this case computed on a three-year basis.

Companies make new capital investments all the time. When they do, they are often aiming for ROIC levels in excess of a *hurdle rate*, typically set at or above their cost of capital. Note that overall ROIC levels, on average or at the margin, have centered in the 17 to 18 percent range. This indicates after-tax ROIC in the 10 to 11 percent range, modestly above the central range of applicable costs of capital, which is roughly 8 to 10 percent. At a 9 percent cost of capital and a 36 percent overall tax rate, a hurdle rate for pretax ROIC would be 14.1 percent (9%/(1−36%)). Only modestly more than half of companies beat this hurdle.[3]

EXHIBIT 8.2   ROIC FOR S&P 500 COMPANIES

Percentile	EBIT/Capital	Three-Year Incremental ROIC
25%	9.6%	4.0%
40%	13.8%	12.5%
50%	17.1%	18.0%
60%	20.9%	24.8%
75%	28.3%	40.1%

EXHIBIT 8.3   ROIC TARGETING SCENARIOS

	Prior Year	New Investment	Forecast
Company One:			
EBIT	1,000	140	1,140
Capital	7,143	1,000	8,143
ROIC	14.0%	14.0%	14.0%
Company Two:			
EBIT	1,000	140	1,140
Capital	3,333	1,000	4,333
ROIC	30.0%	14.0%	26.3%
Company Three:			
EBIT	1,000	140	1,140
Capital	14,286	1,000	15,286
ROIC	7.0%	14.0%	7.5%

In Exhibit 8.3, a cost of capital-based hurdle of 14 percent is used to set ROIC goals for three companies, each forecasting new capital usage of $1,000 and each having true prospects, from existing operations, of zero income growth and zero net capital needs. Company One has ROIC of 14%.

Company Two has high ROIC at 30 percent. It has a goal that falls to 26.3 percent. Company Three has low ROIC at 7.0 percent and a rising goal at 7.5 percent. But the goals are the same, in sense, for all of them—they have the same income gain, the same free cash flow (FCF) and are accountable to the same standard for returns on new investments. Just as the discounted cash flow (DCF) model indicated in Chapter 2, we ignored the irrelevant part of the past.

This ROIC method was an example of *decay* or *mean reversion*, as a forecast assumption. When a company has high results—income growth, ROIC—those results commonly assumed are assumed to revert toward norms due to competitive effects. A typical assumption is that high performance is indeed persistent but fades toward norms over time. That is just what would happen to the high- and low-ROIC companies above if the target-setting example were extended under similar assumptions for years. Their ROIC levels would move toward a long-run trend.

Past performance is often not a very precise guide to the future. That is particularly true in periods like the dicey post-2008-crisis era. Post-crisis, stock prices, and EPS forecasts at many companies suggested past performance did not provide a good estimate of the outlook for the near term. But history can often inform assessments of matters like risk, capital usage, and longer-term growth. Historical variables often do have some persistence, as industries often show stable trends.

From a board perspective, it can be helpful simply to present data on a range of metrics in a compact format. These folks have often experienced the performance histories at issue, so providing a quick recap of the facts can help them level-set their own perspectives on applicable performance norms. When executives and board members disagree about going-forward performance standards, they sometimes hold differing views about the past—what the overall picture was, from the standpoint of a balanced set of metrics, and how it might have compared to relevant standards. In these situations, providing a condensed range of factual comparisons can be useful. And so can the technique of interpreting financial results against stock market performance.

NOT TO INSULT CHIMPANZEES

Analysts commonly publish estimated financial performance for at least the next year or two. Exhibit 8.4 is an example of how such estimates compare for the Fortune 50 company and its large capitalization peers.

The subject company's EPS is expected to fall 1 percent in the current year (F10). The next year's consensus is 8.4 percent growth, and five-year growth is hoped, on average, to be 12.9 percent per year. Since initial growth is lower, the 12.9 percent longer-term growth rate implies a strong EPS growth acceleration late in the period. Peer prospects vary but center on a 12.1 percent growth rate for five years. Next year's estimates range from 82.5 to 110 percent for the subject company, and a similar spread is shown by peers at the median. Comparatively high dispersion in analyst forecasts can be an indicator of real business uncertainty and risk.

Mean estimates should be seen as reasonably well-informed most of the time. The consensus is often well-populated, though each member of the pack may not opine independently from others. Instead, a few leading analysts may be delivering most of the insight. And sell-side bias is a concern. However, consensus EPS forecasts normally do reflect important economic information. As evidence, note they tend to be correlated with stock prices, usually better than past EPS. Similarly, price/earnings ratios based on forecast EPS tend to be more tightly distributed than ones based on the most recent year. Also, when a leading analyst changes an outlook, it often causes a stock price change. If you want to understand a company's stock price using one piece of information, and the choices are historical EPS versus an analyst forecast consensus, you are better off, on average, using the consensus.

Where are analysts getting the information? Much of it comes from management, certainly. Estimates are sometimes seen just to reflect management's public guidance. But even if analysts do nothing more than that, their compilations are a

EXHIBIT 8.4 ANALYST EPS ESTIMATES EXAMPLE

Analyst Forecasts: EPS	Last Year Actual	Current Forecast	Next Year Forecast	Current Year Growth	Next Year Growth	5-Year Growth Rate	Next Year Low (% of Est.)	Next Year High (% of Est.)
Company, Annual Consensus	$2.88	$2.85	$3.09	−1.0%	8.4%	12.9%	82.5%	110.0%
Peer Low	$0.46	$0.36	$0.42	−75%	6%	5.5%	65.8%	104.6%
Peer 25th Percentile	$1.39	$1.05	$1.32	−24%	11%	9.7%	81.4%	111.9%
Peer 50th Percentile	$1.92	$1.56	$1.74	−14%	15%	12.1%	86.5%	117.4%
Peer 75th Percentile	$2.84	$2.43	$2.65	−0%	22%	15.3%	89.5%	120.3%
Peer High	$5.36	$5.57	$6.43	15%	86%	21.4%	94.1%	142.3%
Industry				5.9%	12.5%	11.9%		
Sector				−5.1%	20.3%	11.0%		

Source: yahoo.com.

204

valuable service. It is easier to read a consensus than to sit through all the earnings calls. And when analysts sit through those calls, they do it with an expert ear.

Where forecasts are concerned, longer-term ones should be seen as less precisely informed than the shorter ones. Analysts fuss quite a bit over trying to predict the next quarter. Arguably, that is what they really get paid to do. For longer-term growth rates, one suspects they sometimes "back-solve" them from the stock price. Still, if long-term growth rates were as empty of insight as that—if analysts just used valuation models to reconcile the longer-term growth rate to the stock price—that would be another valuable analytical service. What they would be doing, in effect, is assuming the stock price is economically "correct" and back solving for the earnings growth rate that supports it.

It is not a bad method. In a few pages, in fact, I will recommend that method as one you should consider using. And again, this back solving into a forecast is not being done by a chimpanzee. It is the work of an expert. It is often available for free. Markets react to it, so it meets market standards for information. I will take it, thank you very much. What I may do with it, though, is to assume that it sometimes contains a modest upward growth bias. As remarked in Chapter 5, when analysts have used costs of capital around 10 percent in a big-company DCF model (precrisis), I have assumed that both their discount rates and earnings growth rates each have been a bit on the upper end of the likely range.

INTERPRETING THE ORACLE

Delphi is the ancient site of the famed oracle whose prognostications were sought by kings and generals. These forecasts tended to be rather vague and cryptic. Visitors needed to do some interpretation.

Using analyst forecasts can be a bit similar. The most readily available data often are limited to consensus revenue and EPS forecasts. The corporate-level target-setting task, however, could require goals for any of a dozen other common financial metrics—operating income, net income, ROIC, and so on. Often, you can find such details by digging into all the underlying reports. But those details are not always available for the full set of reporting analysts, so there are fewer data points than one finds for revenue and EPS averages. Sometimes the details are presented on an inconsistent basis from one report to another.

Here are examples of relevant considerations, when translating revenue and EPS estimates into the differing metrics often used in incentive plans:

- As we found in Chapter 6, financing policy can affect performance metrics. High or rising debt can cause a high level of growth in net income and EPS to correspond to lower rate for operating income.

- The growth rate for EPS can be higher still, in relation to core results, if share repurchases are involved. Note that big rates of EPS gain driven by new debt normally are not expected to persist.

- Taxes are big costs, and their forecast conventions can vary. The overall tax rate can often be used to convert net income to pretax income, for example. The marginal rate is more appropriate when calculating after-tax interest costs, as when estimating after-tax operating profit. The accounting provision for taxes can be a more stable basis for projections than the cash tax rate for a particular year. Prospective changes in rates may be an element of the outlook, as well.

- Operational leverage means that operating income can rise faster than gross profit or revenue due to scale effects. Effects are not always permanent, but they may be applicable during the relatively short forecast term of an incentive plan.

- Incentive targets for income often need a corresponding goal for return on invested capital. Here, using incremental ROIC can be helpful (an example appeared earlier in this chapter).

- Translating further into cash-flow-based metrics can require assumptions about future capital usage and depreciation. Company and sector norms can be useful here, stated in terms such as depreciation as a percentage of revenue, the ratio of revenue to capital, or average fixed asset life (gross fixed assets divided by depreciation).

As metrics move farther from revenue and EPS estimates, translating goals becomes a more assumption-driven process with less certain conclusions. At that point, it is a good idea to make heavier use of whatever detailed forecasts are available from analysts or management. Those sources may, of course, simply include forecasts of the incentive metrics themselves, with no translation required. Such results may be of use even if they are available from only a few analysts. They can set out prevailing ratios and forecast conventions for matters like tax rates and capital turnover, doing so in a forecast format that may be more applicable than historical norms. This can provide helpful input when one is translating revenue and EPS estimates—which are comparatively well-populated—into other incentive plan metrics.

MULTIPLE PERSONALITIES

Enterprise multiples can personify a range of different outlooks—high growth, volatile, cash cow, stable earner. They convey information about a company's future performance characteristics. That information should be interpreted in terms of the three main drivers of value creation—income, capital usage, and risk. As seen in Chapter 2, a higher-quality profile of prospective earnings should bring about a higher valuation.

Valuation multiples for the Fortune 50 company and its peers are shown in Exhibit 8.5.

Rising price/earnings multiples by themselves most often suggest an accelerating outlook for growth in income from operations and in its driving effect on other metrics. Falling multiples most often suggest the income growth outlook is contracting. Income growth is only one of the three most general drivers of valuation, however. The others always merit a look:

- *Capital usage.* A lower multiple may stem from lower FCF expectations (e.g., a diminished outlook for incremental ROIC). This would mean that future income growth is expected to be less profitable from an economic standpoint, reducing its current valuation. As one example of how this could play out, consider that lower FCF likely would limit a company's ability to drive EPS with repurchases, reducing prospective EPS gains without affecting operating income growth.

- *Risk.* Lower multiples may stem from higher assessments of risk that raise the cost of capital and reduce the present value of expected financial results. It is useful to consult some risk metrics along the lines of those reviewed in Chapter 5. Implied volatility is a current snapshot of risk. Option pricing models can be used to infer volatility from option prices. Differences between short and longer contracts (or against past volatility) may signal expected changes in the risk outlook. These indicators are of potential use in judging whether a company's valuation multiple is higher or lower than norms due to a difference in risk levels. Other indicators can be compiled as well (beta, leverage, etc.).

A review of multiples should consider the "base" being capitalized; the denominator of the ratio of value to income. Is it a stable earnings year, one that is representative of ongoing earning capacity? Does it reflect a dip in results—for example, a 50 percent drop that requires 100 percent growth before any net recovery is complete? In such as case, a market multiple at twice the norm may simply portend an earnings recovery and not persistently higher growth prospects.

Three general sources of data were examined in this short-format review: historical comparisons with peers in terms of financial results and TSR, analyst forecasts, and market capitalization multiples. If they are consistent, this

EXHIBIT 8.5 CAPITALIZATION MULTIPLES EXAMPLE

Price/Earnings Ratio:	Year End Stock Price/Year End EPS						Most Recent Month Stock Price/EPS	P/E on TTM EPS	This Year Frcst. P/E	Next Year Frcst. P/E
	2003	2004	2005	2006	2007	2008				
P/E Ratio—Subject Company	19.4	23.7	16.7	13.8	12.1	14.0	14.1	7.0	7.0	6.4
Peer 25th Percentile	20.4	18.9	18.3	15.5	10.4	12.7	13.6	14.4	14.9	13.3
Peer 50th Percentile	24.0	20.6	20.8	20.6	14.1	14.8	14.3	15.6	18.1	15.3
Peer 75th Percentile	40.5	33.4	37.0	36.0	24.1	25.7	25.2	24.4	27.3	19.7
Percent Rank	12%	60%	3%	8%	34%	43%	44%			

Enterprise Value Multiples:	2003	2004	2005	2006	2007	2008	Most Recent Month EV/FYE	5-Year Historical Median	Average 3-Year	5-Year
Ratio of Enterprise Value to:										
Revenue—Subject Company	**0.7**	**0.6**	**0.6**	**0.6**	**0.5**	**0.3**	**0.3**	**0.6**	**0.5**	**0.5**
Peer 25th Percentile	0.9	1.0	1.0	1.0	0.7	0.5	0.5	1.0	0.7	0.9
Peer 50th Percentile	1.2	1.4	1.3	1.1	0.9	0.7	0.7	1.1	0.9	1.1
Peer 75th Percentile	2.6	2.7	2.4	2.8	2.1	1.1	1.4	2.4	2.0	2.2
Percent Rank	7%	3%	4%	5%	3%	12%	7%			
Operating Income—Subject Co.	**12.3**	**12.1**	**11.3**	**10.6**	**9.9**	**6.9**	**7.5**	**10.6**	**9.2**	**10.2**
Peer 25th Percentile	13.6	13.1	11.7	11.6	9.8	7.2	8.7	11.6	9.5	10.7
Peer 50th Percentile	19.3	16.6	14.0	14.3	11.9	9.5	9.2	14.0	11.9	13.3
Peer 75th Percentile	30.6	39.4	32.4	24.1	19.0	10.8	13.8	24.1	18.0	25.1
Percent Rank	19%	10%	16%	13%	30%	20%	13%			
EBITDA—Subject Company	**9.5**	**9.2**	**8.9**	**8.5**	**7.8**	**4.9**	**5.4**	**8.5**	**7.1**	**7.8**
Peer 25th Percentile	10.2	10.8	9.6	9.4	7.4	5.1	6.1	9.4	7.3	8.5
Peer 50th Percentile	14.9	12.9	10.9	11.1	9.6	6.2	7.1	10.9	9.0	10.1
Peer 75th Percentile	21.4	27.3	25.8	18.0	12.9	7.7	8.3	18.0	12.9	18.3
Percent Rank	16%	12%	17%	13%	28%	18%	13%			

should lend greater confidence in moving toward a conclusion. Capitalization multiples often convey information that overlaps with EPS forecasts, for example. Trailing multiples are often higher for companies with higher expected earnings growth.

Stability in findings also should, all else being equal, increase confidence. If company, peer, and sector forecasts are markedly different than past results, for example, more weight should be placed on forward-looking indicators such as EPS estimates and the implications of market capitalization. If indications are very mixed, however, it does not mean the average of them is correct. One indicator may be more valid than another.

TSR can be of help in evaluating the general validity of peer comparisons, too. If company share prices have an unusually strong degree of ambient correlation with peer prices, this suggests capital markets see their fortunes as highly intertwined. This means information regarding risks, prospects, and outlook of peers likely is relevant to standard and range setting. Ordinary correlations among S&P 500 companies are 50 percent to 60 percent on average—qualified peers ought to be higher.

Although the example discussed here has focused on target setting, other applications are possible. In the case of a health insurance company, market evidence was used to help judge whether goals could be set properly for incentive purposes. This was at the peak of the 2008 crisis. The client faced real uncertainty about the viability of its future business, given the prospect of industry restructuring under the Obama administration.

When we reviewed market data we found that analysts were not forecasting earnings declines. And forecasts in the near- and medium-term were not highly dispersed, suggesting uncertainties in the three- to five-year time frame were not that high. The stock was depressed and implied volatilities (based on option quotes) were quite high. This did suggest there were indeed very large uncertainties about their franchise over the longer term. But these did not stand in the way of proper target setting for the relevant nearer-term time frame. The consensus was not a sector meltdown, and data indicated that standards could be set practicably for incentive purposes in the nearer-term despite longer-term franchise risks. So, in this case, prospective market evidence was used not only to set targets, but first to address the feasibility of target setting.

To reconcile variances among capitalization multiples, the most thorough method is to fit DCF models to the company's valuation. This can help specify how a company with, say, a higher multiple than peers might trace its valuation premium back to differential rates of expected income growth, capital usage, or risk. That sort of approach is a full reconciliation—it is the general method we examine next.

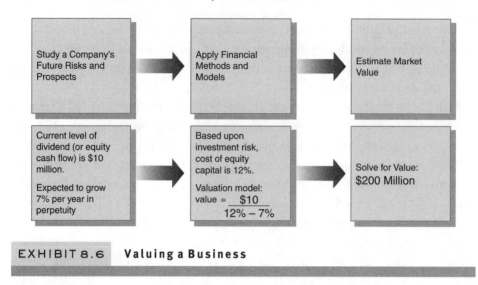

EXHIBIT 8.6   Valuing a Business

FULL RECONCILIATION TO MARKET VALUE

Performance expectations underlie the pricing of a company's shares. We have just gone through an example of a process that consulted capitalization multiples as a source of evidence about the level of those expectations. That process can be expanded into a full reconciliation. That is, goals can be estimated by developing a performance forecast that squares with the company's stock price.

   This involves running the valuation process in reverse—fitting the company's share price to a set of performance expectations. Exhibit 8.6 sets out the essentials of the business valuation process we introduced in Chapter 2. Exhibit 8.7 depicts the general idea of estimating shareholder expectations.

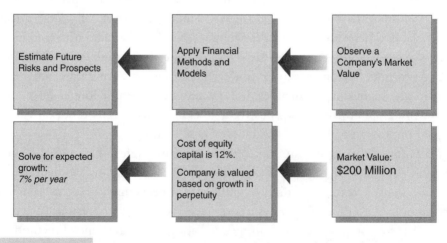

EXHIBIT 8.7   Measuring Shareholder Expectations

This is an alternative to using the budget as the incentive target. It provides an external and shareholder-oriented alternative to a process of internal negotiation.[4] I assisted a large electric and gas utility in setting targets for its incentive plan without using internal budgets, in a process profiled in *CFO* magazine. The targets were based on expectations held by shareholders, ones driving the company's stock price.

Let us consider the executive we used as an example in Chapter 3 and his business unit, which has earnings of $125 million. The debt and equity of the parent company has a value totaling $7.5 billion; that is its *enterprise value*. To figure out the value of the business unit, we need to apportion that $7.5 billion among all the company's business units. If a basic comparison of a group's prospects with those of peers suggests that his has a generally higher income growth profile, lower risk or lower capital requirements, we would value it in the upper end of the range of peer multiples, and vice versa.

The average company in our group's sector is trading at 15 times earnings; assume it applies here. Our market value is $1.875 billion (or 15 times earnings).[5] Note this procedure has not required an independent, absolute valuation analysis. Instead, it starts with a given valuation for the parent company and apportions it roughly among business units. It also does not require us to set out absolute expectations for performance. Instead, it requires a relative assessment of business size and positioning. The absolute process comes next. We do that by assembling a discounted cash flow valuation analysis of the group. (See Exhibit 8.8.)

As input, we review information helpful to judging business conditions and prospects: analyst commentary, management's remarks, historical financial statements, and any forecasts. This helps us set some key assumptions:

- We determine the cost of capital for the group using methods described in Chapter 5 (assume 9 percent).

- For now, we sidestep the process of setting income growth targets for Years 1 through 5. Income is what we solve for, in this example, at the conclusion of the analysis.

- We set up assumptions to govern the income forecast for Years 6 through 10, triggering them based on growth assumptions from Year 5. Forecast assumptions during this time period reflect a general pattern of decelerating growth in income and value creation. In this instance, income growth is assumed to decay toward long-run norms at 15 percent per year, from whatever rate is attained by Year 5.

- We set capital requirements each year for five years based on the assumption they will resemble past capital levels in relation to income (consistent

Simplified Discounted Cash Flow Model

Operating Income, AT

Cost of Capital (WACC)

Total Capital

Enterprise Value

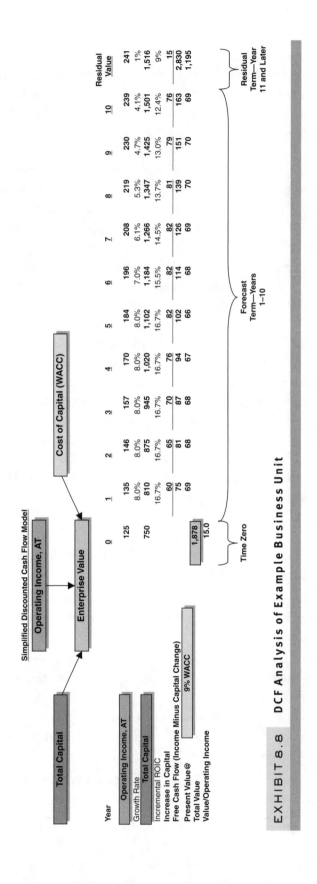

Year	0	1	2	3	4	5	6	7	8	9	10	Residual Value
Operating Income, AT	125	135	146	157	170	184	196	208	219	230	239	241
Growth Rate		8.0%	8.0%	8.0%	8.0%	8.0%	7.0%	6.1%	5.3%	4.7%	4.1%	1%
Total Capital	750	810	875	945	1,020	1,102	1,184	1,266	1,347	1,425	1,501	1,516
Incremental ROIC		16.7%	16.7%	16.7%	16.7%	16.7%	15.5%	14.5%	13.7%	13.7%	13.0%	12.4%	9%
Increase in Capital		60	65	70	76	82	82	82	81	79	76	15
Free Cash Flow (Income Minus Capital Change)		75	81	87	94	102	114	126	139	151	163	2,830
Present Value @ 9% WACC		69	68	68	67	66	68	69	70	70	69	1,195
Total Value	1,878											
Value/Operating Income	15.0											

Time Zero

Forecast Term—Years 1–10

Residual Term—Year 11 and Later

EXHIBIT 8.8 DCF Analysis of Example Business Unit

with about 17 percent ROIC, in this case). During Years 6 through 10, this incremental ROIC performance is assumed to decay toward the cost of capital of 9 percent.

- We use typical methods to value the group at the end of a customary ten-year forecast period. We assume its income will grow 1 percent per year in perpetuity, a rate meant to reflect long-run inflationary expectations[6] (the level of inflation impounded in the 9 percent nominal cost of capital).

At this point, every aspect of a basic DCF valuation scenario has been set out except for the growth rate in income for the next few years. We solve for the growth rate in income over Years 1 through 5 that, when combined with the other assumptions, results in a present value for the group equal to $1.9 billion. That rate is 8 percent, meaning that 8 percent annual growth in operating income over the next five years is implied by the valuation at 15 times earnings.

The result is based on many assumptions, so a prudent step is to go back and reconcile the results with evidence. Exhibit 8.9 depicts some angles available for reconciliation.

One example of a basic reconciliation step is to examine the sales levels involved in the performance scenario. The forecast sales growth rate should be consistent with industry evidence and commentary. Also, the forecast should be reconcilable in terms of the ratio of operating income to sales (operating margin) and the ratio of sales to net assets (capital turnover). The DCF scenario cannot involve a big expansion in margins, for example, unless this prospect is supported by evidence like strong pricing trends or economies linked with growth (e.g., operational leverage). And it cannot involve greatly increased capital turnover

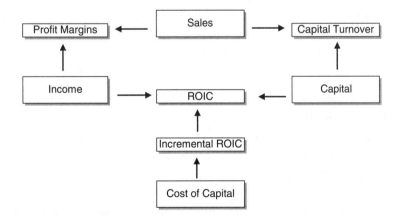

EXHIBIT 8.9   Basic Yardsticks for Forecast Reconciliation

unless supported by scale effects like high initial inventory levels or low initial capacity utilization.

Note that the indicators we are examining are simple ones. There are only three financial quantities involved in the basic DCF forecast: operating income and capital usage, with sales as a driver of income and as a reference point. But, simply by examining the ratios among them, we created many opportunities to validate the forecast against norms.

Results may also be squared with those of other business units within the company and to the assumptions involved in explaining the company's overall stock price. The sum of the business unit DCFs, adjusted for any unallocated corporate costs and assets, should equal the overall company's valuation. At this point, the business unit valuations will have been reconciled to the parent stock price using each of the two most common methods used to value closely held businesses—the market comparison approach (using peer valuation multiples to apportion value among the business units) and the DCF approach (establishing a specific performance scenario for each unit).[7] The forecast for each business unit, as well as the overall system, is driven directly by the expectations and valuation criteria held by the external market. This process leads to performance goals that are supported by market evidence coming from several external sources. The is not an exercise that opens a Pandora's Box of ungoverned assumptions. Instead, the assumptions and results are made to fit into a box governed by market value and market norms for performance.

The general DCF model used in this example has been reconciled to market value as well, using Monte Carlo simulation. Its forecast conventions, "decay" assumptions and other parameters tend to lead to statistical distributions of stock returns that resemble market norms.

Here is what the analysis allows us to conclude:

- 4 to 6 percent income growth over the next few years, combined with other reasonable parameters, does not produce a reasonable forecast, one valued as highly as the company's market value.

- Growth of 10 to 12 percent, in combination with other clear business attributes, would quickly lead to a higher valuation than those commanded in this industry.

- Our finding of 8 percent means that the company should be attaching trend operating income growth targets of roughly 7 to 9 percent per year to the next few years (fixing capital and risk levels at target).

This level of precision can address most of the bigger arguments in the target-setting arena. If the incentive plan is based purely on operating income, then the analysis provides a direct basis for future target setting. If it uses other measures, then the income and capital levels involved in the forecast need to be translated into those other measures.

Projected ROIC can be figured for each year by dividing forecast operating income by capital. Net income can be estimated by projecting future debt policy and subtracting interest expense. Subtracting projected debt from capital, we have forecast equity levels for use in projecting return on equity (ROE). Income, capital, interest, and debt tell us how much cash flow is available to equity holders each year. If we subtract dividends from this at a supportable rate, the balance can be used to determine new share issuances or repurchases. That gives the forecast of outstanding shares that enables us to figure EPS. Pulling in a sales forecast gives us not only sales but capital turnover and margins, and so on.

The expectations-based procedure improves target setting by forcing its parameters into a box called market value. Company value, market valuation parameters, and specific information about business prospects must be reconciled. The traditional process, in contrast, is not only internally focused, but also comparatively anchorless.

Valuation-based targets are helpful in an aspect of budget negotiations, too. Group executives might want to argue for low performance targets, meaning they just want payouts higher than warranted by their performance. The industry vernacular changes a bit from one instance to the next, but the story is the same. They insist they really cannot be expected to generate income that meets peer or investor standards. They need more money for their business, beyond what they are using now to generate low yields. They avoid firm promises, playing up the unknowns that affect any business.

In value-focused companies, these are losing arguments. Why? Because these arguments are tantamount to saying, "My business is not worth much." The arguments reduce to effects on only three value drivers: income, capital, and risk. If their business has a modest income outlook accompanied by big capital needs and uncertainties, they have hit the trifecta of value destruction. Their forecast is on the unfavorable end of all three of the main scales: low income, high capital usage, and a high cost of capital. If the business is not worth much today, then its limited outlook cannot easily fund incentive opportunity. A low value does not testify to a history of high management performance, either.

When targeting is seen through a valuation-based frame, the tactics needed to sandbag end up discrediting the sandbagger. Target setting and valuation are two sides of the same coin. Earlier, we noted the importance of acknowledging information asymmetries and using agency devices to try to turn them to the benefit of shareholders. Targeting is an important place to try to apply such tactics. The approaches set out here are meant to address those asymmetries and to help reveal the truest business prospects.

SETTING TARGETS BASED ON TOTAL BUSINESS RETURN

Another example of a valuation-based approach is to calibrate plans in relation to fixed annual standards for total business return (TBR). Recall that TBR is equal to the capitalized change in income plus free cash flow. Stated as a percentage of beginning value, targeted TBR might assume a level like 15 percent or 20 percent. TBR-based standards are flexible. They allow targeted pay levels to be earned based on the many combinations of business performance that can bring about a particular level of return.

One company set targets for each of ten business units based on a uniform standard of 15 percent TBR as a percent of beginning value. This standard was translated into the goals used in each plan. For example, business units can each earn the same, targeted incentive award based on very different profiles for performance:

- One group has operating income growth of 8 percent per year, leading to valuation gains of 8 percent per year. It has free cash flow equal to about 7 percent of beginning value. TBR is 15 percent.

- Another group grows twice as fast at 16 percent but has modestly negative free cash flow at 1 percent of value. TBR is equal to 15 percent in this case as well.

- A last example is a classic cash cow, providing zero operating income growth, but requiring so little reinvestment that free cash flows equal 15 percent of value.

Actual incentive metrics can differ greatly from one business unit to another. One unit might use revenue growth, operating margins, and ROIC, for example, while another might use economic profit. Their performance ranges would be equal, however, when translated into TBR percentages. The TBR method places the underlying connection between value creation and rewards on a consistent scale. So plans are at once fiscally uniform, supportive of value creation, and specific to business unit circumstance.

Beginning value in this example is set at the greater of capital or capitalized income. Normally, TBR uses income as an indication of the company's value. In this example, capital is used as the default valuation when income is low. This has the effect of asking units that have ROIC below the cost of capital to deliver higher future income growth.

This convention does rely on capital as a basis for scaling performance demands, and we have seen some sources of distortion there. Most come out in the wash under the TBR method. Low-ROIC units usually got there either with recent mergers and acquisitions, big recent investing, or just substandard income yield on resources used. In each case, it is appropriate to demand rapid ROIC gains and the TBR method does that. High-ROIC companies may have some denominator-based distortions from differences in historical capital measurement. The TBR method is not affected by them. In their case, it uses the more relevant figure—current income level—as the basis for valuation, so the unrepresentative capital readings do not find their way into the denominator. And the TBR metric itself, like the DCF model, pays no attention to beginning capital and its issues.

These are simple concepts but they are worth emphasizing. The fact is that they can remedy many of the issues that beset systems for standard setting. When companies try to improve the economic character of their incentive targeting, they often are thwarted at the first turn by capital-related problems. These techniques can solve many such problems.

Exhibit 8.10 summarizes target-setting problems and how they might be addressed within a traditional standard-setting approach. If the traditional system tried to take account of risk, for example, it would be obligated to sort business units into various risk classes (three categories are assumed). It would have to make similar assessments to deal with other matters such as the general role of capital usage in value creation and the weight to be placed on actual historical performance in setting future targets. Exhibit 8.11 shows how these matters are addressed within a TBR-based targeting system.

The traditional system does not take proper account of these important drivers of expected financial performance. The TBR framework handles them in a consistent and implicit way. Risk differences matter greatly when judging business performance, and the TBR system addresses this criterion explicitly through its use of a risk-adjusted cost of capital. All else equal, the TBR approach places higher income demands on riskier business units. The TBR system also takes clear account of capital needs, subtracting them in full when measuring FCF and balancing it against increases in value.

TBR is a resilient framework. However, companies with persistently higher growth prospects may be able to generate outsized returns under the TBR system because, for so many of these companies, neither current capitalized earnings nor capital adequately capture the opportunity cost of capital invested in the business. In such instances, some business units may need to be separated for a time into a few classes based on growth prospects. (See Exhibit 8.12.)

Factor	Effect on Budgeting	Number of Separate Assessments Needed		
		Low	Medium	High
Risk	Higher risk *may* increase goals	1	2	3
Capital needs (FCF)	Higher capital needs *may* increase goals	4	5	6
Actual performance	Praise, gratitude, empathy, scorn, or indifference? Unknown	7	8	9
Investment horizon for new money	Big outlays and deals get fuzzy, negotiated treatment over time	10	11	12
Differing financial metrics	May bollix any chance of consistency	13	14	15
Recently acquired?	Potentially unrealistic goals, metrics, or both (goodwill in or out?)	16	17	18
Shareholder criteria/ expectations	Indirect, inconsistent, or absent	19	20	21
Composition of return: growth vs. yield	Requires separate benchmarking. Relative emphases unrelated to value. Cash yield often ignored	22	23	24

EXHIBIT 8.10   **TBR and Target Setting: Factors Potentially Driving Targets**

Factor	Effect on Budgeting	TBR Treatment	Separate Assessments Needed
Risk	Higher risk *may* increase goals	Adjust WACC (2 or 3 classes) – possibly based upon existing categorization	
Capital needs (FCF)	Higher capital needs *may* increase goals	Explicit focus on new money in goals (e.g., ROIC, EP, TBR)	
Actual performance	Praise, gratitude, empathy, scorn, or indifference? Unknown	Only affects opportunity cost (Capital or capitalized NOPAT)	
Investment horizon for new money	Big outlays and deals get fuzzy, negotiated treatment over time	Captured in typical NOPAT and capital rules	0
Differing financial metrics	May bollix any chance of consistency	Given consistent, proportional treatment in TBR terms. Assumptions may be required in translation	
Recently acquired?	Potentially unrealistic goals, metrics, or both (goodwill in or out?)	TBR only cares about new money (but balance may affect opportunity cost)	
Shareholder criteria/ expectations	Indirect, inconsistent, or absent	Roll up to consolidated, expectations. Drivers are WACC, capital, and NOPAT	
Composition of return: growth vs. yield	Requires separate benchmarking. Relative emphases unrelated to value. Cash yield often ignored	Captures each in proportion to impact upon return and value	

EXHIBIT 8.11   **TBR and Target Setting: Treatment of Driving Factors**

Factor	TBR Treatment	Separate Assessments Needed
Near-term growth variation	Fairly addressed through "ratcheting " effect on goals. Ramp-up in a new business may be covered by use of capital as "value"	0
Compositional differences in return: growth vs. yield	Captured in TBR formula	0
Persistently different growth expectations. Likely, wide variation in valuation multiples	Categorize business units into 2 or 3 general classes based upon longer term growth prospects (easier than doing separate valuations or negotiations). Roll up to consolidated goal	2 or 3

EXHIBIT 8.12   **TBR and Target Setting: Addressing Growth's Effects**

This categorization may take some work. But it is a lot easier to slot business units into one of two or three growth classes than it is to run a full budget-based negotiation to set growth targets for each. TBR-based results, though, will not be as precise by year. But the algorithm can be applied year after year, aligning payouts well with economic performance over time. That should appeal to both participants and owners.

Run Away!

A range of methods can be used to sidestep contentious details of target setting, like Monty Python warriors beating a retreat from the battlefield. Many of these are enabled by use of a flexible framework such as TBR. For example, award sizes can be benchmarked based on the expected values of awards and the economic sharing rates they imply. A management team might simply receive 1 percent of its business unit's TBR, per annual grant, if that figure reconciled with market-competitive long-term incentive values for their jobs and with relevant market figures for dilution. The annual share usage in an option plan is like a gain-sharing plan based on valuation, a "targetless" one. This can be converted into a clear, value-based formula like TBR, then pushed down to the business unit level in any of a range of plan formats.

The TBR grants do involve some assessment of likely performance, just as target setting does. All they require is that the company line up pay outcomes across a broad range of acceptable performance scenarios. But that is easier than zeroing in on any one of them as the target and sparking a specific point of dispute.

Moving pay to the longer term can help make short-term posturing pointless. Annual incentive plans can create an unbroken interest in long-run value creation through the use of persistent year-over-year standards such as TBR targets. Long-term incentives can be quite helpful as well. Saying you should focus on the long run is not simply a platitude, in this discussion. The TBR method enables goals to be refocused on the long-term because it is a notably more manageable and forgiving framework:

- Our earlier example of investor expectations indicated that 8 percent per year was a fair level of operating income goal for a three-year period. Annual targets might be a bit higher or lower than that in any year. But, if they are averaging 8 percent, then they are supported by an important outside indicator, one used often in pay delivery—they are supported by the stock price.

- Also, in these plans, there is no budget-based "relief." All income and capital counts. So some big points of contention—what's in, what's out—are demoted to timing, phase-in, or capitalization questions.

- If a given year's results were calculated too generously, allowing a gain to flow through, for example, the next year's target would tend to ratchet up (e.g., in a TBR-based approach). So, securing a higher payout now simply subtracts from next year.

Methods like TBR have a capital-conscious character than can add important flexibility to preset targets. They can adapt well to effects of new investing or divesting activity. Big outlays or asset sales normally wreak havoc on income forecasts, potentially causing payout distortions and, worse, *ex ante* motivational biases. Having a capital-based counterweight in the measurement system automatically adapts payout opportunity to the new outlook. A favorable asset sale might reduce income but increase ROIC over time, for example. Large investments and M&A might do the opposite. Either could increase payouts based on how the net valuation effects shake out (as noted in Chapter 7, simple phase-ins may be required for larger capital outlays).

Another way to make targets more predictable is to wag the dog—to make financial results themselves less variable rather than making incentive terms more adaptable. Reasonable adjustment procedures can be helpful here. If big, nonrecurring effects are running through income, they should be adjusted. In a TBR sense, that would mean running them through FCF only and not including them in the income stream being capitalized into value. Gains and losses can move income around, too, but their effects on TBR are not disproportionate. Being ready to make a few sensible adjustments when needed is *de rigueur* for several reasons we advanced in Chapter 7. These adjustments also tame financial results so they can be administered in a more predictable range. Using more controllable value drivers is another example of this approach (as discussed in Chapter 6 in the section "Indexation and Immunity").

Plan design choices can have big effects on income variation as well, potentially making financial results predictable in a much narrower range. Using *performance share* or *performance unit* grants, for example, can greatly reduce the variability of earnings when compared to a policy of stock option or restricted stock grants. In an example in Chapter 10, *a typical company reduces its earnings variation by half.*

There are other methods under which flexible, economically fair results can be pursued. Though each of these examples is uncommon, they illustrate potentially useful principles:

- In an example of a choice-based targeting system, participants can choose among award schedules in which higher basic performance at targeted pay levels is accompanied by higher upside.

- A "buy-in" phantom stock plan deal is another example of a choice-based approach, though the buy-in aspect may entrain securities law complications and motivational issues.

- Another technique, known as a "Soviet" incentive scheme, actually stems from methods used to set factory production quotas in the old Soviet Union and to address the sandbagging that was endemic in its planned economy. It is based on a matrix that rewards setting high targets and coming in close to them, with payout proportions favoring the confident people who can deliver.

- Setting income targets based on beginning capital levels is another example of a target-setting algorithm. In one example, goals for income growth might equal a standard, modest percentage of prior year income plus a fair return on any increase in capital during the preceding year. In place, this procedure works similarly to an incentive plan based on the economic profit metric, where the capital charge is assessed against the beginning-of-period balance of capital.[8]

- Using a long-term income trend is a potential approach as well. Each year's goal can be equal to the average of a pre-set trend and the year-over-year growth rate, as shown in Exhibit 8.13. The trend growth rate is 10 percent, allowing targets to be set at the outset for the full three-year period.

EXHIBIT 8.13   SETTING INCOME TARGETS BASED ON TREND GROWTH

Year	3-Year Income Trend	Trend-Based	Growth-Based	Target = Average	Growth, At Target	Actual Income	Income/ Target	Payout at 5:1 Lvg.
				Target Income				
0	100.0					100.0		
1	110.0	110.0	110.0	110.0	10%	102.0	93%	64%
2	121.0	121.0	112.2	116.6	14%	129.0	111%	153%
3	133.1	133.1	141.9	137.5	7%	133.1	97%	84%
Growth Rate	10.0%				Average	10.0%	100%	100%

Each year, the actual target is equal to the average of the trend and an annual target based on 10 percent year-over-year growth. In Year 1, the target is $110, computed either way. Actual income for Year 1 is $102. The target for Year 2 is $116.6; the average of the Year 2 trend figure, $121, and figure indicated by 10% year-over-year growth, $112. Year 2's target requires 14 percent income growth as the company is forced to catch up, in part, with the trend. Year 3 targeting comes off a strong year, so the income goal is lightened to 7 percent.

Payouts are based on performance, varying 5:1 based on how performance varies from target. Payouts work out to be 100 percent on average because both the overall growth rate and the total quantity of income is equal to trend. The actual v. trend method can be applied to TBR targeting parameters as well. Trends would be reset for the next three years. This method takes a bonus plan and turns it into, in effect, a three-year long-term performance plan.

• The shape of the award schedule itself (the payout curve) can have important effects. It determines the range of results eligible for reward and, therefore, whether it sometimes pays to defer or accelerate costs or opportunities. It can also drive the urgency associated with any actions affecting business results. Devised well, it can help to create a continuous stake in results and overcome some of the temptations to manipulate them. A lower slope at the extremes, in the S-curve example in Exhibit 8.14, reduces any temptation to move results into the current year or the next. With lower slopes at the edges, ranges can be expanded to cover a wider range of outcomes, keeping hope alive in the range's extremes without putting too many incentive dollars at play there or resorting to a cap. A higher slope in the middle of the range heightens urgency through the interval over which performance gains are most likely to play out. This increases pay at the highest rate when forecasts are most accurate.

Range and Domain: Setting Intervals for Performance and Pay

Most goal-based incentive plans involve finite performance ranges. A classic one has performance levels ranging from 80 to 120 percent of target and payouts that run from 0 to 200 percent. The payout moves 100 percentage points in relation to target for 20 percentage points of movement in performance, so the plan's leverage can be described as 100:20, or 5:1. Threshold payouts sometimes are set at 50 percent of target or other levels, rather than having payouts start off at 0 percent.

Exhibit 8.14 sets out data on our survey respondents concerning the payout leverage of EPS metrics (59 companies provided details regarding the EPS element on payouts).

Leverage is lower below target because there is often a payout, often 50 percent, at the threshold performance level. Payouts in these cases are already positive at the threshold performance level so they only rise 50 points when performance increases from threshold to target. Above target, however, they rise 100 points most often, from a 100 percent payout level to a 200 percent

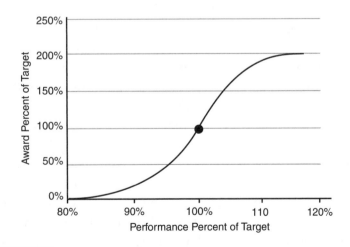

EXHIBIT 8.14   **S-Curve Payout Line**

EXHIBIT 8.15   **EPS PAYOUT LEVERAGE**

	Leverage Ratios	
	Threshold to Target	**Target to Max**
Average	4.9	6.5
Median	2.5	3.9

maximum. So below-target leverage, computed as "rise over run" from threshold to target, is not as high.

Companies typically expect to have performance within the range—not below the threshold or above the maximum—around seven or eight times in a ten-year span. This means an overall in-range probability of about 75 percent in any given year. Applying common, symmetrical performance ranges, this means a 25 percent overall chance of being out of range—12.5 percent on the downside, below threshold, and 12.5 percent above the range maximum.

Our studies of the general variability of business results around budgets or trends suggest that companies are setting their ranges properly to meet this criterion. Given the typical variability around trend for operating income (e.g., a standard error of 15 to 20 percent around a given target), a company would expect its operating income to fall within the typical 80 to 120 percent performance range seven or eight times out of ten. Market practice does appear on average to line up well with company intentions regarding the frequency of out-of-range performance levels. Higher payouts at threshold sometimes entrain a larger chance of nonpayment, and so may cases of recovery from weak earnings.

When setting ranges, you need them wide enough so you do not have performance coming in around thresholds and caps very often. Companies risk some odd incentive effects around thresholds and caps. At the same time, you want them narrow enough that they impart appropriate leverage. One solution to this was described earlier—make sure the company has reasonable processes for handling big, nonrecurring events that otherwise would move results all over the map.

Regarding thresholds, if we saw performance coming in just below threshold we might expect management to pull out all the stops to make a little money this year. Instead, though, they might take a "big bath," accelerating some discretionary spending into this year, deferring certain sales transactions by a few weeks and accruing some reserves a bit more aggressively. If next year's threshold is likely to be set at this year's actual performance (as we might well suggest), this could buy them onto the payout schedule earlier.

What if the plan had a 50 percent payout at threshold? In that case, management might do anything it can to bring in a little more profit this year. Cutting way back on discretionary expenses is an obvious strategy here, although many such cutbacks—advertising and research and development come to mind—risk diminishing longer-run earning power and valuation. The award schedule pays them to do it nonetheless.

Many other scenarios are possible, and they advise against setting ranges that are too narrow, having leverage that is too high, and having great variations in leverage from one region of the payout schedule to another. Unattainable goals can create an "every other year" bonus plan, as participants called it in one case. Goals had been set very high to emphasize high expectations, but the plan made the timing of income more important than its amount.

Now consider what happens if the plan is based on sales and operating income, with a joint threshold on each goal, so that failure to hit threshold on either goal wipes out the whole award budget. Depending on the way the year is shaping up, participants could end up with a very strong encouragement to gouge customers, make unprofitable sales, or shift revenue or expense from one year to the next. If plans use limited ranges at all, then at least some of these scenarios are feasible.

Adjusting ranges at least roughly for variability is a good general solution. Companies with particularly volatile or unpredictable results do tend to have wider award ranges within bonus plans. If a particular company has results that have varied widely around budgets and trends, holding all else equal, that company should have a wider performance range.

As shown in Exhibit 8.16, these data are helpful when assessing the future predictability of results and, therefore, in setting ranges. A company with a regression standard error of 16 percent, for example, would have ranges set at +/−20 percent if it wanted to have a 10 percent chance of either an above-range performance level or one below threshold.[9]

The general procedure to apply these within a set of bonus plans requires:

• *Measuring the variability of business unit results around past budgets or, as an approximation, around a regression trend line of past performance.* Using these results, the company's business units are sorted into two to four categories of variability. Peer company analysis and other sources of benchmark data on business uncertainty may be useful to consult, as well.

• *Using these risk data to construct performance ranges.* (See Exhibit 8.17.) For the more uncertain businesses, a relatively wide range from threshold to maximum performance—like 70 to 130 percent of target—may be reasonable. Very stable, predictable businesses may warrant a range of 90 to 110 percent

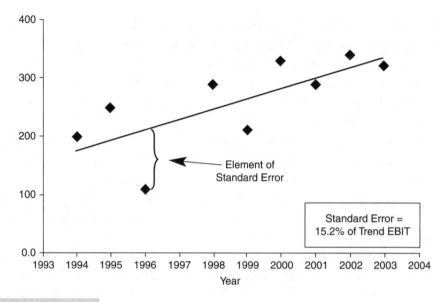

EXHIBIT 8.16   **Historical EBIT versus Trend (Regression)**

of target to move from threshold to maximum payouts, and so may relatively predictable metrics like revenue. An intermediate risk group may employ the typical 80 to 120 percent range.

Under this approach, statistical inferences are used to set ranges that all have roughly the same chances of hitting threshold, target, and maximum award levels. The company's ranges end up being very consistently derived and, at the same time, are tailored to the characteristics of the particular business.

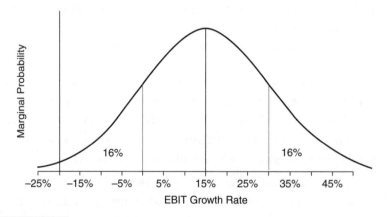

EXHIBIT 8.17   **Distribution of Operating Performance Based on Standard Error of Trend**

The stakes on the bonus range-setting process are greatest in large, complex companies because they have so many business units. That is also where the chances of costly error are greatest because the ability of corporate staff to monitor such important matters is more dispersed. In those cases in particular, it is worthwhile to be thorough and systematic when setting ranges.

To judge performance and set targets, companies often rank businesses against peers or other business units. But not every company has the same chance of hitting a particular percentile for financial performance like the 50th or 90th. Rather, characteristics of the metrics themselves may place a company ahead of or behind the pack. Business conditions at a company might make it strong on FCF, but weak in any race for income growth. The methods discussed in this chapter—targets effectively driven by TBR or by its market version, total investor return—are helpful in stating performance on a consistent basis.

Total shareholder return (TSR) is actually the easiest common metric to benchmark against peer standards. A company's expected level of TSR generally is equal to its cost of equity capital, irrespective of what its past TSR performance has been. Its expected rate of stock price growth is equal to the cost of capital minus its expected dividend yield. A typical company's chance of hitting the 50th TSR percentile of its peer group is 50 percent, assuming the levels of business risk and financial leverage driving its cost of equity capital resemble those of peers.

As noted earlier most bonus plans and performance plans involve limited payout ranges, with 200 percent of the target award being typical as the upper limit of payout. Most often, this is done to control payouts in view of perceived fiscal risk. Unlimited plans do not have a monopoly on fiscal risk, however. Payout caps can be a false friend. They do not by themselves protect the company from unreasonable payouts. As the examples earlier demonstrated, finite incentive ranges are one of the areas in which incentive design choices can lead to business trouble. And, *payouts can be out of hand even when they are well within range.* This can occur for a number of reasons:

- Payouts can be too dilutive at target, and performance levels and goals can be too easy to attain.
- Metrics and award schedules can allow payouts for bad business decisions.
- Granting structures (e.g., end-to-end performance cycles rather than overlapping ones) can encourage hyping short-term pay with unsustainable results.
- Narrow ranges can encourage management of income or simply discourage high performance.

Finite ranges may encourage manipulation of the timing of revenues and costs, fitting wide-ranging business results over time into the narrower interval that is eligible for reward. We need better safeguards. Properly set metrics, targets and ranges are the key safeguards. A range of fiscal controls is set out in the next chapter, as part of the exposition of TBR-based phantom stock plans offering unlimited upside. When companies have properly designed plans, they can expand their upside and make them more compelling without straying into a fiscal danger zone.

Weightings, Award Leverage, and Participant Influence

Performance/award ranges set the payout leverage for each goal. The median leverage of annual incentive plan metrics is around 3.5:1, but actual leverage can vary from 1:1 to as much as 20:1 for the various performance metrics and intervals involved.[10]

High leverage may be used to create a strong incentive to improve results. It may also fit businesses in which the likely range of business results, along with management's ability to improve them, is unusually narrow. Wider ranges and concomitantly low leverage may fit in cases where results are less predictable or performance gains are easier to effect.

Weightings matter, too. Incentive plans may employ metrics that track results at the corporate level, the division level, at intermediate echelons like group or sector, and below the division level in units like profit centers and ventures. Each of these organizational levels can have different degrees of importance, or weight, in the overall delivery of awards.

Leverage is another form of goal weighting. Small changes in business unit results might have large incentive payout effects, while corporate payouts may vary much less. In that case, business unit results are featured more heavily than their weighting would on its face suggest. In this regard, leverage is a stealth variable in incentive design. Within the overall incentive structure, the leverage placed on business unit results (or on any goal) can be more important than the weighting of the goals themselves.

Leverage is the slope of the payout line. We saw earlier that 100 percentage points of gain earned over 20 percentage points of performance improvement achieves 5-to-1 leverage. In computing leverage, the "rise" in income is as important as the "run" of performance by which it is divided. The setting of performance ranges re-enters the discussion when it turns to the subject of leverage. For example, in many businesses, earnings are much more volatile than revenue. Yet, some plans attach the same performance range to both sales and

profit goals. A wide interval, attached to a relatively predictable goal like revenue, lessens the effective leverage attached to that goal. This oversight can be
beneficial though, sometimes reducing inadvertently the payout effects of unprofitable sales growth.

The most important type of goal weighting, however, is individual influence.
If awards under a performance plan are weighted equally on corporate and business goals, then the plan will appear on its face to place equal importance on
them. However, the fact that business unit executives have more influence on
business unit results increases their effective weight. In fact, a typical business
unit bonus plan for executives may be divided into two parts: a functioning incentive plan based on business unit results and a general, corporate results-
sharing arrangement unrelated to their own efforts.

INCENTIVE RISKS, CALIBRATION, AND TESTING

Earlier chapters examined a number of ways in which business risk overlaps with
incentive design, and this chapter has extended that discussion. Incentives can
carry serious risks of decision-making bias, ones that can escape typical governance processes. We have just seen that payout calibration creates risks of a range
of distortions and biases.

These aspects of design have important cost-related risks, as well. First, let us
examine some cost baselines. If a bonus plan costs 5 percent of net income at
target and has 5:1 leverage, then its costs will amount to 25 percent of the next
dollar of income gain. Exhibit 8.18 shows the details behind that scenario and
some others.

If leverage were 10:1, then incremental costs would be 50 percent. Incremental costs can be surprisingly high, and can rise when long-term incentives and
broader-based incentives are considered. In one electric and gas utility, the only

EXHIBIT 8.18   INCREMENTAL INCENTIVE COST EXAMPLE

	Target	High Scenario	Low Scenario
Net Income	100	110	95
Bonus % of Target	100%	150%	75%
Bonus	5	7.5	3.75
Bonus Variance from Target		2.5	−1.25
Income variance from Target		10	−5
Incremental Bonus Cost %		25%	25%

thing preventing marginal costs of variable pay from exceeding 100 percent of marginal income was the fact that the income metric used in incentive plans was stated net of plan costs (this is customary in goal-based plans, and implicit in stock-based ones). Such cost effects should be among the matters studied and benchmarked as part of the design process. They should be the result of explicit choices. Instead, sometimes, the cost behavior of incentive commitments is unknown to senior management and the board.

With all of these design factors moving around, it can be difficult to divine what performance a company is paying for, how strongly, and under what circumstances. These important terms in companies' plans often consist of an accumulation of past, one-off design choices made in response to issues pressing on the company's incentive plans at the time. The result of these decisions, taken together, can be rife with unintended consequences. And the level of expense involved in executive incentives demands some cost analysis, not to mention cost/benefit analysis. That cannot be done without closely examining the inner workings of the plans.

A testing and simulation step should be included in the incentive design process. This step should address the precise workings of the company's plans, the connection between business results and the stock price, and cost and motivational effects across a wide range of possible business decisions and results. This is a key step when reviewing the costs, efficacy, and risks of incentive policy.

■ NOTES

1. Michael C. Jensen, "Corporate Budgeting Is Broken, Let's Fix It," *Harvard Business Review* (November 2001).
2. The Conference Board, "The Conference Board Task Force on Executive Compensation," 2009.
3. Capital increases often are phased in for ROIC measurement purposes, sometimes resulting in higher readings.
4. For an early application of investor expectation measurement to the matter of incentive target-setting, see Stephen F. O'Byrne, "EVA and Market Value," *Journal of Applied Corporate Finance* 9(1) (Summer 1996).
5. Simplified example assumes all corporate costs are fully allocated so unit earnings add up to consolidated earnings.
6. The residual value is equal to final-year FCF, increased by 1 percent, then divided by the cost of capital reduced by 1 percent; that is the present value of a perpetuity growing at a 1 percent per year rate (1 to 2 percent inflation has been a reasonable assumption in the United States much of the time for the past two decades).
7. These valuation methods are described further in Chapter 9.
8. Verbal source of Soviet incentive matrix idea: Mark Ubelhart. Verbal source of "beginning capital" EP method: Scott Olsen.

9. The examples used thus far have assumed that the variance of operating income around trend or budget is normally distributed. Our study of this actually finds the distribution to be somewhat leptokurtic, but we have used the normal distribution nonetheless as a reasonable and convenient approximation. Had we used the actual distributions, the bulk of our conclusions about incentive efficacy and the weakness of traditional methods would have been strengthened because there would have been more, larger, out-of-range observations.

10. Based on our annual incentive plan design studies.

CHAPTER 9

Business Units and Private Companies, Phantom Stock and Performance Plans

Most medium- and large-sized companies are not run entirely from a head office. They have at least three or four business units, and many have dozens or even hundreds of groups, divisions, profit centers, and joint ventures. In the case of a global food and beverage company, we put metrics and targets in place for over 90 profit centers. For these organizations, a single business unit rarely accounts for enough of the results of the parent company to drive them.

Nonetheless, business unit executives get incentive pay based mainly on corporate rather than business-unit results. Long-term incentive grants consist mostly of corporate stock and options. Performance units and shares often are based mostly on corporate goals. Annual bonuses most often reflect a mix of corporate and business unit results. A 50/50 weighting is most common, for a business-unit head. Corporate-level circuit breakers can lessen further the potential impact of unit results.

Overall, the typical business-unit incentive structure is several steps removed from one offering real line of sight (as we found in the simulation presented in Chapter 3):

- Results of a typical business unit are overwhelmed by results of other business units at consolidation time.

- Corporate actions can have big effects, too, raising worries about pay effects of overpriced acquisitions, failed reorganizations, and high levels of expense.

- Stock market volatility consistently clouds the linkage between business results and share prices.

In the far-flung organizations that comprise the bulk of the business world, management decisions taken at the business-unit level are critical to success. Yet, this is where incentives are the least effective. For many business unit executives, an industry competitor's stock has a stronger connection to the value of their own business unit than does that of their own diversified parent company.

Typical short-term bonus pay does not support an ownership mindset, either. Bonus plans may have flawed metrics, counterproductive target setting, schizophrenic award ranges, short-term bias, risk aversion, and, sometimes, risk indifference. The one thing that bonus plans do offer is relatively high line of sight. Considering the other issues, though, high line of sight is not always an advantage. Some of the avenues to bonus rewards involve the destruction of value. It is often better to leave that light under a bushel.

Companies believe that by dividing results between business unit and corporate results, they have created a kind of equality of interests—one that will win support for corporate initiatives and encourage enterprisewide resource sharing and teamwork. The company may achieve these things, but it will not have the bonus plan to thank. If your business unit is one-tenth of the corporation, one dollar fielded for the business unit is worth ten times as much as one for the corporation. In that game, the home team wins every time.

Even in a major group, business unit executives' own results typically drive 20 percent or less of overall incentive pay. The bulk of the value of most enterprises is found within their operating units. So are most of their executive decision makers and, arguably, most of the business decisions that might create value. This is the organizational level where incentive plans ought to be posing their strongest governance and performance effects. They are not, and that is a widespread, ongoing problem in business organizations.

Companies worry that business unit interdependencies will be harmed by separate-company pay. But many business units are fairly autonomous and separable. They are bought and sold all the time, after all. We do see greater usage of business-unit-level long-term incentives (LTI) in cases like ventures, U.S. affiliates of non-U.S. companies and recently acquired businesses. That suggests decision makers are paying some attention to autonomy.

Things like allocated costs and transfer prices are bugaboos, and so are the risks of adverse effects on teamwork and on support for corporate initiatives. Nonetheless, most companies do place some weight on unit results within bonus plans. When they do, they make the unit bonus plan the only element of incentive pay offering any line of sight. If business unit incentives were going to turn the place into a set of warring fiefdoms as a result, they would have done so a long time ago. The typical company should not fear that business-unit pay will open Pandora's box. It has been wide open for a long time, apparently with manageable consequences.

There sometimes are difficulties when managers move from one business to another. But turnover and mobility in senior management are not very high. Executive-level jobs are not occupied by tourists. When someone does make a job transfer, they may retain a trailing grant under a business-unit incentive plan or the grant may be cashed out or converted. That is a bit sticky but manageable.

Unit-level management usually knows more about their businesses than corporate management does. And, within the customary latitude of business unit governance, they are in a position to do more about it. Corporate managers should exploit this informational asymmetry. Without ceding any power, they easily could encourage business-unit managers to do some things they are not really paid to do now:

- Clearly identify their best business prospects.
- Demand the right resources, no more or less.
- Chase only profitable growth and distribute cash when appropriate.
- Balance risks and the long-term like an owner would.
- Chase business opportunities with entrepreneurial zeal.

Typical business unit managers are, in most instances, perfectly qualified candidates for the types of incentives recommended here. In some situations, a decisive money stake in business-unit financial results could be harmful—ones where interdependencies among units, or with corporate, are genuinely high, perhaps, or where the level of autonomy is very low. In these cases, a more limited set of value-driving goals may serve as a better basis for judging management's success than the overall financial results emphasized by most phantom stock and performance plans.

Usually, though, there is a clear gap between the pay structure that a typical business unit's circumstances warrant and the one that executives actually get. What serves investor interests best, in most cases, is to create within business-unit management a decisive financial interest in business success, one oriented toward value creation and toward the longer term.

PRIVATE COMPANIES

The situation of private companies is a lot like that of business units when it comes to long-term incentives. Many private companies hesitate to use actual shares as incentive currency due to a range of legal and funding concerns. At the same time, they often find that public companies are business competitors and rivals in the market for executive talent. They need to compete with the large equity-based incentive grants public companies make. When they do so, their design choices overlap strongly with those of business units.

Even when not concerned so acutely about competitive norms, they are interested in long-term incentive plans because they can help improve business results. A pay package of a given size is designed better, from an owner's viewpoint, if it has some long-term incentives in it. It involves more sustained financial results and more retention effect.

In private companies, owners are not the anonymous, fractional stakeholders depicted in the corporate governance tableau. On the contrary, they are often found right down the hall. And when you are spending too much of their money or otherwise disappointing them, they will often come right up to you and tell you what they think about it. *That* is shareholder activism.

Another thing that private companies have is substantive long-term incentive design experience. On the public company side, expense-free option accounting created a long moratorium on thinking, where LTI design is concerned. Public companies were never obliged to deliver much pay based on long-term goals or to confront fully the measurement, grant mix, and calibration complexities they can bring.

Only a minority of private companies used stock options or actual stock. Many did not pursue expense-free option accounting because they did not pursue bookkeeping tricks at all. There were no public shareholders to fool in the first place. Instead, they strove to run proper phantom stock plans and performance plans. They were pressed not only to compete with public company incentives. They also needed to stay on the good side of owners by being sure payouts were linked to shareholder returns and funded by financial performance. The best practices developed in this crucible can provide solutions for everyone, in the post-expensing era.

There are a number of ways to better encourage the critically important executives found in business units and in private companies. Solutions include phantom stock plans, performance plans and performance share plans that place heavy weight on business unit results. The design methods presented here, particularly for performance plans, are fully applicable at the corporate level in public companies.

PHANTOM STOCK AND SUBSIDIARY EQUITY

Phantom stock plans provide a useful starting point for a discussion of business unit and private company incentives. The range of phantom stock plans used in the market embodies the best and worst of incentive design. If designed well and used in the right setting, phantom stock can create a compelling economic stake in long-run value creation. This can increase greatly the efficacy of management incentives and contribute to success, all in a fiscally prudent and predictable way.

If designed badly or misapplied, a phantom stock plan can be confusing, ineffective, and internally controversial. Even worse, badly designed phantom plans can encourage business decisions that destroy shareholder value and subject the company to inappropriate levels of expense.

A discussion of phantom stock is also useful in illuminating key aspects of incentive plan design that affect other kinds of plans:

- The general structure of overlapping grants and long-run payouts used in other types of long-term incentives at the business unit and corporate levels.

- The potential impact of metrics on decision making.

- Approaches to setting goals and the role that expected performance plays when judging success and delivering pay.

- The strength of the connection of long-term rewards to actual results, with implications for line of sight and for plan funding.

The discussion of business unit long-term incentives focuses on phantom stock plans, but the findings are applicable to many subsidiary equity plans as well.

PHANTOM STOCK PLAN EXAMPLE USING TOTAL BUSINESS RETURN

We will look at an example of a phantom stock plan that uses a particular form of the performance/valuation measure called total business return (TBR).[1] The example in Exhibit 9.1 introduces key terms and features of phantom stock plans and sets up a "straw man" example against which to compare several alternatives cited later. TBR-based phantom stock also is, in its own right, a good solution for many situations. The following is an overview of the TBR phantom stock plan:

- *Basic plan mechanism.* A grant entitles the participant to the TBR generated by a block of stock. A $100,000 TBR phantom stock grant entitles the participant to the return generated by a $100,000 block of stock, in much the same way that a $100,000 option grant delivers the gains on $100,000 in shares. In this case, however, the grant is based on the value of the manager's own division or private company rather than on traded corporate shares.

- *Valuation and TBR computations.* TBR is used to measure the increase in the value of the business over a period of time, plus the free cash flows generated by its operations. For purposes of the plan, the business unit is

Performance Scenario				
Year	0	1	2	3
Operating Income After Tax (OI)	$100	$105	$120	$125
Capital	$1,000	$1,050	$1,100	$1,150
		Grant Term = 3 Years		

TBR Computation	
Total OI	$350
▲ Capital	$150
FCF	$200

Plus

▲ OI	$25
÷ WACC	10%
Value Gain	$250

Equals

TBR = $450

Award Computation	
TBR	$450
Beginning Value ($100/10%)	÷ $1,000
TBR %	45%
Phantom Stock Grant Size	$100,000
TBR %	× 45%
Payout Earned	$45,000

EXHIBIT 9.1   Phantom Stock Grant: Three-Year Example

valued at ten times income (defined as after-tax operating profit). That is, the business is valued using one of the simplest possible approaches: a fixed multiple of income. The TBR plan determines the company's value by making an estimate of how current, actual financial results—if they were to continue for a long time—would translate into a current valuation for the enterprise.[2]

EXHIBIT 9.2   TBR SCENARIO

	No-Growth	Medium	Hi-Growth
NOPAT Year 0	100	100	100
NOPAT Year 1	100	110	125
Beginning Value @ 10% Cost of Capital	1000	1000	1000
Capital Year 0	500	1000	750
Capital Year 1	465	1075	990
NOPAT Increase	0	10	25
Change in Value @ 10% Cost of Capital	0	100	250
Capital Increase	−35	75	240
FCF = NOPAT − Cap. Incr.	135	35	−115
TBR = Change in Value Plus FCF	135	135	135
TBR % of Beginning Value	13.5%	13.5%	13.5%
ROIC	22%	10%	13%
NOPAT Growth	0%	10%	25%

Exhibit 9.1 is a basic example of the plan mechanism. In the example, the business increases its income by $25 million, raising the value of the business by $250 million. It also generates $200 million in free cash flows, so its total business return is $450 million. TBR is 45 percent of beginning value, so the gain on a $100,000 grant is $45,000.

Thus participants share in value creation in a format using a simple valuation approach. This is a straightforward structure and one that offers:

- *Flexibility and consistency.* This form of TBR can take businesses with many different levels of risk, growth, and capital needs and evaluate their results on a roughly consistent footing. Exhibit 9.2 provides examples of companies with strongly differing levels of income growth and return on invested capital. TBR, however, indicates that each business is generating equal levels of return for shareholders. The *total return* format helps in benchmarking pay and performance and addresses many issues that confound traditional performance metrics.[3]

- *Alignment with value-creating business decisions.* Since business investments normally increase the level of capital used by a business unit, investment outlays by themselves reduce free cash flow. Returns on those investments should increase income over time, causing a tenfold increase in valuation. Therefore, ten dollars of new investment must generate at least one dollar of income—a 10 percent return, equal to the cost of capital—to break even in TBR terms.[4]

- *Long-term orientation.* The way to maximize gains under the plan is to max-imize TBR over the long run. One-time increases in income or reduc-tions of expense are valuable. Every dollar counts toward free cash flow (FCF) and TBR, just as it would for a business owner. However, sustain-able gains in income increase TBR by a factor of ten.

Key terms and features of the TBR phantom stock plan can be applied to many kinds of phantom stock and other long-term incentive plans:

- *Grant term.* Grants under plans of this type normally have a three- to five-year term, which is adequate in a prospective sense to directly encourage management's role in value creation. Longer grants—particularly in a formula-based plan like this TBR example—may allow plan liabilities to hit inappropriate levels.

- *Grant frequency.* The plan should last much longer than five years in most settings, but it does so through annual grants with vesting and maturity dates extending progressively into the future. End-to-end grants may encourage management to hype income in a big maturity year. Annual TBR grants, on the other hand, mean that management has a clear financial claim on results in every year of the near, me-dium, and long term.

- *Vesting.* Like other kinds of long-term incentives, these grants vest on a cliff or pro rata basis, most often over their three- to five-year terms.[5] As with other long-term incentives, unvested grants normally are forfeited on voluntary or involuntary termination. Death, disability, and retirement are circumstances in which grant vesting or payment may be accelerated.

- *Change in control.* Corporate stock and option grants normally provide accelerated vesting in the event of a change in control as well as implicit credit for stock price gains on the deal. Though TBR phantom stock grants are analogous in structure to stock-based ones, change in control terms are mixed and situational.

The TBR formula itself describes a default treatment for change in control. If a business unit with a TBR phantom stock grant is sold, the proceeds are treated as a reduction of capital. Income falls to zero, and so does the capitalized value of earnings, so a net TBR gain occurs to the extent the after-tax sale proceeds exceed the pre-deal value of prospective TBR. Participants generally are better off if the sale price is favorable in relation to the economic results that would otherwise have come in and rewarded them over the next few years. That is the same trade-off facing shareholders.

Strictly from an incentive viewpoint, it is a good idea to set change-in-control terms clearly. If the company is unlikely to be sold, but management is concerned about that possibility, then contractual change-in-control protections are a valuable kind of insurance that can be underwritten cheaply. If sale is likely, on the other hand, these provisions encourage management to sell at the best price.

TBR PHANTOM STOCK GRANT STRUCTURE AND LEVERAGE

Phantom stock plans are designed to compete with the equity-based incentive plans used by public companies, especially stock option grants. Phantom stock grants can also be structured like whole shares of stock so participants receive accrued returns on top of the beginning value per share.

Like restricted stock, full-value phantom shares have a greater per-share value than stock options at grant, which enables a company to grant fewer shares and still offer competitive grant value. These grants are used more often when retention concerns are particularly important. Appreciation-only grants—in which awards are based entirely on TBR performance and not on the beginning value—are used in most cases. This is because companies are often seeking to create optionlike performance and award leverage. Discounted grants are possible, too, along with grants that act like premium options, and pay out only when returns exceed some hurdle rate.

Exhibit 9.3 shows hypothetical payoffs on various grant structures that were examined by a realty subsidiary of a diversified company during the design of its incentives. The chart shows equally valued grants of full value phantom stock (exercise price at zero) and discounted phantom stock (exercise price at 50 percent of beginning value), as well as grants with exercise prices at current value and at a 25 percent premium to current value. The full-value phantom stock grant was valued at 90 percent of face value, while the premium, discounted, and standard grants were valued at 15 percent, 60 percent, and 30 percent, respectively.

The discounted and full value grants involve gains (and forfeitable grant value) at many different performance levels. The at-the-money and premium grants, in contrast, are more concerned with leverage and home-run potential. As the exhibit demonstrates, the exercise price on a phantom stock grant is a variable affecting plan leverage, retention power, and dilution. Companies should examine trade-offs like these when structuring phantom stock grants just as when structuring grants of real stock and options.

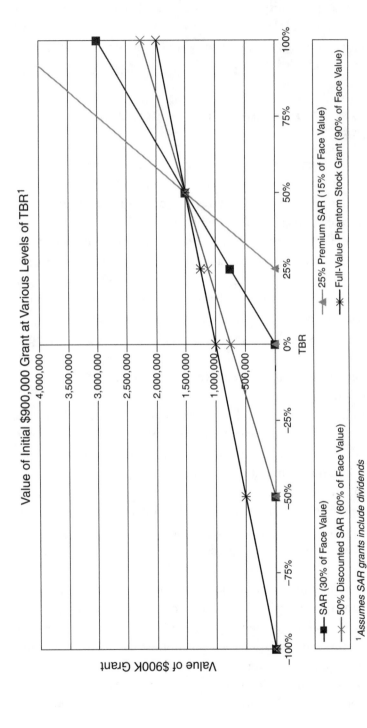

Value of Initial $900,000 Grant at Various Levels of TBR[1]

Value of $900K Grant

TBR

-100% -75% -50% -25% 0% 25% 50% 75% 100%

4,000,000
3,500,000
3,000,000
2,500,000
2,000,000
1,500,000
1,000,000
500,000

— SAR (30% of Face Value)

— 50% Discounted SAR (60% of Face Value)

— 25% Premium SAR (15% of Face Value)

— Full-Value Phantom Stock Grant (90% of Face Value)

[1] Assumes SAR grants include dividends

EXHIBIT 9.3   Setting Leverage: TBR Example

DILUTION GUIDELINES AND COMPETITIVE AWARD LEVELS

A general guideline for use in assessing dilution related to business unit and private company long-term incentives is to keep the face value of annual TBR grants in a range of between 0.5 and 2 percent of company value per year. This is based on typical grant structure, market benchmarking for long-term incentive grants and participant group sizes, with the assumption that business unit long-term incentive grants are the only form of long-term incentive grant made to business unit executives. Companies should keep in mind that other incentive plans—ones at the group or corporate level—may pose financial claims on the results of a given division and thereby enlarge the footprint of incentive costs on business results.

Companies should regard these grant guidelines as an upper limit and not a grant pool. They should set individual award levels based on their own market objectives, competitive norms, and the expected value of the specific financial claims they are creating within the incentive plan.

As a general guideline, a typical five-year grant of TBR-based phantom stock is worth 30 to 40 percent of face value; about what typical option grants are worth.[6] This TBR grant lasts only five years so, holding all else equal, it should be worth less than a ten-year option grant. Offsetting this is the fact that vanilla TBR grants accrue gains from the first dollar of income gain (or free cash flow), while option gains normally hinge on the market's higher expectations for performance. Full-value TBR phantom stock grants tend to be worth around 100 percent of face value.

A company's market value may be far higher than the value indicated by a formula like the one used in this version of TBR. However, this does not mean that phantom stock plan gains under a market-valuation approach will be higher than those under a TBR plan. For a typical company, a TBR phantom stock plan would be expected to generate grant gains at an annual rate of 10 to 15 percent per year. Market-based plans would be expected to generate gains at a more modest rate equal to the cost of capital, but against a larger grant size (e.g., 10 percent of a higher valuation). Either approach delivers customary and reasonable levels of gain for good performance as long as grants are competitively sized in present value terms.

Stock-based incentive grants, when compared to TBR grants based on business-unit results, offer easier administration in certain regards. Stock gains are struck only at the corporate level. Overall granting levels and impacts are easily measured and benchmarked.[7] The greater incentive power of well-designed phantom stock, where fitting, outweighs its higher administrative complexity. At the same time, companies need to be diligent in these matters to avoid unintended levels of dilution. One technique these safeguards rely on is the practice of annual granting, in prudent amounts.

VALUATION APPROACHES FOR THE PHANTOM STOCK PLAN

One of the key requirements of a phantom stock plan is to determine the company's value from time to time. The TBR formula described earlier is just one example of a valuation approach for a phantom stock plan. Many businesses with phantom stock plans simply have their shares valued by an outside expert in order to determine share valuation and gains. They are unlisted companies, for the most part—business units and closely held companies—so they cannot get a stock market quote on their shares.

Market valuation is used more often when the plan uses actual shares rather than phantom stock. The market-value approach allows companies to have equity-based incentives that work in a way most similar to the option and stock grants used by public companies, aligning gains more closely with actual market value than a formula-based plan would do. Liquidity is not as great as with public company options or stock, since shares typically are valued at annual intervals (sale constraints limit liquidity in the public company sector as well). Some companies incorporate quarterly and even daily valuation into their plans by pegging their share prices to those of publicly traded peers. (Exercisability is a more achievable feature under I.R.C. section 409A, generally speaking, when share value is determined by market valuation. Note that dividend payments can complicate this.)

When companies go down the market valuation path, they should use an independent valuation expert. This avoids the administrative difficulty and potential conflicts that an internal market valuation process might engender. Outside valuation can add significant costs. However, having shares valued makes sense in a range of settings. The market-value approach is often chosen when the company is obliged to have shares valued periodically anyway for investor reporting, buy/sell agreements, or to enable use of nonquoted stock in a qualified retirement plan. It can also make sense in private companies that expect to go public within a few years. In some cases, the company may be growing so rapidly or have such volatile or uncertain prospects that a formula-based approach is not seen as useful.

In many other settings, however, market value simply is regarded as a more complete and accurate way of judging management's contribution to value creation and therefore a better basis for delivering incentive gains. Of course, that is the *de facto* stance of so many public companies that use options and other kinds of stock-based incentives as the centerpiece of their incentive structure.

In the stages preceding an initial public offering (IPO), some companies determine their share prices using market appraisals. Use of incentive stock options—tax-qualified stock options under U.S. law—may encourage them to do a good job of documenting the market value used for option exercise prices at the time of grant. Also, the Securities and Exchange Commission (SEC) has looked closely at the valuation basis for option exercise prices in public offerings of subsidiary shares, to ensure an accurate portrayal of separate-company incentive costs.

Where formula-based valuations are concerned, most companies administer these on their own, often with some input from outside advisors. Formula-based plans require adjustment from time to time. However, these are limited in scope and tend to focus on the treatment of specified events, ideally within guidelines established at the time of plan design. Market valuation, however, is compelled to address a broad range of matters affecting future business prospects and risks. This can require many subjective adjustments, creating many potential areas of argument between parent and subsidiary. Often, it is best assigned to an outside expert.

Market Valuation Techniques

Two methods used most often in market valuation of closely held businesses are market comparison approaches and discounted cash flow valuation.

Market Comparison Approach

Under this method, stock prices of comparable public companies are used as evidence of the value of a private company. Recent sales of similar companies—whether in private market transactions or public company takeovers—are reviewed as well, along with available data on any relevant asset sales or licenses (e.g., sale of bank core deposits). Capitalization multiples are then compiled, ones relating various measures of business performance and scale to company valuation. Some examples are:

- Market value of capital to sales, gross margins, capital, operating income, or cash flow, or EBITDA (earnings before depreciation, interest, and taxes)
- Market value of equity to net income, equity cash flow, or book value of equity

A multiple for the subject company is determined based on how it compares to companies in the peer group in terms of the quality of its performance and other factors driving its economic earning power. We examined these dynamics closely in Chapters 2 and 8. This process may result in a valuation at, above, or below the median of the peer group multiples.

Discounted Cash Flow Valuation[8]

We examined this method as well in Chapters 2 and 8. A detailed forecast is developed for the company's financial results, typically for a period of five to ten years. Cash flows distributable from operations—free cash flow that can be paid out of the company after satisfying its reinvestment needs—are computed for each forecast year and then discounted to present value at a discount rate that takes into account the company's degree of business risk. The "residual" value of the company—that part of its value that is based on cash flows expected in years beyond the forecast term—is estimated as well and discounted to present value. The overall value of the enterprise is equal to the present value of free cash flows during the forecast term, plus the present value of the residual.

Results of different market valuation methods are normally studied together in a process of reconciliation. This makes sure the basic drivers of value in the industry and the company's own performance and prospects are reflected properly in the overall value. If the compensation program requires a determination of the price per common share, this is computed by doing the following:

- Subtracting debt and preferred stock value from enterprise value, leaving the value of common equity
- Assuming there is a single class of common stock, per share value is computed by dividing the overall value of common equity by the number of outstanding common shares

DISCOUNTS FOR LACK OF MARKETABILITY AND CONTROL

The valuation may be adjusted further in a private company situation. In particular, the share price may be reduced by a liquidity discount, or discount for lack of marketability. Relevant benchmarks for this discount have for many years ranged widely but averaged about 35 percent of the share price.[9] Some marketability discount applies at the time of a private placement, for example, since shares at that time do not enjoy the full liquidity of publicly traded ones. Any such discount would be small, however, since private placements tend to be undertaken in cases in which a liquidity event such as an IPO, resale, or redemption is expected within a few years. The premise of the valuation normally is a minority interest, so a minority discount also may be needed to reverse out any control premium implied by the discounted cash flow valuation scenario or by market data on any control transactions of comparable companies.

The valuations used to determine IPO prices tend to be stated on an "as if public" or "when issued" basis with no so discount subtracted. As a practical matter, however, much analysis of share price and investment returns that is done in pre-IPO and private placement situations takes no explicit account of discounts for lack of marketability or minority interest status. Rather, analysis tends to focus on eventual share price valuation in a future IPO or sale and on cash flows during the holding period, backing into levels of estimated return based on the price to be paid now. Effects of marketability and control—as well as their risks—presumably are addressed within the structuring of these financing transactions as well as in the investment returns expected from them.

VALUATION ACCURACY VERSUS INCENTIVE EFFICACY

Specific trade-offs affect the decision of whether to use market valuation or a formula-based method to value a business for incentive purposes The valuation method—the connection between management actions, business results, and rewards—is, after all, the engine of the phantom stock or nonpublic equity plan.

Market valuation is the most accurate approach, better in terms of valuation accuracy and timeliness than the alternatives that compose the balance of this section. However, market valuation can be the approach with the highest administrative cost due to the appraisal fees involved. It also tends to involve the lowest degree of line of sight—the least tangible perceived connection between what incentive plan participants can do, how it might affect market valuation, and what they might get paid. Gains under many stock-based plans are unconnected to business unit management's actions for two main reasons:

1. Business units often don't have much influence on overall results.
2. Stock prices move around for many reasons unrelated to consolidated performance, particularly during the one- to five-year time frame that matters so greatly within an incentive plan.

Using a business unit equity plan—whether based on phantom or actual equity—addresses the first and more serious of these issues by focusing on performance and value creation at the business unit level. However, if market value is used as the basis for reward, the second problem may persist. The plan will reflect not only the results produced by the business unit, but also the vagaries of market valuation. Valuation formulas, by contrast, link rewards directly with actual business results, not with the unrelated portion of market stock price movement. The TBR plan, specifically, is driven by the portion of value creation that management can affect (income and capital) without a lot of susceptibility to market factors (e.g., shifts in the cost of capital or in market expectations for future performance).

Companies wishing to impose clearer and more compelling linkages between actions, success, and pay often pursue one or another of the formulaic alternatives to market valuation. These companies offer fully competitive long-term incentives. At the same time, they achieve other design goals like providing clear line of sight in their incentive plans and linking pay strongly with actual results over the long run. Formula-based approaches, properly structured, also have a funding advantage. In such cases, costs can be calibrated closely because actual income and cash flow levels drive value and incentive payouts.

RECONCILING AND FUNDING MARKET VALUE AND FORMULA VALUE

When well constructed, valuation formulas align with market value over time. The difference between market value and a typical formula valuation is greatest when company valuation diverges greatly from a modest multiple of current earnings. When a company expects exceptionally high growth, current earnings are very low in relation to expected future earnings. At such times, valuation multiples are high. A low multiple usually means earnings are regarded as slow-growth, unsustainable, or especially risky. Free cash flow enters into the equation as well. Companies with highly distributable earnings tend to be valued, all else equal, at higher multiples.[10]

These valuation gaps subside over time as the company's actual performance plays out. When multiples are particularly high, for example, they often reflect hopes for income growth expected over the next few years.[11] The formula-based plan, in such a case, will show a rapid rise in value as income actually grows. It tracks value and returns over time in proportions similar to those indicated by market appraisal. In these high-growth cases, care must be taken that the run-up in earnings does not distort the formula valuation or cause inappropriate payouts. Here are some examples of how companies addressed these issues:

- A start-up subsidiary expected high levels of growth in earnings and cash flow, ones likely to cause the company's cash-flow-based valuation to rise greatly over time. The company simply made lower grants than it otherwise would have, ones still competitive in present value terms since their prospective gains made them quite valuable.

- A travel and marketing services company expected a big rebound in earnings from the levels prevailing just before adoption of a TBR plan. The beginning capital level was used as a representation of value at the outset rather than capitalizing an earnings level seen as a low outlier.

Big differences between the market-based and formula approaches lie in the timing of value creation and the standard of proof applied. The former approach follows a market value rule, connecting pay with timely and accurate market values. The latter connects it with value-creating financial performance only as it is earned. The formula-based plan effectively says to management, "Show me the money." This is a reasonable demand in view of senior management's decision-making role and the medium- to long-term time frame of many of their actions.

The distinction between market and formula valuation is important to plan funding as well. Market valuation can increase phantom stock gains well beyond a level warranted by current financial results. That means plan costs may become intolerably high in relation to company earnings and the company's current ability to pay. And, if financial results eventually disappoint, market-based plans may have paid out big gains based on anticipated performance that did not happen.

Public companies face these same concerns with option and stock plans, since the costs are borne by owners in the form of cash used to repurchase shares, of share dilution, or both. But for nonpublic companies or business units, gains normally must be paid in cash, so funding can be a more acute concern. Formula valuations tend to tie plan expense accruals and payouts more closely to company earnings and cash flows, lessening the concerns about funding.

This linkage to actual results is not foolproof. Financial results can be volatile, hard to interpret, and subject to manipulation in the short term. It is risky to have a lot of money riding on any one year's results, for example, and well-designed plans do not. Suitable terms can ensure plan gains and costs align closely with value creation over time:

- Making multiyear grants—typically between three and five years in overall length—so pay is based on sustained performance. Limiting grants to five or six years is prudent to prevent liabilities from compounding beyond anticipated levels and to prevent large batches of exercisable grants from overhanging the results of any one future year.

- Using annual granting and multiyear vesting, so that exercise or maturity dates are spread over several years.

- Using the ending value each year as the basis for cash-out and also for setting the exercise price for future grants. This has a ratcheting effect on goals, requiring that gains in earnings be sustained to deliver high payouts on many grants over time.

- Administering grants with close attention to annual share usage. As mentioned earlier, grants amounting to between 0.5 to 2 percent of value annually tend to keep plan liabilities in reasonable proportion to owner gains while providing competitive grants to a normally-sized management participant group.

- Subtracting plan cost accruals or share dilution effects before calculating earnings and share value. This procedure smoothes out fluctuations in income, valuation, and plan gains, particularly when grant overhang is high. Absent the subtraction, large increases in income and value could cause plan costs to spike.

So, the important choice between market versus formula valuation is not simply a question of the cost of annual appraisals. Rather, the choice also may depend on factors like applicability of valuation formulas, timing of when value creation is recognized, funding and cost concerns, and the overall effect on line of sight and plan design efficacy.

Anti-dilution clauses are needed irrespective of which valuation method is used. These can take a range of forms. The FCF computation involved in TBR is one example. It tracks the investor money going into and out of a business. A $100 million capital infusion by itself simply reduces TBR by $100 million, so management is affected by dilution in proportion to that felt by owners. Capital transactions can also affect share value through share issuance or redemption, real or phantom. Another solution is simply to subtract net capital infusions from any value gain, as in the *net gain* format used in incentive plans of some corporate start-ups. In plans based on the value of equity, these matters can be adjustments to *net debt*, or debt net of cash, which is subtracted from enterprise value.

MARKET-INDEXED AND PERFORMANCE-BASED VALUATION FORMULAS

Some companies use indexing to produce a daily or weekly share valuation in a private company. For one window manufacturer, for example, shares undergo a full valuation annually using a traditional appraisal process. Values are updated daily based on movement in an index of industry peers, with new financial data on the company and its peers used to reset valuations on a quarterly basis.

Indexing can be used as a valuation method by itself. Market-indexed valuation provides a kind of compromise between formula valuation and market valuation. In one simple example, the company is valued at a multiple of income determined by an industry peer group. This method gives management directly observable credit for improving results (income) while also being responsive to valuation trends for similar companies.

More complex formulas may be devised to address specific business circumstances. A privately held catalog retailer valued itself based on a market-determined multiple of earnings or revenue, whichever was higher. This enabled the company to bear downturns in profitability related to marketing campaigns geared toward longer-run business growth.

The incentive context in which indexing is applied most often is in incentive plans in which awards are earned (or vested or accelerated) based on relative total shareholder return (TSR). These plans normally are used by public companies that can measure their TSR from a stock market perspective. (Comments on this method appear in Chapter 10.)

Since indexed methods normally involve multiples based on explicit performance measures like revenue, EBITDA, or income, they provide some explicit instructions on how to create value. For example, increasing income typically increases value. This is a positive attribute in terms of line of sight. Still, this area requires great care. The indexing algorithms, if badly designed, can create many situations where management is paid for poor performance. Also note that indexers bear market-value-based repurchase liabilities while still private. These costs may or may not be funded easily by current financial results.

Valuation multiples used in incentive plans can be made to vary not only based on market movements, but on company performance. Exhibit 9.4 is an example used in a captive finance subsidiary of a manufacturer. This company's phantom shares are valued as a multiple of earnings, but the multiple varies based on net income and return on equity.

The multiples were established by:

- Performing statistical analysis of peer company valuation multiples, isolating the incremental impact of return on equity (ROE) and earnings growth on price-earnings (P/E) ratios. This analysis provided the target multiple, helped set target performance levels, and guided the general range of valuation multiples to be used.

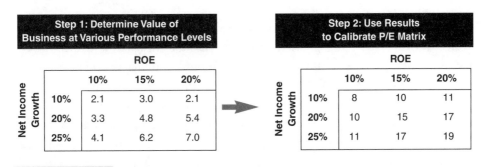

EXHIBIT 9.4   TBR and Incentive Design: Phantom Stock Based on P/E Ratio

- Constructing a discounted cash flow model that syncs up financial performance scenarios with the range of multiples indicated by the regression analysis. The exact P/E multiples used to populate the matrix were generated by running scenarios of the discounted cash flow (DCF) model.

This general approach can be applied to many industries and metrics. An example in the independent power industry featured valuation multiples earned based on operating cash flow and gross capital usage. As in the case of the captive financier, valuation multiples were generated using discounted cash flow scenarios, ones that set the company's value at each performance scenario (i.e., at each cell in the valuation matrix). The high-growth, low-capital scenarios involved larger free cash flows and bigger gains in income and, therefore, higher valuations.

At the same time, these methods require that high performance be sustained over a period of years and that related valuation gains be proved, in effect, before being fully rewarded. The valuation scenarios satisfied both these requirements:

- They allowed for multiple expansion and contraction. This involved a forecast assumption that a company with high earnings growth would be able to continue that growth for a time.[12]
- They used those higher expectations as conditions for payouts on later grants. If expectations were not met, multiples would contract.

This method picks up the stock market's expected-performance dynamic without the market noise. In each of these scenarios, business valuations could expand greatly based on actual results. So each of these plans delivered potentially strong award leverage and payouts. Compared to the fixed-multiple approach used in most TBR plans, these methods are a bit more like market valuation, allowing for the possibility that a high-performing business could attract a high valuation multiple, one well ahead of its current performance level.

The upside and its fiscal risks are moderated by higher performance expectations and the ratcheting goals they create. Under this plan and other well-designed ones, payouts are not persistently high unless management consistently beats reasonable performance expectations. Those are the circumstances under which companies create extraordinary amounts of value for owners. Those are the only circumstances warranting extraordinarily high incentive awards for management. A pure market valuation-based plan, in contrast, or one simply using a high, fixed valuation multiple may pay out systematically for growth expectations that are never attained.

Companies sometimes wish to create wide play in valuations and gains as a way to create greater plan leverage and motivational power. In such cases, performance-based adjustments can be a more prudent path than a market-indexed plan since the latter may write a blank check based on the market's vagaries.

EBITDA AS A VALUATION YARDSTICK

EBITDA is used commonly in some industries as a valuation yardstick. It tends to be strongly related to enterprise value. It is quoted commonly in buy/sell contexts. As discussed in Chapter 6, EBITDA is also referred to as pretax operating cash flow (the "A" is a vestigial feature since goodwill amortization was discontinued under generally accepted accounting principles [GAAP]). Phantom stock plans using EBITDA normally value the enterprise at a multiple between five and ten. Multiples are often fixed, but sometimes are indexed to a comparable set of companies. Gains or losses in value normally are adjusted by adding free cash flow (FCF) or by subtracting net debt at each valuation date. In the latter case, the result is an equity valuation rather than a valuation of the overall enterprise.

EBITDA should be used with care within incentive plans. It does not take account of the financial claims that taxes and asset replacement can pose on owner income, so it does not provide enough information to judge whether a particular business decision creates value. EBITDA-based formulas may encourage the company to make investments with low, value-destroying economic yields.

For example, if a company is valued at eight times EBITDA, then an investment that reduces FCF by $1 million (or increases net debt by $1 million) would have to produce EBITDA of $125,000 to break even in terms of total return. So the formula in that case would impose a threshold EBITDA yield on new investment of 12.5 percent per year.[13]

In this example, EBITDA is computed before taxes and before any provision for recapture of investment in wasting assets (e.g., before depreciation charges). To increase value, a company needs to get returns on investment at least equal to its cost of capital. A 12.5 percent return, once adjusted for taxes and for recapture of most kinds of depreciating assets, is not high enough to create value and may actually be negative.

Such plans directly reward management for many kinds of value-destroying decisions, particularly in the short term before short-lived assets reach their replacement dates. Lower EBITDA multiples reduce these risks, but many of them remain a concern even with multiples as low as four or five.

EQUITY-BASED INCENTIVE PLANS BASED ON BOOK VALUE

Small-company phantom stock plans sometimes use book value as the basis for valuation. This is also the method used, in effect, in many professional services firms owned by partners or principals. Book-value plans typically reward the participant for increasing stockholders' equity accounts by accumulating earnings for shareholders. They may pay dividends as well.

Like the TBR approach, this method is based on actual financial results, accreting value only to the extent they have been achieved. However, book value gains do not take into account whether participants have increased the earning power of the business during the measurement period. Rather, they simply reward accumulation of earnings irrespective of whether earnings are rising or falling. Falling earnings tend to mean a falling valuation, so these plans carry the risk of paying out substantial rewards even if performance suggests destruction of value. They also may underreward companies with value-creating earnings growth.

Book-value plans do not necessarily attach a complete or consistent cost to the use of capital and may reward results that do not create value. Since book earnings drive book value plans, they reflect the hodgepodge of issues involved when computing equity-based metrics such as net income, earnings per share (EPS), or ROE. They may ignore any cost for the use of equity capital, miss the impact of financial leverage on that cost, or both. Like other dangerously incomplete methods, book value plans offer the advantage of being simple and familiar.

Phantom and subsidiary equity plans usually have anti-dilution clauses protecting plan participants and sponsors from some serious risks:

- They protect against the possibility that the business's owners will pay out a lot of money in dividends or otherwise withdraw capital, reducing earning power and value.

- Correspondingly, they prevent capital infusions from inadvertently enriching participants.

TALE OF THREE CITIES

The nature of the business certainly has some impact on incentive design. Often, though, companies in the same sector will make different choices. The controller of a volatile phosphate business, for example, reviewed incentive norms from peer proxy statements and found they were all handling the same volatility issue in different ways.

Three energy-generation companies provide an example of the range of choices here. The first was a wholly owned subsidiary of a utility. It put in a phantom stock plan whose valuation was driven by performance as tracked by cash flow from operations and cash flow return on gross investment. Payouts were calibrated based on scenarios of a DCF model.

A stand-alone public company chose to measure results based on the value-based metric cash value added (CVA). A third, a 50/50 venture between an electric utility and a private investment fund, actually designed three approaches:

1. A cash performance plan based on return on invested capital (ROIC) that crashed due to misspecified standards

2. A market-value-based phantom stock plan that ran into unusual technical hurdles

3. A formula based phantom stock plan using an EBITDA multiple

And, along the way, it seriously considered book value. In another case, a private company reviewed many designs and targeting approaches in its efforts to apply some consistency across its varied businesses.

Once you know a company's industry, you know a lot about its challenges and prospects. But there are still many unique and genuine considerations that may affect its incentive design choices. We just saw three companies in the same sector make different decisions about incentive design. Leadership's preferences often have a driving role, with company experience with past pay plans often being a decisive factor.

ADJUSTING VALUATION RESULTS

Whether value is determined by appraisal or formula, care must be taken to see that the earnings base being capitalized into value is representative of continuing earning power, not distorted by temporary blips or downturns. In indexed plans, the same needs to be true of the multiple arising from the peer group. This tends to be less of an issue since peer-group composite multiples are less volatile than company income. Peer multiples are often computed as a peer group's average or median (the interquartile mean is available as well as evidence of central tendency).

Further smoothing in the market-indexed plan design, as well as many others, may be accomplished through devices such as the following:

- Capitalizing trailing average earnings of the company and its peers
- Establishing alternative minimum or maximum valuations based on net assets, equity, sales, and so on
- Placing a maximum range on capitalization multiples or on rates of valuation movement per measurement period ("collaring")

These adjustments tend to spread out the timing of price movements, making them depend more fully on sustained financial results without limiting the valuation ultimately attained. Current earnings or cash flows can be adjusted directly if they contain a large temporary or one-time element.

In these cases, the *total return* format of many formulas provides guidance on how to adjust. Acquisition outlays, or one-time losses, for example, tend to run through the FCF computation only—all at once or over two or three years—so that management's performance in TBR terms reflects these hits only once in total. In contrast, general variation in income has a capitalized, multiple impact on valuation, since it tends to affect not only the current year but also income expectations going forward. The plan's general architecture (e.g., overlapping multiyear grants, iterative subtraction of plan accruals from income) does a lot to regularize gains over time.

Financial results may need adjustment to deal with unusual company circumstances. One of the energy companies mentioned earlier provides an example. The company held various percentage interests in many power plant investments. Consolidation rules could have distorted measurements of capital, pulling all the debt of a 51 percent-owned investee onto the books while eliminating all the debt of a 49 percent-owned venture. We devised a proportional consolidation approach for this company's incentive plan, one in which its capital levels reflected its exact percentage share both of investee assets and obligations.

The captive finance company's incentive plan provided another example of how a company's circumstances may require an adjustment. The measures used in the plan—net income and return on equity—are ones affected by variations in financial leverage. This factor was a potential source of volatility and bias within the plan, so results were restated pro forma to reflect a targeted, fixed capital structure. A similar plan used in a district power business, on the other hand, had no such provision since management insisted that debt levels were fixed by certain financing constraints. Shortly after implementation, management figured out a way to overcome those constraints, greatly increasing the plan's gains as a result. The parent company promptly canceled the plan. In that case, everyone involved would have been better off if the plan had been adjusted in some reasonable way as we had recommended.

PERFORMANCE PLANS

Performance plans are the other main type of long-term incentive plan used in business units and private companies. These plans come in two main varieties:

1. *Performance unit plans.* Also known as performance cash plans, these provide cash awards based on attaining long-term performance goals.

Basically like bonus plans in structure, they tend to be based entirely on financial performance in relation to preset goals, to have finite payout ranges, and to be based mainly on corporate-level performance. When we cite performance plans and performance shares as business–unit incentives, we are referring to plans whose metrics are set at least partly on business unit results. The term performance "unit" refers to the fact that some such plans have in the past been denominated in "units" whose value might vary based on financial performance, inflation, or other factors.

2. *Performance share plans.* These allow participants to earn shares of the parent company based on attainment of preset goals. These basically are performance unit plans denominated in shares rather than cash. They provide a fairly straightforward means of encouraging long-run success for business units. At the same time, by using stock, they maintain a firm link to parent company success. If subsidiary shares are available for use in an incentive plan, then these may be delivered in a performance–share format as well.

Performance plans have much in common with phantom stock. Their general architecture involves many features of phantom equity or subsidiary equity plans like overlapping grants, staggered vesting, and maturity dates and, when designed well, proper connections between financial performance and executive rewards.

We do not need to embark on a fresh discussion of the ingredients of performance plan design at this point. Rather, the steps in performance plan design already have been covered in this book's earlier discussions of metric selection, target setting and range setting, and the term and vesting of long-term incentive grants.

Performance plans can emphasize value creation in the same terms as a phantom plan that uses a valuation formula. The TBR-based phantom stock plan presented earlier can be converted into an equivalent performance plan, as one example. This approach involves the following:

- Making performance plan grants each year, ones with a total term of three to five years and either ratable or cliff vesting (overlapping three-year cycles are by far the most common approach for performance plans)

- Setting up an award schedule involving a linear connection between TBR and cash payout, with zero payment at zero TBR and a long interval on the upside

In the example in Exhibit 9.5, awards are earned based on earnings before interest and taxes (EBIT) and ROIC. Payouts are set in 1:1 scale to TBR.

EXHIBIT 9.5   **TBR-BASED PAYOUT SCHEDULE**

TBR at Each Performance Level

	20.0%	452	820	1,084	1,281	1,435	1,579	1,694
Three-Year	**16.0%**	350	683	921	1,099	1,238	1,369	1,472
Compound	**13.0%**	278	586	805	970	1,099	1,219	1,315
EBIT	**10.0%**	208	492	695	**847**	966	1,077	1,165
Growth	**7.0%**	142	404	590	730	839	942	1,023
	4.0%	79	319	491	619	719	813	888
	0.0%	–	213	366	480	569	653	719
		12.5%	**15.0%**	**17.5%**	**20.0%**	**22.5%**	**25.5%**	**28.5%**

Three-Year Average ROIC, After Tax

Payout as a % of Target (and TBR as a % of Target)

	20.0%	55%	95%	130%	150%	170%	185%	200%
Three-Year	**16.0%**	40%	80%	110%	130%	145%	160%	175%
Compound	**13.0%**	35%	70%	95%	115%	130%	145%	155%
EBIT	**10.0%**	25%	60%	80%	**100%**	115%	125%	135%
Growth	**7.0%**	15%	50%	70%	85%	100%	110%	120%
	4.0%	10%	40%	60%	75%	85%	95%	105%
	0.0%	0%	25%	45%	55%	65%	75%	85%
		12.5%	**15.0%**	**17.5%**	**20.0%**	**22.5%**	**25.5%**	**28.5%**

Three-Year Average ROIC, After Tax

Here is how it works. First, we figure out what TBR is at each level in the TBR performance matrix. Exhibit 9.6 shows the TBR computation for the targeted performance level and the threshold and maximum levels.

Targeted EBIT growth is 10 percent per year and ROIC at target averages 20 percent. At this target performance level, TBR is $847 million:

- EBIT after taxes grows at 10 percent per year from $160 million to $213 million. Using a 10 percent cost of capital, this $53 million income gain is valued at $530 million for TBR purposes.

- FCF is $318 million. Year 3 EBIT is $213 million, so if ROIC is 20 percent then ending capital is $1,065 million ($213/20 percent = $1,065). Capital rose by $265 million from its initial $800 million level.

- Cumulative after-tax EBIT of $583 million, minus the $265 million change in capital, equals FCF of $318 million. TBR is $847 million, equal to the gain in value plus FCF.

The top performance scenario has TBR at twice the targeted level. Payout for this performance level is set at twice target. TBR at threshold is 100 percent below target, earning a zero payout. Other scenarios drive payouts similarly,

EXHIBIT 9.6	TBR DETAILS AT TARGET, MAXIMUM, AND THRESHOLD PERFORMANCE		
	Threshold	**Target**	**Maximum**
Growth in EBIT	0.0%	10.0%	20.0%
After-Tax Return on Invested Capital	12.5%	20.0%	28.5%
Operating Income (After Fixed Tax Rate)			
Year 0	160	160	160
Year 1	160	176	192
Year 2	160	194	230
Year 3	160	213	276
Change in OI After-Tax	–	53	116
Change in Value (@ 10% WACC)	–	530	1,165
Beginning Capital	800	800	800
Ending Capital (Based on ROIC)	1,280	1,065	970
Change in Capital	480	265	170
Cumulative OI After-Tax	480	583	699
Minus: Change in Capital	480	265	170
Equals: Free Cash Flow	–	318	529
TBR = Change in Value Plus FCF	–	847	1,694

with 50 percent above-target TBR leading to a payout at 50 percent above target, and so on.

This example creates a one-for-one linkage between TBR and pay, and it does so across a wide range of performance levels. If payouts at target were $8.5 million, for example, they would represent 1 percent of TBR at target and at every other performance level.

The plan's matrix format is a bit complex, but many plans use payout tables with two driving metrics. The plan's basic payout and performance ranges can be set out as simply as shown in Exhibit 9.7.

TBR is driven by FCF and operating income, and the plan just examined can be described just as easily in those terms. The target payout of $8.5 million equals 1 percent of FCF plus 10 percent of the change in after-tax operating income. The same formula gives the payout at every performance level. If a columnar table were preferred, then payouts could be shown for various levels of operating income and FCF, in a simple two-column schedule. Operating income and capital usage could be arrayed the same way, with payouts predicted by a formula or set out in a simple table. Under any of these methods, payouts would be governed by the same underlying connections between TBR and value.

If a company captures basic economic trade-offs like these and applies them to pay, it will have a better functioning rewards structure than most.[14] This example happens to be struck at the business-unit level, but the technique applies equally at the corporate level. Performance plan designs do not always capture the key economic trade-offs. In fact, typical performance plans are bedeviled by

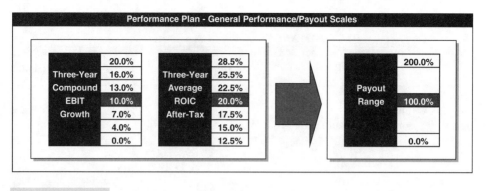

EXHIBIT 9.7   **Performance Plan: General Performance/Payout Scales**

the same design issues that affect bonus plans. Their traditional metrics and negotiated targets create a range of situations in which management can be paid well for decisions that actually destroy value.

An example of a traditional design of a performance plan, using the same operating income and ROIC metrics used earlier, can be seen in Exhibit 9.8. In this case, payout ranges are set in typical symmetrical fashion against the performance ranges used earlier. This matrix works exactly the same way as another traditional format—separate payout schedules for the ROIC and OI metrics, weighing each equally in the overall payout computation.

Note that 100 percent payouts are possible in both the top-left and lower-right corners of the schedule (most payout percentages are omitted, for simplicity). But we know from the TBR analysis that those scenarios have very different results for owners. The upper-left corner has very high income growth, which certainly is valuable. But it was accompanied by very high new capital demands in the business, ones that generated very poor returns (even after taking into

		Payout as a % of Target (and TBR as a % of Target)						
		12.5%	15.0%	17.5%	20.0%	22.5%	25.5%	28.5%
Three-Year Compound EBIT Growth	20.0%	100%			150%			200%
	16.0%		100%			150%		
	13.0%			100%			150%	
	10.0%	50%			100%			150%
	7.0%		50%			100%		
	4.0%			50%			100%	
	0.0%	0%			50%			100%

Three-Year Average ROIC, After Tax

EXHIBIT 9.8   **Typical Payout Calibration Example**

account the phase-ins commonly used to buffer the impact of big investments and mergers and acquisitions). This is miserable economic performance. The rate of return on the huge new outlays is only 5 percent. But it pays out at 100 percent in the traditionally arrayed matrix.

The opposite corner also pays out 100 percent, this time since it has zero income growth but maximum ROIC. To get to that ROIC level, however, the company had to pay out enormous FCF from operations—as in a very favorable divestiture. We saw similar issues in the "two wrongs make a right" example in Chapter 6. The traditional plan does not recognize this, though, again because it ignoring the decisive effects that capital usage has on value creation. Goal-based incentives should be set carefully. Even this traditional-looking example can skew decision-making strongly and under many circumstances.

VALUE-BASED INCENTIVES VERSUS PRIVATE EQUITY INCENTIVES

Companies financed by private equity are an interesting category of private company to consider. They take positions in ordinary businesses and sometimes turn them into great performance for investors, so their incentive practices warrant some attention. High performance has not been a persistent rule for the private equity sector, of course. When it occurs, though, it sometimes is attributed to closer governance by the owner group and to more effective incentives for senior management. Equity participation tends to be limited to a few top officers who are committed for the duration of the deal.

The long-term incentive stakes created in a business financed by private equity, in contrast to more typical approaches, tend to be:

- Tied to events—deal formation and exit—rather than to periodic granting.

- Comparatively illiquid during their expected lives, with liquidity often tied to the targeted exit strategy.

- One-time in nature, effectively accelerating long-term incentive stakes that might otherwise have accumulated over time through periodic granting.

- Partially purchased by management, with amounts affected by individual resources and risk tolerances rather than being set based on desired reward policy.

- At least where the buy-in portion is concerned, usually not subject to the customary employment-related vesting of long-term incentive grants (some firms are said to impose forfeiture of gains on purchased shares).

- Often limited to a small group of top officers rather than a more broadly defined group of key management decision makers and contributors.

- Riskier, being affected strongly by the high levels of financial leverage normally involved in the deal.

This distinctive approach has contributed in some cases to high performance for private equity investees and to high risk-adjusted returns to their investors. Executives usually hold relatively big stakes in a private equity-owned company and they earn big gains when things go well. The potential for very high payouts almost always is a feature of such deals.

Because of this upside, private equity financiers often think their investee incentive deals are generous. But that is not clear, from a normal market perspective. One must properly compare the partly bought, front-loaded, and risky nature of management's interest in a private equity deal with the more typical annual granting of long-term incentives by public companies. Equity stakes for individual executives should be annualized, reduced by the value of any interest bought, valued appropriately on a risk-adjusted basis at the time of grant, and offset against the more parsimonious salary and bonus plans that sometimes prevail in these deals. After these adjustments are completed, equity interests often are found to be roughly comparable. Private equity stakes may be higher, but not dramatically out of the normal range.

Here is a quick reconciliation of private equity investee pay and ordinary market pay norms. Take a company that posts good economic performance over five years: a 10 percent return to all debt and equity investors, consisting of free cash flow for debt paydown and interest expense as well as increases in enterprise value. This company provides a benchmark private equity yield in the upper teens:

- A $1 billion investment, with total returns compounded annually at 10 percent per year, reaches $1.61 billion at the end of five years.

- $700 million in debt, at a 6 percent after-tax debt cost, reaches a value of $940 million when compounded annually to the same date (interest expense capitalized, for computational convenience).

- The ending value for equity holders is $1.61 billion minus $940 million, or $670 million. That is a 17.5 percent annual return on the initial equity of $300 million.

Let's say management bought three percent of the shares and received twice that amount in stock option grants or "override" incentives. Management would own 9 percent of the upside through its purchased stock and its granted incentive interests. Its gain would be 9 percent of $370 million, or about $33 million. That is more money than a few top officers normally make on their option grants in five years. But their salaries and bonuses tend to run at least a bit lighter than they would in the more typical corporate setting. And a third of their gain owes to their buy-in. Their buy-in may be intertwined with other terms, but it can be separated for analytical purposes. So we have $22 million in gain on the "long-term incentive grant" part of the deal. The other $11 million of management's gain is a return on the $9 million investment and not "pay" at all.

What pay would one otherwise have? If this billion-dollar company were financed by normal amounts of debt, it might have $750 million in equity. Let's say it granted one percent of its equity each year, as stock options, to the limited top officer group who would participate in a private equity deal. If grants were held five years on average, typical option holdings would amount to five percent of equity, or $37.5 million. Matching the $22 million in private equity incentive gain would require a rate of stock price appreciation a bit under 10 percent per year. That is good performance, but hardly extraordinary.

Private equity stakes look pretty big at first glance. But those stakes are not necessarily generous if they require a large buy-in and involve a particularly performance-contingent stock option or override structure. When equity percentages like 20 percent are quoted, they often are the incremental stake at the top of the performance scale rather than the overall, share-equivalent value held by management. A deal offering a far lower percent stake actually might be more generous, if it is an outright grant of full shares.

The comparison of typical pay with private equity pay lends us this general guidance:

- This sector's pay strategy is that having a concentrated, leveraged stake in business results can focus management more strongly on business success. This presumption is applicable at many businesses, irrespective of how they are financed.

- Companies can create this kind of financial stake without increasing pay. By restructuring existing pay to concentrate on business unit results, companies can create a stake for senior management that is close to what they would receive in a buyout transaction (aside from the part they receive by buying into the deal).

- Private equity deals involve buy-in, but so can incentive plans. If participants wish to hold a greater stake, they can take elective actions like putting off option exercises and share sales, deferring gain into accounts that appreciate on a phantom share basis, or taking bonus potential in phantom shares instead (again, I.R.C. section 409A is a factor here). If they want to lever things up as in a private equity deal and put their own money at risk, they can buy large amounts of stock financed by personal borrowings.

The economics of such deals can be created without an actual buyout transaction and without heavy debt levels. They can be created in phantom form, and higher award leverage can stand in for the financial leverage connected with high debt levels.

Private equity success does not depend on milking the company for cash flow and underinvesting in long-run earning power any more than public company success flows from an opposite set of biases. The structure of these deals provides credit for FCF and for valuation gains, a productive emphasis on "total return" that can be designed into many types of plans.

WHERE THE RUBBER HITS THE ROAD

For many companies, business units are where the rubber hits the road. That is where their company's value, opportunities, detailed business knowledge, and key decision makers are concentrated. If they are to get business results from the enormous amount of money they spend on executive incentives, they must overcome hesitancies about having serious incentive pay at the business unit level. And, as in private companies, they have to work a bit harder at metric selection, targeting, and value-based payout calibration. This chapter has set forth the reasons why many companies should go down this road for business-unit pay and has provided examples of how to do it prudently and effectively. Along the way, it has exposed a range of approaches applicable to not just to business units but to corporate-level measurement in private and public companies.

■ NOTES

1. TBR's definition and structure were set forth in Chapter 7 along with those of other value-based metrics. TBR-based solutions to target-setting were described in Chapter 8.
2. This "capitalized operations value" or "warranted value" concept is described in Chapter 2. It is the residual valuation method used in the basic valuation model set forth in that chapter. The multiple of 10 used in this example corresponds to a cost of capital of 10 percent.
3. This is part of the flexibility of "total return" frameworks as demonstrated in Chapters 2 and 8.
4. Ten percent is the threshold in this example when the cost of capital is 10 percent. This simple version of TBR is an approximation of valuation effects, and of the economic threshold for value-creating investment decisions. Effects are not precise, as noted in Chapter 8, but function well on balance within the overall context of the plan.
5. Unlike stock options, grants under formula-based phantom stock plans typically no longer permit participant control over exercises due to limitations under I.R.C. section 409A. Attorney David Kelly of Minneapolis notes that exercised amounts can simply

bear interest at some reasonable rate until payout at the original maturity date, sidestepping the section 409A problem.

6. That is based on annual TBR of 12 percent, a 10 percent discount rate, and a 3 percent annual likelihood of forfeiture.

7. Stock-based incentives do involve many legal and technical issues, but these do not go away when a company replaces part of its stock-based pay with operating incentives like TBR phantom stock plans. Dilution may fall under the stock-based plans, but the bulk of other issues remain active. Making more kinds of incentive grants, on top of stock-based grants, does make matters more complex.

8. Discussed in Chapter 2 in detail.

9. See Shannon P. Pratt and Robert Schweis, *Business Valuation: The Analysis and Appraisal of Closely-Held Companies*, (Hoboken, NJ: John Wiley & Sons, 2005).

10. For more information, see Chapter 2.

11. The effect of medium-term expectations on stock prices was covered extensively in Chapter 2.

12. The forecast assumed that high performance would degrade over time to industry norms, consistent with the DCF forecast conventions noted in Chapter 2.

13. A similar example was reviewed in closer detail in Chapter 6.

14. The "two wrongs make a right" example from Chapter 6 worked this way as well.

CHAPTER 10

Using Stock to Create Effective Incentives

This chapter is about using stock as an incentive medium within executive compensation programs. That is a big topic. There are many, many designs in the marketplace, each with its own context and rationale. If we surveyed all that, we would end up sifting through a lot of one-off, situational ideas. Many of those do not travel well, and most do not keep. They often go away quickly when you ask, "What problem is this meant to address?"

Google the term *incentives*. You will get quickly to dozens of different approaches, and new ones a week later, making one think the "incentive" notion of executive incentives is something that moves around a lot. The meaning of the term *executive* seems fluid as well:

> Gone are the days when exciting things like strategy, expansion, and deal making were the CEO's main focus. Today's CEO must devote considerable time to the less enviable tasks of planning layoffs, restructuring operations, closing plants, exiting geographies, eliminating product lines, and getting clients to pay their bills on time.[1]

This was fair enough, at the early 2009 citation date. But chief executive officers (CEOs) always spent time on unpleasant stuff. And matters like deal making had their stresses, let us not forget, including the risk of huge losses and share price implosions. That will be true next year and the year after. Really, officer jobs have stable scope, authority, and generalized content. They have stable incumbency, too. Tenures have shortened, but many of these same people were on the payroll ten or more years ago. They were not exclusively imperial CEOs or charismatic CEOs in the past, nor blood-letters today. Studies of CEO traits show that these folks focus on execution, pushing relentlessly to get the ball over the line. They find things they can do successfully—methods that work for them—and they repeat them over and over.[2] The basic characteristics of stock will not change, either, and neither will the general exigencies of governance.

The situation is not so unstable. So, a company should not have to sift through scores of incentive approaches to get the structure right, and the set of alternatives should not be jumping around that much over time. This book is meant to help evaluate *all* the ideas, from the standpoint of the rather stable criteria that ought to drive incentive policy. That means focusing on things like the basic characteristics of stock, payout leverage, and targeting implications, not this month's editorial hot-button or technical dodge.

Companies should think in very basic terms about what they are trying to accomplish with incentive pay. There are things that stock can reasonably be expected to do, in the context of rewards, and others it cannot. We make a review of those efficacy-based considerations at the outset of this chapter. Then we apply them to stock-based incentive design approaches.

Technical compliance is a big deal with stock-based pay in particular, and it does drive changes to designs. But this book is not a reference text for tax or legal requirements. Rules could have changed the day after this book went to print. As one astute chief financial officer (CFO) said to a design team, "Let's get the economics right and then address the accounting."

FROM THE TOP

Stock conveys a bundle of legal rights that differ in content from other incentive media. Stockholders have a perpetual interest. They can vote on important matters. They have an undiluted right to any dividends and they will share in any change in control. Shareholders own the place, and the board works for them. Stock is a kind of property, like real estate. It does not merely seek to encourage an ownership mindset—it *is* ownership.

A goal-based incentive plan, on the other hand, is an employee pay arrangement. Normally it can be regarded as a contingent promise to deliver cash or shares in the future. It can be very engaging, certainly, but it is not as weighty a concept as legal ownership.

Still, stock-based incentives do not function as a performance incentive, in a material cause-and-effect sense, for most of senior management. But they do provide very relevant feedback on the performance of the CEO and a few top officers. Top officers are the ones with the biggest impacts on the three big value drivers—long-run income, risk, and commitments of investor capital. Stock prices react sensibly to these drivers—as the discounted cash flow (DCF) model would, by and large. And top officers can often see pretty well how the market is judging what they do. It might take some work to interpret the stock price, and it might appear senseless at times. Executives might not always like the message. But, most of the time they can take steps to interpret the price and see where they stand as well as what they have to do to get in better stead.

Stock performance provides a basis for imposing real stake and accountability at the very top, one that can be exploited heavily in the structuring of pay. At this level, executive stock ownership and retention requirements extend accountability farther, over time, into a kind of *economic clawback* arrangement.

You may by now have noticed this book has a heavy goal-based orientation. Part of that is simply because it is intended to help with the difficult work of goal administration, in a world where that subject matter has large and rising stakes and complexity. But much is because most senior managers cannot push the stock price. We need to apply proper goals, if their incentives are to be effective. When we turn to the CEO, we have a different balance. In Chapter 4 we saw that many commentators think the CEO and all others at the top ought to be accountable not only to stock performance but to clear and proper long-term goals. For the CEO, though, stock-based performance feedback is already doing much of the heavy lifting. So we do not need to lean as heavily on an apparatus of goals to properly judge and reward people at this level.

Stock valuation is a performance-discounting device. It allows companies to outsource to the stock market part of the work of executive performance evaluation and incentive payout determination. It can be difficult, for example, to connect bonus designs with performance that drives shareholder gains. Many companies do not do that work. They risk racking up big bonus costs while shareholders are on track for losses. Performance plans often have the same problem.

The direct way to fix this is not simply to avoid goal-based pay and revert to stock-based incentives. That would short-circuit incentive effects for almost everyone. We have seen instead that goal-based incentive problems should be fixed directly through better metrics, targets, calibration, and the like. Still, using shares as award currency can be a big part of the system.

Performance shares provide a good illustration of the balance. In a performance unit plan or a bonus plan, cash pay obligations are set directly by achievement of goals. These goals may or may not have been set, and payouts may or may not have been earned, in a high-quality way. In a performance share plan, by contrast, award potential is denominated in shares. Good results mean more shares earned, but those shares are not worth as much if those results have not enriched shareholders. A participant might earn 150 percent of the targeted number of shares but, if the stock price attains only half its expected level, that 150 percent payout is worth only 75 percent of the targeted value. Balancing these two effects is helpful in many scenarios:

- If plan design or calibration is poor, the 150 percent payout may have been inappropriate. In that case the share price reduction has helped limit consequences of bad design. The better solution is, of course, better design.

- If the overall stock market simply fell, however, as many companies experienced with the 2008 financial crisis, then participants experience a drop in the value of shares earned. This is a measured response, since the grants still reward executives for doing their part by generating strong financial results. It is a better outcome, generally speaking, than underwater options.

- If financial performance and the stock price are high, then stock has affirmed the quality of financial results and provided additional upside leverage. This multiplier effect creates an overall degree of leverage that often resembles that of option grants. And it permits goal ranges to be a bit wider and easier to administer.

Stock prices are forward looking. Achievement of goals, however, is something seen only through the rear-view mirror. That is another reason stock prices might move in one direction while financial results are still moving the other way. Stock prices reflect hopes about the future, and judgments about how well the company is positioned for it. Again, this provides feedback well suited to the most forwardly-focused positions in the house—top officers.

Forward-looking stock valuations are helpful to incentive policy for the broader senior management group, as well. We took some trouble in earlier chapters to demonstrate how we can set solid business goals that most of senior management can influence, and to run them in a framework oriented toward the medium- to long-term. Many of these methods are based on a "warranted value" convention, one that accords credit to management for valuation gains demonstrated by actual results—not just hoped-for future gains that are baked into the stock price. Having awards set in shares can help goal-based plans be more responsive to the outlook, raising payout values when things look good.

And, let's remember, company stock is trading all the time. The stock price is a constant arbiter of results and the outlook, and that is a helpful thing no matter how you structure incentive pay. Goal-based incentive plans, in contrast, are more challenging to communicate in the interim. Companies are doing well, really, if they can provide timely quarterly updates.

Stock can reward management for potentially valuable actions not handled well by operational goals. These might include debt/equity ratio changes, effects of risk reduction during a performance cycle, favorable moves in terms of dividend or repurchase policy, or ongoing changes in the timing and terms of acquisitions. This means you can outboard complex matters like these from corporate-level goal measurement, instead relying on the stock market to incorporate their effects into the stock price.

We will see shortly that goal-based pay can create a very substantial hedge against variation in financial results. Goal-based plans put management in front of shareholders in the queue for risk. Incentive plans absorb a large part of the earnings variances that would otherwise affect shareholders fully. Stock-based pay has substantial risk-sharing aspects as well. Making an option grant on 2 percent of the company's shares will limit shareholder costs, pretax, to 2 percent of shareholder gains until exercise. And it does so under a wide range of business performance and share price gains (though losses are not shared). A stock grant has dilution consequences that are scaled across a wide range of performance levels. Retention grants often are denominated in shares rather than cash, creating some risk-sharing effects even when the main goal is simply to pose some exit costs. The best hedge for executive pay costs, however, is to encourage better performance and actually get it.

Overall, stock can fulfill a range of important functions within the rewards system, not only for management, but the broader workforce. Stock can be effective within broader efforts to create a sense of affiliation and engagement.

OFF TO THE RACES

Relative total shareholder return is total shareholder return (TSR) in comparison to a group of peer companies or a stock index. Performance plans are sometimes designed to deliver cash or shares on this basis. Relative TSR naturally handicaps the individual company's performance against the general business conditions and expectations affecting a group of business peers. In this regard, it delivers rewards based on a "pure play" measure of management performance. If assessed against the general market rather than a peer group, relative TSR still does the valuable service of stating company TSR on a basis net of general market movement.

As peer metrics go, TSR goals are the easiest to set. Expected TSR is equal to a company's cost of equity. Expected TSR performance against peers should be equal to the 50th percentile, assuming company business risk and capital structure are similar to those of peers. Reasonable goals for typical financial metrics like operating income or sales growth, in contrast, could be equal to any percentile of the peer group for a given company.

Relative TSR is admired as a resilient and complete way of looking at a business's performance for its owners and zeroing in on management's contribution. Performance plans using relative TSR do not do well in terms of clarity and line of sight, however:

- For management simply to know how it is doing under such a plan, it needs a handle not only on what the company's stock price performance has been but also on what it has been for peer companies.

- To understand that picture, participants need a sense of what has been driving stock performance in the industry and what role each management team has played in it. Only then can they gain a sense of the management performance contest the plan means to emphasize.

- For the plan to be at all informative, management needs to know what it can do to improve the stock price. TSR against peers, just like the company's own stock price, is silent on that critical matter.

- For the plan to be effective in a prospective sense, participating executives need to have an impact on its outcomes. For people aside from the top few officers in the company, relative TSR plans do not meet this criterion. After all, relative TSR plans involve no line-of-sight business goals.

Relative TSR plans may align gains more closely with a company's specific performance, but that is not always the case and, in any event, there are other ways to get that done. We find that there typically is a large degree of stock intercorrelation among sector peers. But there is also a lot of correlation among all kinds of stocks in the stock market, so general market movements are the main things being "immunized" in a relative TSR approach. Stock price correlations among S&P 500 companies, for example, tend to average fifty to sixty percent.

Executives, as a rule, do not need shelter from the vagaries of the stock market, particularly as their multiple and varied incentive opportunities play out over time. Moving pay toward goals has an immunizing effect, we have noted, when it strips out market noise. And the incentive signal–to–noise ratio improves greatly when measured over time. Relative TSR is often is less helpful here. What it does, to an extent, is simply to trade one form of market noise for another.

Relative TSR plans may pay out big awards when actual stock price performance has been poor, but not as bad as that of peer companies. Rather than being the cream of the crop, as one colleague puts it, such results might be the "cream of the crap." Many boards will balk at the prospect of paying for negative results simply because they are relatively less negative. And if this low end of the payout scale is clipped, the plan may simply be uncompetitive.

Most companies are in charge of their destiny, in the end. Relative TSR plans should be seen as a special-purpose incentive device, suited best in the few cases where exogenous influences on profit are so large that heroic measures should be taken to correct them. For most companies, these plans commit the same sins as stock options. They do not come with instructions on how to create value, and they do not connect with actions of almost anyone in senior management.

Some mechanical issues with TSR measurement warrant noting:

- Just as in measuring the performance of investment managers, relative TSR results are very sensitive to the performance period chosen and, in particular, to the beginning stock price at that date. The solution is to use a structure of overlapping grants with uniform terms and measurement dates.

- To the extent percentile measures or rankings are used, results can be affected by discontinuities in the range of peer results, making the award scale lumpy and jumpy. A TSR gain of 1 percent in one interval of the award schedule might have the same award impact as a 5 percent gain in an adjacent interval. This can be addressed by standardizing the range of peer data and making inferences about relative performance against a smoothed distribution, rather than against the unadjusted range of peer data points. This method takes into account the dimensions of peer performance that are important when establishing a ranking—central tendency and dispersion—in a more effective way. This technique is applicable in most peer-based measurement situations, not just those involving TSR.

- Whether percentile rankings are used or not, there are target-setting issues that concern the spread in TSR results of the company and its peers. A plan that pays out maximum awards for attaining TSR of a certain number of points above the peer median, for example, might work out to be inappropriately easy to reach. In such a case, it might also create extremely high leverage and incremental dilution within a small range of company stock price changes. Thresholds set at the peer median simply create a 50 percent chance of nonpayment. Targeting at a level far above the 50th percentile devalues award opportunity, a bit like issuing a stock option with a premium price. Award schedules in such plans need to be tested carefully, just as with plans using financial goals.

Performance plans can also be based on financial metrics that are compared to those of peer companies—measures like earnings per share growth. The motives created by these plans resemble those associated with TSR plans, but they are likely to remain less prevalent due to greater measurement issues.

Indexed stock options have strike prices that rise or fall in tandem with peer company stock prices or with the value of a stock market index. These plans have a lot of the same relative performance dynamics as performance plans based on relative TSR. They enlarge gains when a company's stock price does well against an index or peers, and vice versa. They raise a range of technical issues, however. Companies wishing to go down this general path look to relative TSR much more often.

PROS AND CONS OF MAJOR APPROACHES TO STOCK-BASED INCENTIVE DESIGN

We looked at relative TSR plans first here since they are a big subject. And we covered many forms of long-term incentives (LTI) in earlier chapters, like subsidiary equity, phantom stock, and performance plans reflecting business-unit performance. Now we will survey the mainstream range of stock-based incentive approaches in terms of their pay/performance dynamics (but not in technical terms like taxation, accounting, disclosure rules, or securities laws).

We have said a fair bit already about stock options, restricted stock, and performance shares and units, as well. As someone in the habit of retelling stories will say—this time, I will keep it brief:

- *Options and stock appreciation rights (SARs).* They offer payout leverage, flexibility, and a direct connection with shareholder outcomes. But they often involve a miserably inefficient trade between issuer and recipient. Gains tend to drift upward over a period of years so they are not particularly concentrated on the pivotal one- to three-year time frame in which we are hoping to drive the best decisions. And few people can affect the stock price anyway.

  They are obviously going to work best for top officers at the corporate level. They will also continue to be a good fit in certain settings (e.g., high-tech start-ups) in which they capture prospective performance and its valuation effects more accurately than other approaches. Options should not be used as the centerpiece of the executive rewards system for the several dozen to several hundred executives in the senior management group. They are most fitting as incentives, in the strict sense, for the CEO and just a few other officers at the top.

  SARs work like options, sharing stock gains until exercised. They may pay out in cash or shares. Various SAR approaches have been favored over the years due to situational advantages in matters like share usage and financial accounting.

- *Restricted stock grants and units.* These can help create retention incentives, and they do align executive wealth with that of shareholders. They do not pose very difficult valuation problems, either. If someone receives $100,000 in typical time-vesting restricted shares, they probably will not discount it wildly below that figure. Holders may accrue dividend payments, so there is less of the anti-dividend bias that options may carry.

  But restricted shares do not have sharp enough performance teeth. The fact of the matter is that restricted stock grants can allow executives to walk away with a lot of valuable shares even when their performance has for years been mediocre. When used, grants to top officers should be made performance-contingent enough to qualify for deductibility under I.R.C. section 162(m), in any event. Otherwise the after-tax cost of affected grants will increase by more than 50 percent.

  Stock units often are used rather than actual shares. As with SARs, stock units sometimes offer technical advantages (e.g., deferral of individual taxation beyond the vesting date).

- *Performance share and unit plans based on financial performance.* These are grants of stock or cash that are earned or vested over time based on company performance against preset goals (rather than market-based metrics like relative TSR). Dividends may be accumulated and paid on performance shares. In a corporate world properly faulted for short-term thinking and insufficient attention to risk, basing a lot of pay on well-built long-term goals is one of the best paths for restructuring incentives. And we have seen that denominating such grants in shares can help align plan outcomes more closely with owner interests. However, administering a goal-based plan can be complex.

ALL-IN-ONE

A performance share plan can be set up to act as a combination of all three of these approaches. It also applies the kind of performance contingencies sometimes enacted to qualify grants for tax-deductibility under I.R.C. section 162(m). This is worth a look, since it shows that the ordinary alternatives can be combined, mixed, and matched in a range of ways. Consider Exhibit 10.1 in which all of a company's LTI is issued as three-year performance share grants.

Payouts on a $100 target grant are shown on the right in the exhibit. The exhibit has a threshold payout level equal to 50 percent, one that is earned by exceeding a modest threshold performance level (assigned a 90 percent probability of achievement in this example). That is a lot like making a restricted stock grant equal in size to one-half of the targeted number of performance shares (one with a three-year look-back grant contingency). Payout leverage on the plan is set within a relatively low 50 to 150 percent range, but effects are high since this leverage applies to all of long-term incentive potential. Stock prices are assumed to move between 5 percent and 15 percent annually over five years, so performance variances have compounded consequences on the ending share price (performance share payouts occur after three years, taxes and dividends are ignored, and stock gains are assumed to run for five years in total).

Performance Calibration			Payout Estimates			
Perform./ Target	Probability		Payouts	Stock Gain	Value/ Target	$ Gain on $100 Grant
80%	90%		50.0%	28%	64%	$ 63.8
90%	70%		75.0%	44%	108%	$ 107.7
100%	50%		100.0%	61%	161%	$ 161.1
110%	30%		125.0%	80%	225%	$ 225.3
120%	10%		150.0%	101%	302%	$ 301.7

EXHIBIT 10.1 Payout Scenarios for Performance Share Grant

Performance Shares		Restricted			% of One-	
Payout %	Payout $	Stock	Options		Total $	Grant Mix
	33.3%	33.3%	33.3%			
0%	$ -	$ 42.5	$ 27.6		$ 70.2	110%
50%	$ 23.9	$ 47.9	$ 43.6		$ 115.3	107%
100%	$ 53.7	$ 53.7	$ 61.1		$ 168.4	105%
150%	$ 90.1	$ 60.1	$ 80.2		$ 230.4	102%
200%	$ 134.1	$ 67.0	$ 101.1		$ 302.3	100%

EXHIBIT 10.2   Payout Scenarios for Long-Term Incentive Mix

This approach to LTI granting has a high level of exposure to share perform-ance and financial performance. Retention effects are present in all but 10 per-cent or so of scenarios.

It also has effects similar to making separate, equally weighted grants of re-stricted stock, performance shares, and options. Exhibit 10.2 shows an example of performance shares in which leverage is more normal, the option grant size is $100 ($33 in value divided by a valuation at 33 percent of face) and the restricted share element is made contingent on the same threshold financial performance used in the performance share grant.

Estimated payouts at various levels are quite close to the earlier example. Close to threshold, for example, the 33 percent restricted stock grant plus the 16.7 percent performance share threshold (50 percent threshold, against the one-third weighting attached to performance share grants) add up to be close to the 50 percent overall threshold in the first plan.

Stock prices could move differently from these estimates, of course. But this example shows that there is a testable pay/performance profile within the overall LTI structure, one that has goal-based and stock-based elements. The compari-son shows that a desired performance profile can be pursued in a range of ways. And this particular example has some merits worth noting:

- This method avoids making restricted stock grants at all, thereby avoiding the pay-for-performance criticisms they bring. It carries the retention benefits of restricted stock except in the case of very low performance, in which case shareholders would probably like to get their shares back, anyway.

- It does not issue option grants and therefore does not create dilution that may trail on for as many as ten years. Rather, it concentrates effects of goals and stock performance into the critical medium term. This is assisted by using continually updated, overlapping grants (and through the forward-looking valuation mechanism of shares).

- It makes the overall incentive structure very strictly accountable to goals. So it is not a proper choice unless the company will make well-studied and proper choices about metric and goals, administering them in an adaptive way over time.

- It is meant to use simple and achievable goals, administered over broad performance ranges. The goals themselves may not have very high payout leverage, but the fact that all LTI gains ride on them makes them quite important. And potential stock movement brings leverage up further.

- The plan is denominated in whole shares—in relatively stable award currency. And it is based wholly on clear, plausible goals. Participants should find such a plan compelling and understandable enough that they will not ignore or discount it.

This plan does not require three different types of grants in order to reflect balanced performance criteria and to be adaptive and flexible. If the share price falls when internal performance metrics were genuinely strong, for example, management will still earn valuable awards.

LET THEM EAT RISK

The performance share approach shown in Exhibit 10.1 delivers all long-term incentive pay in a variable cost format. This approach has another effect beyond those cited so far, a very large one that many find surprising. This approach may reduce earnings variation by 50 percent. That is a bookkeeping effect, but it flows from the fact that performance plan participants stand to buffer substantial real risks for owners rather than simply sharing them. This reduces risk for shareholders to a very substantial extent, one hard to attain using alternatives like hedging strategies.

In Exhibit 10.3, an example public company makes long-term incentive grants with value totaling around 1 percent of the value of its equity each year. If the company's price-earnings ratio is 15, these grants add up to 15 percent of earnings, or around 10 percent when they are stated on an after-tax basis. If the grants were stock options or restricted shares, they would normally be expensed

EXHIBIT 10.3	PERFORMANCE SCENARIOS WITH STOCK OPTION AND/OR RESTRICTED STOCK GAINS		
Net Income	$ 80.00	$ 100.00	$ 120.00
Net Income Variance from Target	−20.0%	0.0%	20.0%
Annualized Option/Stock Expense, after Tax	$ 10.00	$ 10.00	$ 10.00
Net Income after Option or Stock Expense	$ 70.00	$ 90.00	$ 110.00
Net Income Variance from Target	−22.2%	0.0%	22.2%

EXHIBIT 10.4	PERFORMANCE SCENARIOS WITH PERFORMANCE SHARES OR UNITS		
Net Income	$ 80.00	$ 100.00	$ 120.00
Net Income Variance from Target	−20.0%	0.0%	20.0%
Annualized Performance Grant Expense, after Tax	$ -	$ 10.00	$ 20.00
Net Income after Performance Grant Expense	$ 80.00	$ 90.00	$ 100.00
Net Income Variance from Target	−11.1%	0.0%	11.1%

over their vesting period (33 percent per year, say). Since grants are made every year, amortization of three years' grants is underway at any given time; the annual run rate of expense stays at 10 percent of earnings. When earnings rise or fall, the subtraction of this large, fixed cost has the effect of increasing the variability of earnings.

Performance shares and units have very different effects. These plans allow participants to earn shares or cash, respectively, based on the attainment of performance goals. In Exhibit 10.4, income at 80 percent of target means no award is earned. The performance unit or share grant will result in zero expense over its life. Earnings at 120 percent of target means 200 percent of the targeted payout is earned, with expense rising in tandem (other outcomes normally are interpolated). The reduction or increase in incentive expense, when performance deviates from target, substantially buffers the impact on book earnings.

Earnings variation was reduced by 50 percent, from plus or minus 22.2 percent to plus or minus 11.1 percent. What happened to the larger, earlier variances? Management ate them. Management absorbs risk under goal-based plans, so the stream of financial results going to shareholders is made less risky. This is not quite the same thing as a stock grant, which starts out by diluting shareholders. And it is not quite the same thing as an option grant, which is more like a gain- and risk-sharing device.

Performance plans reduce operational leverage. Pay is an operating expense, like rent or utilities. The size and behavior of these costs affects the size and risk of the operating income stream itself. Goal-based long-term incentives are economically different commitments than purely stock-based ones. Goal-based payouts put management in the chow line in front of shareholders, when the risk is being served up. From an economic standpoint, the payout risks of purely stock-based incentives take effect a couple of steps later in the valuation chain, when earnings are being valued. Variance-reducing effects can be carried several steps further upstream, when goal-based performance units or shares, or formula-based phantom stock, are struck at the business unit level.

The performance leverage of these grants flows through the books as well, in a process that also tracks the economic effects of performance plan grants. Awards in the performance-based plan vary by 100 percent in relation to target, when performance varies by 20 percent, so leverage is 5:1. Awards may be 10 percent of earnings at target, but 5:1 leverage means they fall so fast when income is below target that they mitigate the earnings reduction not by 10 percent but by 50 percent. They attenuate earnings gains similarly, so the overall framework smoothes out spikes and troughs in reported earnings.

Effects are large. That is because executives, through their interests in typical incentive plans, are substantial claimants on business results. They bear disproportionate upside and downside, taking on risk that otherwise would be borne solely by shareholders. As it happens, the reality of this dynamic does not show up in the books unless the grants are based explicitly on company financial performance. Then, the variable presentation of expense, together with the explicit link to financial results, creates the book hedge.

Stock option grants create substantial award leverage, but their costs are fixed under current rules. The more modest variability of gains on a restricted stock grant also is presented as a fixed matter. For heavy users of stock options and time-vesting restricted shares, moving heavily toward performance-based long-term incentive pay can greatly shift the fixed/variable profile of book expense.

Performance share gains actually vary based not only on hitting performance goals but also on share price performance. However, under current U.S. rules, share price movement, post-grant, generally does not affect expense. This means that performance share expenses are set in predictable proportion to the financial results that drive gains on such grants. So performance share grants, like grants of performance units, can create a formal hedge.

Performance shares have an additional book benefit, when compared to plans denominated in cash. The share-price element of the expense is fixed at grant, so later increases in share price do not cause expenses to rise. This means expenses at target can be expected to be about 20 percent lower on average, over the life of a typical three-year grant, than they would be on a cash-based grant with similar present value.

Under APB 25, the "fixed" or "grant date" accounting treatment for options was seen as a good thing, but that is because those terms really meant "no expense." Variable accounting for performance-based plans, however, usually meant recognition of a substantial expense. The trade-off was not so much about the fixed versus variable nature of the cost, but rather the overall amount of expense. Under ASC 718 (formerly FAS 123(R)), the distinction between fixed and variable costs should be regarded in the more customary business terms—variable costs that are scaled to performance, all else equal, will reduce the variability in earnings.

Accounting advantages are not the main reason to consider using more performance-based pay. Our review has shown that performance grants provide an excellent way to improve the efficacy of incentive pay. The goal-based apparatus of such grants, properly designed, can encourage value-creating business decisions in the clearest terms. That is particularly true when compared to stock options and time-vesting restricted shares, whose gains are affected by few and perhaps understood by fewer. Goal-based plans, in contrast, can be devised to place a clear bounty on the long-term results of successful business actions. They can do so at the corporate, group, divisional, or profit center level. And, when made in the form of performance shares, they maintain strong concurrent linkages to the share price.

Most companies would find it very costly to take actions that greatly reduce earnings variability. It would also be difficult to restructure toward a more heavily variable-cost profile. With upgrades in incentive pay design, it can be done at negative cost, since business results can improve as a result of having more effective incentives. And the share price may benefit from the notable degree of risk reduction. Performance-based long-term incentives do not merely reduce the variance in earnings or reduce profit and loss expense. They can improve business performance over the long run by creating clear, effective, and compelling incentives to take those actions that create most value over time.

PURELY STOCK-BASED LTI APPROACHES

One chemical industry client moved to restricted stock and options as LTI grants, indicating they simply did not favor performance plans. The CEO did not see it as a motivational aid he could use with his senior management team. The company had used a performance plan in the recent past and had real difficulty. Most committee members cited difficulties or hesitancies as well, ones to them outweighing the basic benefits of goal-based grants. I noted that the rising prevalence and interest in performance plans do not by themselves compel them to take any action in that direction.

Companies should not just shift the pay mix out of stock options and into traditional performance share plans without first improving their metrics, designs, and target-setting methods. We have seen that traditional approaches can cause pay-related bias in company business planning, encourage income manipulation, and simply pay out good money for bad business results. Increasing the load on this vehicle without improving its balance simply increases the likelihood that it will end up in the ditch.

I could have argued at length in favor of high-quality goal-based LTI, but the company did not appear to me to be prepared to commit to the right steps at that time. I did not think my advisory role in that particular situation was to try to up-end matters. This is not one-size-fits-all subject matter, and big changes were not fitting in that situation.

The following is an example of a contrasting view of how far one should go with motivational initiatives—from a magazine headline:

Talent Is Everything. It's not enough to hire good people and keep them happy. You need to refashion the entire organization around them.[3]

The entire organization? Shouldn't, say, tractor dealers be located near farms, even if their "talent" wants to live in SoHo? Perhaps we could all lighten up. Let us put aside this book's goal-based pay agenda for the moment. Instead, let us focus on performance effects that can be sought with stock and option granting by themselves.

We will review effects of some basic choices about matters like grant mix, grant frequency, and grant size determination. In Exhibit 10.5, five stock/option mixes are presented with payouts shown across a range of gain levels.

The all-option line has the highest upside leverage, of course, but carries the largest motivational risk in the event of modest or negative price movement. It

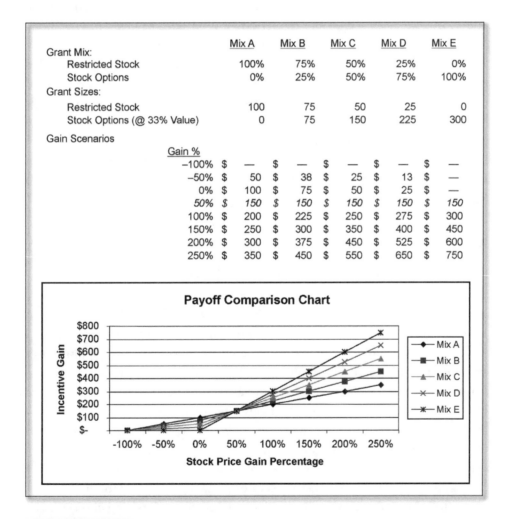

		Mix A	Mix B	Mix C	Mix D	Mix E
Grant Mix:						
Restricted Stock		100%	75%	50%	25%	0%
Stock Options		0%	25%	50%	75%	100%
Grant Sizes:						
Restricted Stock		100	75	50	25	0
Stock Options (@ 33% Value)		0	75	150	225	300
Gain Scenarios	Gain %					
	−100%	$ —	$ —	$ —	$ —	$ —
	−50%	$ 50	$ 38	$ 25	$ 13	$ —
	0%	$ 100	$ 75	$ 50	$ 25	$ —
	50%	*$ 150*	*$ 150*	*$ 150*	*$ 150*	*$ 150*
	100%	$ 200	$ 225	$ 250	$ 275	$ 300
	150%	$ 250	$ 300	$ 350	$ 400	$ 450
	200%	$ 300	$ 375	$ 450	$ 525	$ 600
	250%	$ 350	$ 450	$ 550	$ 650	$ 750

Payoff Comparison Chart

EXHIBIT 10.5   **Payout Scenarios for Various Grant Mixes**

also uses the most shares, but share usage comparisons should take that into account. The all-stock line for Mix A has the lowest pitch in its performance/payout curve. That one is all about retention. The others show various combinations in which downside protection is being traded off against upside leverage.

Using some mix—rather than making persistent use of an all-option or all-share mix—seems prudent for most companies. Involving shares in the mix is, of course, more effective for retention, perceived value, and general resiliency in the face of the stock downtowns that very often occur. Options add leverage and create more exciting overall gain prospects. When the pay structure has some whole shares in it, it is not only about upside. Such moderation should be helpful, when concerned that an upside-only structure will turn management into risk-seeking privateers.

Companies sometimes apply the same mix up and down the organizational ladder. But we often see people farther down the ladder having a heavier stock mix, with more stock option exposure as one nears the top.

Some of these moderating effects of grant mix could, in theory, be handled with discounted stock options. They are in-the-money at grant so they should invite less discounting. And they may create a better trade-off between leverage and retention than either stock or options alone. But discounted options are troubled by technical and shareholder concerns. One of these is I.R.C. section 409A, but it does permit use of discounted options so long as exercise does not accelerate payout. The grant in that case would be a *European option* exercised only at expiration.

KEEPING THE HORSES IN THE BARN

Control over exercise is a valuable feature of options, though. It permits executives to adjust their holdings based on their risk tolerances. It enables potentially valuable tax planning. And it conveys a valuable sense of control.

Some proposed designs involve cashing out options or optionlike interests at a fixed date. This seems to be in reaction to concerns about executive control over exercise timing, presumably about selling based on inside information before a big stock price drop. However, executives' ability to exercise at will is constrained by matters like window periods after earnings releases and by stock holding requirements. In the worst scenarios, their ability to cut and run is stemmed by the threat of litigation and prosecution as well. They do have some control over the timing of their trades, but that does not necessarily mean they can game the system. The stock market normally displays good foresight, and it is hard to beat. Executives do not display notably superior timing choices based on their insider status.

In any event, if we are sure that executives will manipulate their timing of exercises and we shut that door, we ought to consider whether other doors are still open. And they are. Top executives can manipulate the stock price with the timing and content of information releases. They can also manipulate financial reporting choices, as well as a range of business decisions. These can affect the stock price, potentially, at any date of sale, purchase, grant, exercise, or vesting. Focusing on option exercise constraints is like worrying about whether one horse will get out through one open barn door. The solution is good overall design, one creating compelling interests in sustained business performance and value creation and one requiring material and persistent share holdings. To do that is to keep all the doors closed and all the horses in the barn.

Premium options could have figured into the earlier list of granting and pay-out alternatives, but few companies these days are reporting a desire to create leverage at levels higher than those imposed by at-the-money option grants. Per-formance plans can employ share price hurdles as ways to get cash or shares as well. They are ignored here, though, since their basic linkages from stock price performance to pay can be conveyed using more typical stock and option grant combinations.

Companies often have a lot of premium options outstanding, though, and that was especially so post-crisis. A ten-year option issued three years ago, one whose exercise price is 20 percent below today's stock price, is like a seven-year option issued today, fully or mostly vested, with a strike price at a 25 percent premium. If a company has a lot of these outstanding, it might just want to make restricted stock grants for awhile. That creates an overall payout schedule with downside cushion, full-price-range exposure, and lots of upside.

Some companies argue that a good time to make option grants is when the price is low, since there could be a large subsequent run-up. But option grants may be particularly wasteful at such times. They actually tend to be quite expensive due to high volatility, but valued poorly at such moments by many participants. Near the market low in March 2009, we estimated implied volatility levels on Dow Jones Industrial Average stocks by looking at two-year call quotes. Implied volatilities averaged about 55 percent. This means executive stock options for many companies would be valued at 40 to 50 percent of the stock price. When risk is high, how many people would give away a share and its downside protection in exchange for only two or two and one-half options?

Putting aside the option trade, we should note there is also no guarantee of a stock bounce-back. A sudden 2 percent rise in the cost of capital due to the risk premium could really kill a stock price, for example, but only cause its predicted growth rate in equilibrium to increase by 2 percent per year (Chapter 2). What one is really asserting, when looking for a big bounce-back, is that markets are in a disequilibrium that is driving inefficient stock prices. The stronger general assumption is one of market efficiency.

We have examined TSR and stock price patterns for a range of periods in the past, looking for any pattern of stock bounce-backs. Our general finding is that the range of year-over-year performance levels for stocks is about the same whether the preceding year had a stock price drop or not. The commonly-assumed bounce-back actually is, on average, a dead-cat bounce. This sort of finding has been confirmed for decades by the many academic studies showing zero serial negative correlation in monthly or longer-term stock returns, and the many studies finding market efficiency more generally. Stock prices snapped back nicely beginning in March 2009, making recent stock-based incentive grants look pretty good pretty quickly. But a several-sigma move like that is not reliable in the context of persistent granting.

To the extent any bounce-back occurs, having lots of underwater options means having lots of upside leverage. Many companies were in this position after the 2008 financial crisis, as we have noted. At October 17, 2008, for example, a little over two-thirds of the Fortune 500 companies had underwater stock options overall; their weighted-average exercise prices were above the stock price.[4] From a starting point like that, making a restricted stock grant seems like a better idea than issuing more options. It results in an overall financial position that has more balance—a durable, valuable interest combined with a steeply pitched upside payout curve.

There are some other arguments for moderating stock-based leverage, or at least creating a longer downside range, in all kinds of markets. There is some evidence that CEOs with heavy stock option holdings are more likely to make risky acquisitions. There is a ton of evidence, of course, that most acquisitions fail. Companies whose CEOs hold large blocks of stock, on the other hand, are significantly less likely to go for big, risky deals.[5] Stock exposes its owners to the full spectrum of upside and downside, while stock options, appearing on their face to be about upside only, may well encourage top management to gamble too freely with other people's money. This does not mean that companies should ditch stock options as an incentive device for the CEO. But it obviously does invite them to think through the risk implications of the overall incentive mix.

GRANTING AND LEVERAGE

Grant frequency can have some effects on the risk profile of ordinary equity granting. Proponents of a "wealth leverage" perspective have argued for, among other things, less-frequent option granting than the annual cadence used almost all the time.

EXHIBIT 10.6	ACCELERATED GRANT SCENARIO

	Annual Granting				
	Year 1	Year 2	Year 3	Total	PV Front-Loaded
Grant Value	$100.0	$100.0	$100.0	$300.0	$273.6
Option Grant Size @ 33% Value	$300.0	$300.0	$300.0	$900.0	$820.7
Stock Price Growth Rate	Gain Scenarios at Year 5				
5.0%	$ 82.9	$ 64.7	$ 47.3	$194.8	$ 226.7
10.0%	$183.2	$139.2	$ 99.3	$421.7	$ 501.0
20.0%	$446.5	$322.1	$218.4	$987.0	$1,221.4

Exhibit 10.6 shows how this can have the effect of increasing leverage beyond the levels involved with annual granting. Front-loading three years of grants creates a bigger interest on the ground floor, paying off sooner and more intensively. That is true even in this example where the accelerated grants were discounted 10 percent per year as a *quid pro quo*. The front-loaded approach holds management's feet to the fire as well—if the stock price falls, they will not get option grants at the new, lower price in later years.

This subject attracted stronger interest in an era that was pre-expensing, pre-tech crash, pre-2008-crisis, and pre-lost-decade of large-cap returns in the United States. The world is a different place now, and it is not as hungry for risk as an element of incentive granting. In the current frame, the idea that annual granting could *dollar cost average* executive holdings is not a great cause for objection.

The wealth leverage math is worth a look, however, in the current outline because we are examining ways in which basic methods for granting purely equity-based LTI awards might calibrate risk and return. That perspective tempts one to consider front-loaded grant strategies. But, if the share price or performance falls and the big grant goes underwater, will the company really go on for years without functioning incentive or retention effects? Whether the board feels forgiving or not, it might do the practical thing and step up with some retention stock grants or bump up the pace of granting. With that scenario on the menu, it is hard to argue that promised leverage will really occur. With front-loading, any such contingencies and going-forward grant plans need to be considered at the outset.

A last leverage illustration concerns fixed-share grants. This is another long-standing subject of discussion, but one that is active today. In an example of fixed-share guidelines, the number of options or shares to grant each year is set at the outset of a several-year period. More typical variable granting means examining the value of an option grant each year when translating competitive LTI guidelines into grant sizes. Exhibit 10.7 shows an example based on options.

EXHIBIT 10.7   FIXED VERSUS VARIABLE GRANT GUIDELINES

	Fixed Guidelines		Variable Guidelines	
	Year 1	Year 2	Year 1	Year 2
Grant Value	$ 60.0	$ 60.0	$ 60.0	$ 60.0
Share Value	$ 18.0		$ 18.0	$ 24.0
Option Value @ 33%	$ 6.0		$ 6.0	$ 8.0
Shares Granted	10.0	10.0	10.0	7.5

Options are worth $6.00 in Year 1, so meeting a competitive guideline value of $60 means issuing ten options. If guidelines are fixed, that ten-share guideline is used for several years. Under the variable approach, the second year grant is determined based on the option value current at that time. In this scenario of a rising share price, the number of shares granted falls. Fixed-share guidelines cause more shares to be granted, creating potentially larger gains when shares are rising in price. This is a way of using the basics of granting, again, to set leverage at desired levels. Here again, though, there are practical limitations. If the share price falls a great deal, the company will not necessarily use the value-based method's results if it leads to overly dilutive granting. Instead, it might choose to limit the number of shares granted as a way of limiting dilution (as many companies did following the 2008 crisis). The share limit in that case is, in effect, a fixed-grant guideline.

EQUITY-BASED INCENTIVES IN VENTURE-STAGE COMPANIES

This is one of the contexts in which stock-based incentive grants by themselves are most effective. In many venture-stage companies, it is just unproductive to try to set long-term goals for pay purposes. Here more than in most situations, preset goals may get stale and risk turning counterproductive. Companies also tend to be short on cash for incentive pay or any other purpose. And, as we will see, getting more cash can have a high cost.

These deals can be complex, though, since they often involve more than one round of financing before initial public offering (IPO). Exhibit 10.8 sets forth a simplified scenario that demonstrates the general mechanics. The business was started up by a parent company that put in cash and other assets worth $50 million in total. The company is seeking an early-stage venture partner and is putting in place equity-based incentive grants.

In the first round of financing, it wants to take on a 33 percent venture partner. The parent company's interest is worth $50 million and a partner buys in for

$25 million, so the valuation is $75 million post-investment (or post-money). Pretransaction, the company issues equity-based incentives on 10 percent of its shares: 3.33 percent in restricted shares and 6.67 percent in stock options. Exhibit 10.8 shows that when the new partner buys in, the parent's percentage interest drops by one-third and so does that of management. No *make-whole* grant of any kind is made; incentive participants make money when the parent does, on these grants, and no gain has yet been realized.

The company moves along successfully and the valuation doubles. More cash is needed for growth, though, so the company takes on more investors, selling a further one-third interest in a second financing round. This transaction makes it apparent that there has been a $10 gain in stock value and related gains on option and restricted stock grants. The stock price doubles again at IPO to $40 and attains a $50 level later on, so gains increase further.

Over the course of the transactions, parent and management stock control fell by two-thirds. There were more than $450 million in equity gains earned in this example, but the parent company only kept $200 million of them. If it had been able to put off financing rounds until later when value was higher, it might have kept a larger part of the gains for itself and venture management. First-round investors earned gains of $100 million on their $50 million investment, for example, effectively causing founders and management to pay 200 percent interest on that source of cash.

However, it might not have been able to grow and succeed without the partners and their cash. This is a situation in which the underlying equity value gain over the full course of events had a highly leveraged effect on payouts. It was also a situation, though, in which interim share price movements had a big impact. This deal, using purely equity-based incentives, created a highly leveraged incentive program. It made clear that succeeding to the greatest possible extent with the resources one has, and taking in new money at the best times and terms feasible, have leveraged impacts on one's gains.

OWNERSHIP EFFECTS

Stock ownership requirements demand a minimum commitment to share ownership. After events like Enron and the more recent financial meltdown, investors want to see executives in a position to take big losses if things go south after bonuses have been paid and options exercised. There is some empirical evidence that companies with low levels of ownership (under 5 percent or so) have poorer performance. Research covering 60 years of data has indicated that the wealth leverage effects of accumulated stock and option holdings have had the effect of increasing firm performance.[6] These are reasons to consider taking steps to increase ownership if current levels are weak.

EXHIBIT 10.8 Venture Stage Equity Incentive Grants: Dilution and Growth Impacts on Initial Grants

Scenario
10% First Year Grant
2:1 Options:Stock

Valuation Effects of Deal on Enterprise (millions except per-share amounts)

	First Round of VC, Acq, or Partners			Second Round			IPO and Later Gains			
	Now	Round 1 Effects	After	Before	Round 2 Effects	After	Before	IPO Effects	After	Later Gain
Valuation Increase (before financing)		33.3%			33%					25.0%
Percent Sold (after financing, pro forma)	100.0%		33.3%	100.0%		33%	100.0%		25.0%	
Value of Equity	$ 50	$ 25	$ 75	$ 150	$ 75	$ 225	$ 450	$ 150	$ 600	$ 750
Shares (oust or issued)	5.0	2.5	7.5	7.5	3.8	11.3	11.3	3.8	15.0	15.0
Value per Share	$ 10.00	$ 10.00	$ 10.00	$ 20.00	$ 20.00	$ 20.00	$ 40.00	$ 40.00	$ 40.00	$ 50.00
Percent Owned by Parent	100.0%		66.7%	66.7%		44.4%	44.4%		33.333%	33.3%
Value of Parent Interest	$ 50		$ 50	$ 100		$ 100	$ 200		$ 200	$ 250

Impact on Value of Initial Restricted Stock Grant (thousands except per-share amounts)

	First Round of VC, Acq, or Partners			Second Round			IPO and Later Gains			
	Now	Round 1 Effects	After	Before	Round 2 Effects	After	Before	IPO Effects	After	Later Gain
Initial Restricted Shares **3.33%**	167		167	167		167	167		167	167
Value of R/S Grant	$ 1,667		$ 1,667	$ 3,333		$ 3,333	$ 6,667		$ 6,667	$ 8,333

Impact on Initial Option Grant Gain (thousands except per-share amounts)

	First Round of VC, Acq, or Partners			Second Round			IPO and Later Gains			
	Now	Round 1 Effects	After	Before	Round 2 Effects	After	Before	IPO Effects	After	Later Gain
Option Strike Price **6.67%**	$ 10.00		$ 10.00	$ 10.00		$ 10.00	$ 10.00		$ 10.00	$ 10.00
Initial Optioned Shares	333		333	333		333	333		333	333
Option Grant Size	$ 3,333			$ 3,333			$ 10,000			
Option Gain Amount	$ —		$ —	$ 3,333		$ 3,333	$ 10,000		$ 10,000	$ 13,333

Gains to Parent, Other Investors and Partners, and Management

	Parent	Rest. Stock	Options	Opt & R/S
Outset	100.0%	3.33%	6.67%	**10.00%**
Round 1	66.7%	2.22%	4.44%	6.67%
Round 2	44.4%	1.48%	2.96%	4.44%
IPO, Later	**33.3%**	1.11%	2.22%	3.33%
% of Original		33.3%	33.3%	33.3%

Investor Gain

Parent	200.0
First-Round Investors	100.0
Second-Round Investors	112.5
IPO Investors	37.5
Total	$ 450.0

Scenario Gains

		%Parent Gain	%Total Gn
R/S Gain	8,333	4.17%	1.85%
Option Gain	13,333	6.67%	2.96%
Total	$ 21,667	10.83%	4.81%

EXHIBIT 10.9	TYPICAL REQUIRED LEVELS OF STOCK OWNERSHIP AS A MULTIPLE OF SALARY

CEO	5.0
COO	4.0
CFO	3.0
Division Head	3.0
EVP Level	3.0
SVP Level	2.0
VP Level	1.0

Source: Equilar, Inc.

Ownership guidelines are stated most often as a percentage of salary. Exhibit 10.9 shows median multiples reported by Fortune 250 companies, arrayed in percentage of salary terms. Companies often impose share retention guidelines as well, requiring, for example that a percentage of after-tax option gains be held in shares.

Option holdings normally are not included in the definition of stock ownership. This could, in theory, lead executives to exercise stock options and retain the shares received after tax. This actually would decrease stock exposure, greatly in most cases. If companies do not consider option-based share exposure to be "ownership" for purposes of stake and accountability, they might want to stop granting options.

Ownership requirements may cause the wrong side of the risk coin to show its face. As noted in Chapter 5, investors have high levels of liquidity and can diversify easily. Executives do not. This is not something to apologize for, of course. Investors give executives power over the enterprise and a large stake in success. Companies require them to hold illiquid business interests, ones they can't diversify to nearly the extent their financial advisers might prefer. However, at some point—somewhere between a couple million dollars of stock exposure and a few tens of millions for the range of people we are talking about—adding more exposure arguably goes beyond the point of diminishing returns. That is, the personal risk levels involved simply create risk aversion rather than encouraging the balanced risk-taking involved in business success.

A Whole New Ball Game

Vanilla, fixed-price stock options have lost their place as the centerpiece of the incentive structure for company management. These complex instruments, offering little cause-and-effect incentive to most of the people who receive them, became extremely popular due to their fictitious "no cost" portrayal in company profit and loss statements. Options now comprise between one-third to one-half of the market LTI mix, closer to the weighting they merit based on their advantages in matters like leverage, linkages to shareholder gains, and flexibility.

Stock-based pay generally, however, has not been on any path to revocation, particularly for top officers of public companies. When choosing which stock-based vehicles to use, companies have for years been much more discerning. Companies no longer slather the management workforce, or the entire workforce, with stock options every year, without rigorous thinking about what this approach costs and how it might contribute to business results.

▪ NOTES

1. James M. Citrin, "The Job Isn't the Same as It Used to Be," *The Conference Board Review* (May/June 2009).
2. David Brooks, "In Praise of Dullness," *The New York Times*, May 18, 2009.
3. John Hagel, John Seely Brown, and Lang Davison, "Talent Is Everything," *The Conference Board Review* (May/June 2009).
4. Source: Equilar.com.
5. An example is W. G. Sanders, "Behavioral Responses of CEOs to Stock Ownership and Stock Option Pay," *Academy of Management Journal* 44 (2001): 477–492, in which CEO stock option grants are positively correlated with (risky and often economically unsuccessful) acquisition activity, and block share ownership by CEOs and outsiders is negatively correlated with it. A large number of studies document poor corporate performance in the area of mergers and acquisitions. The book *The Synergy Trap*, by Mark Sirower (New York: Free Press, 2007), sets forth his research and summarizes much work by others.
6. See R. Morck, A. Shleifer, and R. W. Vishny, "Management Ownership and Market Valuation: An Empirical Analysis," *Journal of Financial Economics* 20 (1988): 293-315. Also, George-Levi Gayle and Robert A. Miller, "Has Moral Hazard Become a More Important Factor in Managerial Compensation? Paper provided by Carnegie Mellon University, Tepper School of Business in its series GSIA Working Papers with number 2005-E58.

CHAPTER 11

The Medium Is the Message

One of the platitudes of incentive design is that proper communication of incentive plans is pivotal to their success. What is said less often, though, is that the plans themselves are important communication media. When we talk about communication of incentive plans for senior management, *the medium is the message.*

Formal communication initiatives will not work if the plan design itself is ineffective. If an incentive plan does not pay out based on things people can affect, then no number of seminars or brochures will make that plan an active contributor to business results. You cannot talk, write, or gesticulate your way around incentives that are infeasible, weak, or diffuse. If you do not shut down the linkages between bad business decisions and incentive rewards—either through the terms of the plans themselves or through other governance tools—then you bear a risk of value destruction, irrespective of how often your training programs warn against it. Multimedia rollouts do not help when none of the media conveys credible messages.

Money, on the other hand, talks. Senior management knows that better than anyone. Well-designed incentive plans speak for themselves. If your company wants to communicate about performance, you should take business goals and incentive plan terms that are clear, use them to create compelling financial stakes in long-term business success, and grant them to people who are in a position to do something about it. *That* is saying something.

As they say, "You can't not communicate." If you do not convey a clear set of messages, people will supply their own. Nature abhors a vacuum, and executives' natures do, too. They each have a standing set of presumptions about what is and is not rewarded in businesses generally and, normally, a fairly precise sense of the ground rules in their current setting. They are not novices, after all. They attained a lot to get where they are. The traditional incentive structure creates a vacuum. It does not draw a compelling linkage from high quality business decisions to rewards. When silent, vague, or implausible, incentives invite executives to fill in their own messages, maybe cynical ones, and risk creating a mediocre, careerist view of how the company really works.

Here is another valid principle of corporate communication: Leadership's actions are more important than formal communication media. Newsletters, brochures, and seminars often carry little real persuasive power. What really matters is when leadership gets behind a new initiative and clearly communicates that support to employees. The most important communications within a company are handled directly by the chief executive officer (CEO) and a few other top leaders and are expressed most compellingly with actions rather than words. In the context of a senior management incentive plan, it is critical for the CEO to demonstrably support the "deal" that the incentive plan creates. And for good reason. Effective incentive pay plans for the broader senior management group can improve company performance and stock value. No matter what form future incentives take, the CEO will have lots of money riding on the company's stock price. That is why Chapter 1 is written directly to the CEO, pointing out how implementing proper incentives can improve business performance, shareholder wealth, and rewards for top officers.

INCENTIVES AND FINANCIAL GOVERNANCE

Many of the big changes proposed in this book—metrics, target setting, business unit valuation, and other explicitly financial features of incentive design—lie directly within the purview of the finance function. Since incentives are about encouraging good business decision making by rewarding actions that create value, there is a lot of overlap between this mission and the work of the chief financial officer (CFO). In practice, incentives really ought to make the CFO's job easier, and there are many ways in which a proper incentive structure can support key responsibilities of the finance function. Unfortunately, it does not always work this way.

Budgeting

The typical, negotiated incentive structure hurts decision making. It creates short-term bias, it may instill risk aversion, and it sets up adverse interests where there should be alignment. Better methods for incentive design and target setting can encourage a longer-term focus and a balanced view of risk, at the same time uniting the financial interests of the parties. Examples include setting targets based on shareholder expectations, using various financial algorithms to set targets consistently each year, and applying value-based methods to performance measurement and plan calibration. These methods use consistent external standards for target setting rather than letting pay-related goals create a set of one-off disputes between corporate and each business unit. And these plans create shared upside since each party is rewarded for the same stream of economically profitable results.

Long-Range Planning

This process can suffer from many of the same problems as the annual budget, enlarging the risks of biased resource allocation. In a target-setting process framed by shareholder expectations or other value-based criteria, a business unit manager who maintains, "Things are very uncertain in our sector, I can't promise much income growth, and I need a lot of investment," is really saying something else to corporate leaders and to peers: "My business isn't worth much."

Various kinds of phantom stock and performance plans can be very helpful, since they connect pay with achievement of long-run goals, making it difficult for management to continually defer promised performance gains into the out years of "hockey stick" plans. These plans also can help put companies with differing performance on a fair and comparable footing for judging success and delivering rewards. Under the total business return (TBR) cited earlier, the rewards in a company with high growth and big capital requirements might be similar to those in a company posting more modest growth but highly distributable income, provided each has growth and yield levels adding up to the same level of TBR.

This approach can result in truer, better-informed business planning. It encourages business unit management to fully expose their insider views of business prospects as they position the unit for growth or cash yield (each of which can bring payouts). This technique has another virtue. It sidesteps some difficult aspects of the target-setting process since it does not require the company to set hard and fast goals (e.g., separate goals for growth and return on invested capital [ROIC] in a bonus plan) for each business unit.

Investment Evaluation

Incentives can provide full accountability for the use of capital, for business risk, and for long-run returns on investments in the company. Then, managers know they are spending their own money when they propose big capital outlays, initiatives, or acquisitions. They have no incentive to inflate forecasts at the time of deal approval and little ability to defer accountability. This behavior can be reinforced by using value-based designs that clearly account for capital when setting incentive targets under any of several methods and that lengthen the effective time frame of the company's incentive structure.

Financial Education

Well-designed incentive plans can help educate the management workforce about the basic connections between business results and value creation. These linkages—which we boiled down to the interplay among long-run operating income, the use of capital, and its cost—are ones that finance executives would like to see the broader management group applying in many things they do. Value-based incentives reinforce financial training because they reflect the basic value drivers clearly, and they make the training message compelling in money terms.

Cost Control

Incentives can create a clear entrepreneurial interest in business success. This encourages management to spend money as if it were its own. Outlays are seen from a "best bang for the buck" viewpoint, and costs offering no return are cut out quickly. Companies can use consistent target-setting methods each year. They can use incentive plan designs that create a stake in business results that is clear, continuous, concrete, and long-term. Under either method—or when using both—participants understand their financial interests are like those of an entrepreneur.

Financial Performance Evaluation

The inconsistent, incomplete nature of many traditional financial metrics confounds the basic performance assessments they are supposed to enable. These metrics often fail to disentangle the effects of financial leverage, historical and future capital usage, risk, and other factors. One example of a solution is the suite of TBR solutions we applied to measurement, valuation, and target setting. They recognize both the growth in a business's income and the amount of free cash flow it generates. TBR redresses an unusual number of the issues that can crop up in incentive plans. It is unaffected by financial leverage, taking into account only changes in capital and reflecting business risk directly. It enables more meaningful benchmarking of a company's financial results and their effects on enterprise returns.

Financing Decisions

Incentive plans ought to encourage the broad management group to focus on operating performance—on the things they can affect most strongly. Instead, plans tend to make the entire management workforce a stakeholder in financing decisions, as well. That is because pay often is affected strongly when the finance function makes decisions about things like debt levels, dividend policy, share repurchases, leasing, joint venture structuring, and initial public offerings (IPOs). In a certain number of cases, such pay concerns can put undesirable pressure on finance. In almost all cases, the plans interpose financial policy between the company's operating results and its pay outcomes, reducing line of sight and efficacy. Many incentive plan formats—generally, those setting targets and measuring performance from a total capital perspective, tracking enterprise returns in one way or another—can remove the effect of capital structure from pay and link it more strongly with the operating results that most of management can drive.

Risk Management

Incentive methods have important effects on company risks, as well. They can encourage senior management to take a balanced view of risk, one that creates the most value for shareholders. In this regard, their impact on risk is like their impact in many other areas. They encourage the broader senior management team to take the perspective of the finance function, which in this case means taking account of business risk as investors would.

Incentive plans are an invisible hand guiding many, many decisions in all areas of the business. Financial management cannot participate in every business decision, but it would like to see the principles of finance and value creation reflected consistently in actions of the broad management group. The company's incentive structure may be the CFO's best opportunity to do this.

Overall, value-based incentive designs should change the finance function's focus within the enterprise. The current finance role still is too much about policing and control at a tactical level—deflating some forecasts and removing sandbags from others, unwinding bias and gamesmanship, directing attention to the basic financial rules of business success. Finance is too often a bulwark against the negative impulses of the enterprise and the people in it. Incentive plans based on valuation can help position this critical function to guide economic behavior positively, and through it the broader affairs of the enterprise.

HUMAN RESOURCE PERSPECTIVES

This book has been about how the compensation arrangements run by human resources (HR) can be used to get better business results throughout the enterprise. This is one of the areas where HR often leads change, collaborating with the CEO, CFO, and board to make much better use of the stock and cash consumed each year by executive incentive plans.

The gains are low-hanging fruit, as performance initiatives go. And HR often does this, proactively, in an area experiencing ongoing changes. But both finance and HR will have to deal with some complex challenges to get it done properly. Work being done explicitly by the stock market—business target setting, performance evaluation, and pay delivery—will be taken back within the company to make the system more effective.

We may deal with a lot of complexity during the design process. But, when it comes time to roll out the incentive plan, we have to simplify the plan's description to the greatest extent possible. Typically, this means conveying to participants that they have a big claim on company value that they can influence in some simple and direct ways.

Well-designed incentives ought to make HR's job easier, even if setting up the plans is harder than running an option-only grant approach. Effective incentives enhance company systems for performance management and rewards and their effects on attracting, retaining, and motivating key people.

HR is an especially process-astute function, and executive pay design has many process considerations. In Aesop's fable "Belling the Cat," a meeting of mice voted that a bell should be tied around the neck of the local cat, so that they would always be warned of his approach. The meeting foundered, however, when the issue became exactly which mice were to be delegated to do the belling. Sound familiar? Care to act as the messenger, when it comes time to call out poor-quality performance standards and dilutive incentive practices? Is your consultant up to it?

An unflinching incentive design process is important to success when it comes to senior management incentives. The design process needs to provide thorough, decision-quality information to top management and the board, including the pros and cons of the incentive changes being considered. More acutely focused incentives might lead to more challenging relations with the broader senior management team. They can point back at senior management, exposing decision-making flaws and business errors that often go right to the top. This is a good thing for the business and its owners. Valuation-based incentives are about getting business gains by correcting flaws in business decision making. The design process should go looking for trouble, because that is where the gains are to be found.

The CEO and board need to be well informed about the pros and cons of new incentives to understand how they are likely to play out in their company's particular situation. If they hold an incorrect or incomplete picture, disappointment is a real risk, and so is failure. Executives and boards need to consider whether new incentives are likely to offer gains in their particular business situation, taking into account the possibility that gains may come from sources they do not know. If they're quite certain that these methods will not deliver, they should pass.

Many incentive plans have been hampered by problems associated with the process used to design and roll them out in the first place. Many suffer from lack of imagination in their basic design, poor commitment among participants, and little continuing support once they are in place. A proper design process takes steps to engage stakeholders and pursue decision quality:

- State the precise role that incentives will play within the overall system of governance and rewards.
- Pursue input from a wide group of people.
- Involve senior leadership and the board at proper junctures.
- Infuse the design project with high-quality information.
- Develop real, actionable design alternatives to choose from.
- Evaluate alternatives in terms of how well they meet objectives.
- Apply formal simulation and testing tools to the design of the overall incentive structure and its components.
- Bring expertise, experience, integrity, and independence to the process.
- Commit to an implementation plan and execute it.
- Communicate the plan fully to all participants on an ongoing basis.
- Review plan design and efficacy periodically.

A successful rollout certainly does not require full unanimity nor full trust. Unanimity is an unsuitable goal. An incentive structure that pleases everyone will be ineffective, too expensive, or both. And trust is built over time. Situations of low trust typically mean that past incentive plans have been changed a lot or otherwise discredited. That is a good starting point, in a sense, because it increases the potential business gain from doing things right.

Aspects of the process can be streamlined. Proactive principles for incentive pay are meant to distill the real choices involved in effective incentive design. If you are going down this path, you do not need to grapple with the general question of how incentives should work in the senior management group or the basic characteristics of measurement and pay delivery. That is stipulated up front. The role of management is to maximize value creation, and incentives should support such efforts in clear and compelling terms. Effective incentive design is about how to bring such propositions to bear in a particular company's setting.

Over time, the design and administrative processes should try to achieve stability, even permanence within the incentive structure. The basic drivers of the incentive structure have a long shelf life, after all, since the principles of performance, valuation, and governance are stable. One of the distinctive features of an approach based on enduring principles is that it is never repealed:

- *Senior managers are in the decision business.* The essence of their role is not defined by a particular market, like the one for electric utility services or haircuts, nor by a particular set of business conditions. Their specific, unique, and enduring charge is to make business decisions on the part of shareholders.

- *Senior management's product, in the end, is business results that create value for owners.* That is true for a single-line business just as it is for a conglomerate, or even a private equity fund that continually enters and exits businesses.

- *Investors always have had measurable standards for performance and return.* These standards are reflected in capital markets, which judge the success of management teams that run the affairs of business on their behalf. This was true in corporations hundreds of years ago and is still true today.

When asked about his investing methods, Warren Buffett continues to cite 1940s author and analyst Benjamin Graham on fundamental security analysis, whose principles include many of the basic assertions of this book. Business conditions change all the time, though, and so do the structures and fortunes of companies. Management teams turn over from time to time while shareholders can come and go on an hourly basis. Strategies change, and so do business buzzwords. But the underlying connections between management and owners are not transient things. The incentives that formalize these ties need not be either:

- The basic moving parts of value creation—long-run operating income, capital usage, and risk—apply in all business conditions. Incentive plans that flow from these basic drivers do not need continual redesign.

- Metrics themselves can be set up to endure, flexibly, through a range of business conditions. The metric TBR, for example, automatically captures the benefits of business investment and growth when favored by market opportunity, and cash yield when not.

- The mechanics of proper incentives are flexible, as well. With each new grant under a long-term performance plan, the company can re-sync goals based on changes in performance expectations or the cost of capital.

- Basic adjustments can handle the effects of big acquisitions, divestitures, or volatility in operating results without disrupting the incentive system or interrupting management's financial interest in long-term business success.

- Unpredictability, volatility, and cyclicality can be addressed in the target-setting, range-setting, and measurement aspects of plan design.

Company incentive plans get changed all the time, diluting their credibility and contributing to a short-term focus. This, combined with other design flaws, has created a norm in which most of senior management does not have a plausible financial claim on its own results over time. Better approaches are flexible over time and across a range of business conditions. This enables companies to have more permanence in their pay structures, making them more credible and effective.

The formal communication process for management incentive plans poses its own sizable set of issues, but this is an area in which improvements in the typical company's practices are easily envisioned and made.

Participants in many incentive plans do not have a strong sense of how various decisions may pay off. Companies should run seminars at least yearly regarding goals and how to reach them. A spreadsheet model can be devised for just about any plan, one that tells exactly what will be earned at various performance levels and the impact of specific business decisions and scenarios on those performance levels. Armed with such information, participants can easily figure out what they will be paid for various results they might pursue. There is nothing wrong with this because well-designed plans are meant to affect business decision making. They're probably doing this analysis anyway, so the company may as well make it easy.

Business decisions are supposed to create value for shareholders, and results of most decisions can be converted rather simply into a valuation estimate. Linkages between business decisions, business results, and value creation should be made clear in plan communication. This ought to be a compulsory step for any company making use of stock-based incentives, but it is particularly useful for those using goal-based incentive plans that flow from a valuation perspective.

Incentives are valuable at the executive level—and so is total pay. The value of each pay element, as well as the basis for earning awards under incentive plans, needs to be made clear through effective communication.

Again, keep in mind that many of the communication problems with executive pay—the issues causing real dissonance—do not relate to communication, but to design. Executives are smart. When they are unhappy about pay, they often have real, design-related reasons for being unhappy; in those cases, propaganda does not help. True communication problems, as opposed to flaws in design, tend to stem from basic failures to communicate the value of what executives have, how it might pay off and what they can do about it. First, fix the design problems. Then, tell them what incentive opportunity they are getting, what it is worth, and how they can earn it. At that point, the medium is the message.

Glossary

Accumulated depreciation (AD)   A balance sheet account that records the cumulative amount of depreciation for an asset since its acquisition.

Agency theory   The branch of economics concerned with management of shareholder-owned companies in which shareholders are obliged to hire professional managers to run the company on their behalf (as their agents).

Capital asset pricing model (CAPM)   A formula that describes the connection between the risk of a security and the return investors expect from it. The model was developed by economists Jack Treynor, William Sharpe, and John Lintner.

Cash value added (CVA)   A cash-based version of the metric economic profit (EP). (See Chapter 7.)

CFROGI   Cash flow return on gross investment. (See Chapter 6.)

CFROI   Cash flow return on investment. (See Chapter 7.)

Discounted cash flow (DCF)   A method for estimating the value of a business by making a projection of future cash flows from the business's operations and discounting them to present value. (See Chapter 2.)

Earnings per share (EPS)   Net income available to common shareholders (after subtracting preferred dividends) divided by the number of outstanding common shares. (See Chapter 6.)

EBIT   Earnings before interest and taxes. (See Chapter 6.)

EBITDA   Earnings before interest, taxes, depreciation, and amortization. Under U.S. generally accepted accounting principles (GAAP), since companies no longer amortize intangible assets, the "A" part of EBITDA is vestigial. (See Chapter 6.)

Economic profit (EP)   Also known as residual income or economic value added. (See Chapter 7.)

Employee stock ownership plan (ESOP) A type of retirement plan in the United States in which company shares are held as retirement assets for employees.

Financial Accounting Standards Board (FASB) The independent organization that promulgates financial accounting rules for U.S. companies.

Forecast-term income Income projected to be earned during the explicit "forecast period" or "forecast term" in a discounted cash flow (DCF) analysis, normally a period of five to ten years.

Free cash flow (FCF) Cash flow that can be distributed from a company's operations and used to satisfy the claims of investors by paying dividends, repurchasing shares, paying interest costs, or paying down debt. (See Chapter 2.)

Hockey stick plan A forecast of poor near-term business results that are rationalized by expectations of large improvements in performance three to five years in the future.

Incentive A monetary inducement for employees to take actions meant to benefit the company and its shareholders.

Incentive stock option (ISO) A tax-qualified stock option under U.S. law.

Initial public offering (IPO) The act of a company selling its shares to a large number of investors and listing them on a stock exchange for the first time.

Leveraged buy-out (LBO) The purchase of a business, typically by an investor group including company executives, financed mainly by debt.

Long-term incentive (LTI) An incentive plan that measures performance and pays out rewards over time cycles exceeding one year.

Net income Revenue minus all expenses, including taxes. (See Chapter 6.)

Nonqualified plan A retirement plan that does not qualify for favorable tax treatment under U.S. tax law and is not subject to the statutory reporting and funding requirements. Participation in such plans typically is limited to a select group of highly compensated employees.

Optics A vernacular term for the general appearance of executive incentives from an external perspective like that of a shareholder or regulator.

Performance unit plan A plan that pays out awards based on measured performance against goals over a period of more than one year. (See Chapter 9.)

Phantom stock plan   A long-term incentive plan that does not involve the use of actual company shares, but is based one way or another on share price performance. (See Chapter 9.)

Premium option   A stock option whose exercise price is higher than the market value of the shares at the time of grant. (See Chapter 10.)

Real value added (RVA)   A residual income measure—like cash value added—that has been adjusted to take account of inflation that has occurred since company assets were placed in service. (See Chapter 7.)

Return on capital employed (ROCE)   Operating income after tax divided by capital employed (debt plus equity). Generally equivalent to return on invested capital (ROIC) or return on net assets (RONA). (See Chapter 6.)

Return on equity (ROE)   Net income divided by stockholders' equity. (See Chapter 6.)

Return on invested capital (ROIC)   See Return on capital employed.

Return on net assets (RONA)   See Return on capital employed.

Shareholder value added (SVA)   An estimate of how current financial performance contributes to the overall value of a company. (See Chapter 7.)

Total business return (TBR)   A two-part performance measure that tracks how much a business has increased in value and how much income or cash flow it has generated for its owners. (See Chapters 2, 7, 8, and 9.)

Total investor return (TIR)   Like total business return, but stated more precisely in market-value terms. The amount of the increase in the value of an enterprise plus the free cash flows it generates. (See Chapter 2.)

Total shareholder return (TSR)   Capital gains plus dividends earned on a stock investment.

Value-based management (VBM)   Using principles of corporate finance and valuation in a prominent and explicit way in business processes, usually encouraged by value-based incentive plans.

Variable accounting   An accounting treatment for many cash-based incentive plans—one in which variable incentive expense is accrued, depending on estimates of what the plan eventually will pay out to participants.

Weighted-average cost of capital (WACC)   The overall rate of return that a company needs to earn on its investments in order to compensate its debt and equity investors for the risks they bear. (See Chapters 2 and 5.)

Index